CRIME AND PUNISHMENT IN TUDOR ENGLAND

CRIME AND PUNISHMENT IN TUDOR ENGLAND

From Alchemists to Zealots

APRIL TAYLOR

First published in Great Britain in 2023 by
PEN AND SWORD HISTORY
An imprint of
Pen & Sword Books Ltd
Yorkshire – Philadelphia

Copyright © April Taylor, 2023

ISBN 978 1 39907 166 6

The right of April Taylor to be identified as Author of this work has been asserted by her in accordance with the Copyright, Designs and Patents Act 1988.

A CIP catalogue record for this book is available from the British Library.

All rights reserved. No part of this book may be reproduced or transmitted in any form or by any means, electronic or mechanical including photocopying, recording or by any information storage and retrieval system, without permission from the Publisher in writing.

Typeset in Times New Roman 11/13.5 by
SJmagic DESIGN SERVICES, India.
Printed and bound in the UK by CPI Group (UK) Ltd.

Pen & Sword Books Limited incorporates the imprints of Atlas, Archaeology, Aviation, Discovery, Family History, Fiction, History, Maritime, Military, Military Classics, Politics, Select, Transport, True Crime, Air World, Frontline Publishing, Leo Cooper, Remember When, Seaforth Publishing, The Praetorian Press, Wharncliffe Local History, Wharncliffe Transport, Wharncliffe True Crime and White Owl.

For a complete list of Pen & Sword titles please contact
PEN & SWORD BOOKS LIMITED
George House, Units 12 & 13, Beevor Street, Off Pontefract Road,
Barnsley, South Yorkshire, S71 1HN, England
E-mail: enquiries@pen-and-sword.co.uk
Website: www.pen-and-sword.co.uk

or

PEN AND SWORD BOOKS
1950 Lawrence Rd, Havertown, PA 19083, USA
E-mail: uspen-and-sword@casematepublishers.com
Website: www.penandswordbooks.com

Contents

Acknowledgements vii
Introduction viii

PART ONE

Justice from the Romans to the Tudors 2
The role of superstition in the justice system 10
The Power of the Press 14
Prisons in England 21
Population 24
Policing in Tudor England 27
Punishments 34

PART TWO

Crimes and Cases 60
Alchemy 61
Animals 63
Begging 66
Blackmail 70
Blasphemy 76
Coney-Catching 79
Defamation 81
Embezzlement 84
Fraud 87
Gangs 91

Heresy	95
Insurrection	102
Infanticide	106
Infidelity	110
Juvenile Crime	114
Kidnapping and Abduction	116
Larceny	120
Murder	122
Nuisance	135
Organised Crime	138
Poaching	140
Poison	141
Prostitution	146
Quarrels	149
Recusancy	151
Riots	156
Scolding	159
Sedition	161
Sexual Offences	164
Spying	172
Sumptuary Laws	180
Theft	185
Treason	187
Uprisings	193
Vagrancy	196
Witchcraft	204
Xenophobia	211
Zealots	214
Afterword	217
Select Bibliography	219
Endnotes	222
Index	242

Acknowledgements

Nobody writes a book in isolation without help from others in some form or other.

I would like to thank the editorial team at Pen & Sword for their constant help and advice. The Pen & Sword writing community have also given me support and encouragement, for which I am immensely grateful.

Thanks are also due to Luke Shackell, Kings Lynn Archivist, for his help in trying to identify offenders in Norfolk, and the Norfolk Record Office for their help in directing me to possible sources of information.

Like most writers, I have a small band of people to whom I turn when things are not going well and who also share in my small triumphs. Their support is always instant and unstinting. I call them Team Taylor. So, thank you Nicky Griffiths, Joan Mulqueen, Janet Shell, and my long-suffering – occasionally *very* long-suffering – husband, Paul.

Writing this book has often been a soul-searing experience so I must thank all my friends at my local church, who have frequently put their hands on my shoulder and said 'We're here.'

This book is dedicated to Paul, Mum, Dad, and 'the bruvvers'. United we stand!

Introduction

In the humorous 1930 book *1066 And All That* by Sellar & Yeatman[1], the authors describe the seventeenth-century English Civil War as being between the Roundheads – Right but Repulsive – and the Cavaliers – Wrong but Wromantic. One could easily say that about the Plantagenets and Tudors. The Plantagenets, in the form of Edward IV – Illustrious but Indolent – and the Tudors in the form of Henry VII – Insincere but Industrious.

There have been some very strange, inhuman laws passed in England's green and less than pleasant past. None more so than in Tudor times. And throughout the research and writing of this book, again and again we come up against what I call the 'Eve Factor'. The original sin committed by the first woman and thus punishment being administered to all her descendants down to the present day. One of the most horrendous penalties was for poisoning your master or mistress. Richard Roose discovered this at the cost, not only of his life, but the method of him losing it. More of him later.

As a caveat to that level of brutality, laws in continental Europe were infinitely more savage in some ways and very strange in others. It was not uncommon for pigs that had run over children to be put on trial. Nowadays, the parents of the child would be castigated in the press and any other children put on the At-risk Register. Then, they just hanged the pig. However, England's reputation for being a nation of animal lovers still held because there are no documented cases of animals being put on trial in Tudor England, although there are a couple of apocryphal tales.

When Henry Tudor, Duke of Richmond, waded ashore on 7 August 1485 at Mill Bay in Pembrokeshire, with his ragbag army of mercenaries, his sole ambition was to oust Richard III and take back the throne for the House of Lancaster, which he duly did at the Battle of Bosworth on 22 August. He declared himself King Henry VII. Ever a wily operator, Henry changed the official date of his accession to the day before Bosworth thus, in one fell swoop, making everyone who fought on the Yorkist side traitors and achieving a huge land-grab in consequence. This was simply a precursor to methods he would use to swell the royal coffers and reinforce

Introduction

the Tudor dynasty. Although Henry had fled to France after the Battle of Tewkesbury in 1471, the taint of bastardy in his lineage rendered him in many eyes to be ineligible to succeed to the English throne.

Having been in exile for half his life, the 28-year-old could not have realised how fractured the rule of law had become in late fifteenth-century England. Neither could he know how inconsistently it was implemented throughout the country. In truth, after thirty years of the Wars of the Roses England was a mess. So much so that the monarchs instituted what Hall called 'needful despotism, supported by the people.'[2]

The nation's primary requirement was for strong law that would heal the wounds of the previous thirty years of strife.[3] Although this was by no means the foremost of Henry's problems, it was something he could ill-afford to ignore. So, while the Tudor era is best known for Henry VIII, his six wives, some very high-profile executions, and religious schism, what Henry VII put in place to improve law and order meant that by the time of the death of his grand-daughter, Elizabeth I, in 1603, the law, whilst still showing anomalies, was on a more consistent footing.

The main problem with the legal system in 1485 was that not only was it interpreted in different ways in different parts of England, but the whole edifice was riven with corruption.

The other major problem the historian faces is the sparsity of county records. Taking the incidence of homicide, for example, in Middlesex, original records were damaged and incomplete, and this skews the statistics.

Likewise in Nottinghamshire, coroners' records from 1530–1558 indicate a homicide incidence of 38 per million per year, whereas it has been posited the truer number to be 148 per million per year. The other surprising, or perhaps suspicious, feature of the Nottinghamshire records is that there is a total absence of any cases of infanticide.[4]

The aim of this book is to present the story of the Tudor dynasty through crimes and their punishments in an accessible way, giving accurate information. Where possible, there will be case studies, some more amusing than others.

What this book is *not* is a presentation of dry, dusty, and dense facts; rather, it is a dip-in-and-out book to enable the reader to understand the way of life between 1485 and 1603 by reference to its legal system, its criminal fraternity, and the consequences for felons.

Where relevant, monetary amounts in the text have been adjusted to 2021 values using the Bank of England Inflation Calculator.

There will also be *Tavern Talk* (see below), various snippets of Tudor information, not necessarily related to crime, spread throughout the book.

I have purposely not made these gory, since you might be enjoying a pub meal. But you could celebrate the book by drinking a *Bloody Mary*!

Tavern Talk:
The Wars of the Roses (1455-1487) is also called the cousins' war since it was fought by the Lancastrian side of the family with their emblem of the red rose and the Yorkist side with their emblem of the white rose. In 1486, Henry VII, the last Lancastrian claimant to the throne and victor of Bosworth Field, married Elizabeth of York, Edward IV's eldest daughter. Thus was the Tudor rose born with a red outer and white inner.

PART ONE

Justice from the Romans to the Tudors

It is fitting that my introduction began with the future Henry VII wading ashore in Pembrokeshire in 1485. Approximately 1500 years earlier another would-be conqueror waded ashore on the other side of England. Dover to be precise, except that Caesar was met by a furious mob who persuaded him to scramble back aboard his ship, and land himself and his troops elsewhere on an empty beach. This is now thought to be Pegwell Bay on the Isle of Thanet.

What did the great Caesar find when he finally made it ashore and, more importantly, what did he bring with him? Many readers will be aware of the scene in Monty Python's *Life of Brian* where John Cleese asks 'What have the Romans ever done for us?'[1] That has, in truth, been a very hotly debated issue for historians.

The basic principles of Roman law

1. It should be written and transparent with checks and balances. In other words, everyone should know what the law is and it cannot be changed on the whim of a ruler or a judge.
2. The law should treat everyone equally.
3. The law of the State applies only to that State's citizens. Foreigners have no rights unless a treaty has been agreed with their nation whereby they are protected under the law.
4. 'Unwritten law' – what we now call 'custom and practice'.
5. An accused person is presumed innocent until proven guilty.
6. An accused person has the right to face his or her accuser and offer a defence against the charge.
7. Guilt must be clearly established beyond any reasonable doubt and using solid evidence.
8. The burden of proof rests with the accuser.

9. Any law that seems grossly unfair can be rejected. This is the basis for what is now considered 'fair and reasonable'.
10. There must be a system of checks and balances, vetoes, a separation of powers, regular elections, and a set time limit on the length of any position or administration.[2]

Roman law had a widespread effect in Europe and whilst this impact in England was less so, it was still significant.

In Europe, Roman law was used to meet changing social needs. In England, it was implemented to build a new nation. The principles can be traced back to Greek democracy but the Romans interpreted them in a practical way. Ulpian, who held office in York, was a great legal authority and Roman jurist. It is to him that we owe the custom of a majority verdict if the jurors are unable to come to a unanimous decision. In England these tenets remained in force, largely unchanged, until the Norman invasion in 1066.

Most sources agree that around 476 AD the Roman Empire was in trouble from the Germanic armies of the north. However, one source, Zosimus, reports that the Emperor Honorius sent Britain a letter saying they must look to their own defences. Britain was its furthest outpost, having at various times between 30,000 and 125,000 soldiers garrisoned across the country (out of a population of around three million.). Approximately 9,000 were stationed on Hadrian's Wall. The English garrisons were gradually abandoned, but the Romano-British stayed and were driven by the invading Saxons into the west.

The Romans instituted Latin for their legal documents and started schools for the sons of nobles. Some phrases are still in use today, including:

> Ad hoc meaning 'for this purpose or occasion';
> alibi 'in another place, elsewhere';
> bona fide – 'good faith';
> caveat emptor – 'let the buyer beware';
> corpus delicti – 'body of the offence';
> flagrante delicto – 'in the very act of committing the crime';
> pro bono – 'for the good', describes services performed free of charge;
> sine die – 'without a day assigned for a future meeting';
> status quo – 'present state'.

Even workmen such as bricklayers and tilers knew a smattering of Latin, as evidenced by words scrawled on tiles and bricks. One such was 'Austalis dibus XIII vagatur sibi cotidim' which roughly translates as 'Augustalis has been off on his own for a fortnight'.[3]

As previously mentioned, what the Romans left Britain in terms of social and legal issues has been the subject of some seriously rancorous debates. There are those who argue Rome could not have been the rulers in Britain for 400 years without leaving something besides roads, towns, and a wall.

Others are equally certain Britain threw off all the Roman shackles as soon as the overlords stepped into their boats to go home. What does appear to be true is that Britain fell into the Dark Ages and only began to come out of them when Augustine arrived to spread his doctrines.

It is from the Saxons that we have the term *felon (fell* and *one)*. In other words, a person of terrible evil or ferocity, who is likely to corrupt others with their behaviour.

Some tenets of land law, the law of wills and the workings of the Saxon shire-moots – the equivalent of a county assembly – all have their basis in Roman law.

The Emperor Constantine decreed in 325AD that Christianity was the state religion and this, naturally, applied to Britain. After the Romans left, it was not until St Augustine visited Canterbury with a group of Benedictine monks in 596AD, that the link between the English and the Roman Church was reinstated. This was vital because the courts that dealt with most crimes were church courts.

King Aethelbert was also greatly influenced by St Gregory, known as 'the Roman of the Romans'. Aethelbert framed his laws in the Roman way. Before the Norman invasion, the law of England was the *Romani*, which basically means law as defined by the clergy. Although this has, of course, changed considerably, we owe the law of conveyancing to the *Romani*. The Anglo-Saxon 'Land Book' states that is of 'Italian origin'. An understanding of Roman law was the basis of law from the time of Aethelbert to the time of the Norman invasion and was taught in the Cathedral School in York.[4]

Aethelbert was the first king to put laws in writing and this set the custom for the future. He used wergild to base the amount of compensation or fines transgressors had to pay. His laws included:

> If a man lies with a nobleman's serving maid, he shall pay twelve shillings compensation.
>
> If a man lies with a commoner's serving maid, he shall pay six shillings compensation.

> If one man slays another, the ordinary wergild to be paid as compensation shall be 100 shillings.
>
> If one man slays another, he shall pay twenty shillings before the grave is closed and the whole of the wergild within forty days.
>
> If a homicide departs from the country, his relatives shall pay half the wergild.
>
> If an ear is pierced, three shillings compensation shall be paid.
>
> If an ear is lacerated, six shillings compensation shall be paid.
>
> If an eye is knocked out, fifty shillings shall be paid as compensation.[5]

In 827 King Egbert united the Angles and Saxon tribes to create 'Angle Land' or England.

King Alfred, famous for driving out the Danes as well as allegedly being less than skilful in the kitchen, visited Rome in his youth. He formed 'The Laws of King Alfred', picking parts of previously laid down laws that he considered were beneficial to the nation. Previous laws had dealt in the main with theft and trading, but Alfred's laws included the breaking of oaths, injuries and sexual offences.[6]

King Canute ruled England from 1016-1035. He also visited Rome and put many statutes into law, becoming known in the process as 'the greatest legislator of the eleventh century'.

The Anglo-Saxon dynasty was reinstated in 1042 with the accession of Edward the Confessor. Having spent many years in exile in Europe, he, too, was keen to maintain the influence of Roman law. The laws Edward enacted are important. He was revered by the nation as a whole, so when the Normans invaded, they agreed, as a sop to the English, to uphold the laws Edward had put on the statute books. It was these laws that form the basis of the law we have today.

By the time William the Conqueror defeated Harold on Senlac Hill, not only was there a solid base of law in England, much of it based on the Roman model, it was also highly influenced by the moral code of Christianity. That said, England still has some remnants of the Anglo-Saxon law laid down by King Aethelbert in 600AD, basically the Writ and the Jury.

William I (1066-87) retained the Shire Courts and their administrative authority. Each area was split in shires and hundreds. The shire was a larger entity than the hundred, and ruled over by a shire-reeve, who later became a sheriff. A hundred was administered by a bailiff who was appointed by the shire-reeve. There could be several hundreds making up one shire in the same way that different villages, towns and cities make up our shires today. This resulted in a great degree of decentralisation. The shire-reeve was not a judge, but the president of the group of people administering legal affairs for the shire. He was the representative of the king and would hear writs.

William, who appears to have been a very able administrator, set about introducing order and method to the legal system. His right-hand man was Lanfranc, later made Archbishop of Canterbury. Lanfranc was an accomplished scholar and lawyer, trained in Roman law. His ability to argue his case was such that few people could best him in legal discourse. He was a vital component in the development of English common law.[7]

Lanfranc's successor at Canterbury, Anselm, had numerous quarrels with King William Rufus (1087-1100) and Henry I (1100-1135). Anselm began the move away from the law being dependent on the monarch to it being administered by chancellors. This also gave real power to the clergy in all legal matters, irrespective of whether the issues were sacred or secular.

King Stephen (1135-1154) was very much opposed to the way the study of civil law was spreading. However, he was an affable but ineffectual king and his opposition soon faded. From his reign onwards the teaching of Roman law and Canonical law became prominent.[8]

One of the basic tenets of law Henry II (1154-1189) gave England is the assise of novel disseisin, which is an action to recover lands from which the plaintiff has been ejected. It was a speedy, logical procedure for the recovery of property and was responsible, more than any other law, for giving English freeholders security of tenure.

Despite all the foregoing, the concept of common law still did not exist in England until Henry III's Chief Justiciar, Henry de Bracton, wrote a treatise citing specific cases. This became the foundation of the current English legal system. It also provided a basis of study to enable legal administrators to acquire the art of legal writing and advocacy.

The influence of the law of England as set up by Bracton was such that almost five centuries went by before there was another lawyer able to write competently about the English legal system.

The central core of Bracton's view was that even the monarch was subject to God and the law. Nobody argued this more eloquently than Sir Thomas More in his trial in 1535. His crime was treason because he had refused to sign Henry VIII's Oath of Supremacy, and refused to acknowledge the king as head of the church. More declared that the indictment was 'repugnant to the lawes of God and his holie Church'.[9]

Magna Carta

Most people think of Magna Carta as simply a peace treaty between King John and his disaffected barons. However, it was much more.

The beginnings of Magna Carta really lie with Thomas Becket. Becket had been a close colleague and ally of Henry II who made him his chancellor and, as such, Becket wielded a huge amount of legal power. Henry then decided he could gain power over the church as well as the state by making Becket the Archbishop of Canterbury. What Henry had not bargained for was that Becket would become a poacher turned gamekeeper, to the extent that he even wore a hair shirt under his vestments.

He refused to accept Henry's order to limit the power of the church and increase the monarch's power over the clergy – the Constitutions of Clarendon. Henry was furious and tried to put Becket on trial for treason. Becket fled to France but later returned to Canterbury.

At the now infamous Christmas feast in his castle in Bure in Normandy in 1170, Henry never said 'will no one rid me of this turbulent priest?' Henry's disillusion with Becket was expressed as 'what miserable drones and traitors have I nourished and promoted in my realm, who failed to serve their lord with such shameful contempt by a lowborn clerk!' One can imagine a modern-day newspaper editor preferring the snappier 'turbulent priest'.[10]

Of course, Henry was himself very insecure having not actually been born royal, merely a count. He only gained the throne through his mother, the Empress Matilda (sometimes called Maud), daughter of Henry I. Stephen's own son, Eustace, who appears to have been pretty good at soldiering but not much else, was killed in 1153 while plundering the abbey at Bury St Edmunds. This happened just in time for Matilda to agree with Stephen that she would give up her own claim to England so long as her son inherited the throne when Stephen died, which he did the next year in 1154.

However, I digress. Let's look at King John (1199-1216), as already mentioned, a very able administrator when he was not lolling in bed with his mistresses or plotting vicious revenge against perceived slights. He was prone to lengthy periods of indolence and then frenetic periods of action. It is possible that today he might be diagnosed as bipolar.

Pope Innocent III compelled John to accept Stephen Langton as Archbishop of Canterbury. John retaliated by seizing church property. Langton, a firm believer that every man is subject to the law, joined John's revolting barons and that led directly to the ceremony at Runnymede in 1215.[11]

Magna Carta tried to establish firm foundations for the equal administration of justice by those in power, including the king, because John was one of the worst offenders. He agreed to the terms simply because he had no intention of abiding by them.

Some of the clauses of the original Magna Carta are of its age, such as removing fish weirs on the Thames and preventing heirs being married to someone of lower social standing. Four clauses still remain in the British legal system today. Namely that the 'English church' shall be 'free and shall have its rights undiminished': that the 'city of London' may 'enjoy all its liberties and ancient customs'. Then the two really important ones; the ban on arbitrary detention and giving everyone the right to trial by jury.

There were three more Magna Cartas after 1215; in 1216, 1217 and 1225. Most of their clauses have been repealed. However, despite the nobles only being concerned with themselves and caring nothing for the common man and woman, Magna Carta established that nobody, including the monarch, is above the law.[12]

From all the foregoing, sprang the different court systems. The Court of Chancery was rooted in the belief that the monarch is the fount of all justice. However, since the monarch could not hear all cases in person, the King's Courts came into being. From these came an important element of English law – judges deciding classes of suits (lawsuits), but always in the name of the monarch. Which is why cases are always referred to as Rex/Regina vs the name of the defendant.

These suits could involve petitions where common law could not provide a remedy, or whichever remedy was available was inadequate. The suits were heard in the Chancellor's Court. However, by the time of Edward III, following the Roman manner, these petitions were addressed directly to the king.

Up until the time of Sir Thomas More, most chancellors had been churchmen. The general opinion was that ecclesiastics and clergy, having been trained in the tenets of civil law and being of the church, were the perfect people to hold that office. This was also because most people in authority believed that those who were not of the clergy did not have sufficient training, gravitas or courage to alter any of the rules if that became necessary. Shades of Becket and More, who stood up to their monarch and died for it.

All these precepts stemmed from the original Magna Carta, but, and it is an important but, most monarchs altered, added to, and subtracted from the Chancery Courts and canon law to make the legal system fit their purpose.[13]

A large part of the penitentiary laws – those that state the sinner must make amends for his crime and thus reform himself and save his soul – led directly to the building of prisons. Although prisons have not always been used for the purpose of reform, today their main raison d'être is that the punishment is the loss of freedom and, whilst the prisoner is incarcerated, every attempt is made to make him or her reform.

Tavern Talk:

The Tudor dynasty could easily have been the Meredith dynasty. Doesn't have quite the same ring, does it? The 'father' of the dynasty was Owen Tudor. In its Welsh form, Owen's name was Owen ap Maredudd ap Tewdwr. It is believed that as a young man he joined the household of Henry V as a servant. After Henry V's death from dysentery, his queen, Katherine of Valois, was sidelined in the upbringing of their baby son, Henry VI, by his father's brothers. Owen and Katherine fell in love, married and had children, all of whom were half-siblings to King Henry VI and one of whom, Edmund, became Henry VII's father.

The role of superstition in the justice system

In the twenty-first century the most pervasive element of our lives is the Internet and, leading from that, social media. The fact that some anonymous keyboard warrior can sit behind their keyboard spewing hatred and fakery has yet to be addressed effectively. These pronouncements uploaded to a publicly accessible platform feed the basic human instinct of fear for personal safety, whether that be on medical or legal issues or modern fables.

It is the speed with which rumours/news/warnings et al go global that is becoming an anxiety to authorities worldwide because this misinformation becomes a source of power to the originators, but that power is in the perception of those who believe it. Which is why certain national leaders could say the moon was made of green cheese and that would be believed. Anyone not believing it would be an enemy holding heretical views. Precisely the opinion held by mediaeval and Tudor monarchs.

Sin and crime became almost synonymous, and the emphasis on public humiliation, usually processing to church to voice penance, was a powerful weapon wielded by the church at every opportunity. The church fought superstitions by designating a saint or saints to each day of the year.

Sorry, have to digress here again. Whilst on the subject of saints, George has not always been the patron saint of England. He didn't come on the scene until the reign of Edward III in the fourteenth century. Before that, it was Edmund, king of the East Angles, who, in AD 869 clashed with a horde of Viking warriors at Thetford.

Legend has it that Edmund was offered the choice between dying or ruling as a Viking underling. He refused to be an underling and was tied to a tree before being beaten and killed. His body was then beheaded and the head thrown into a bramble bush.[1] This was possibly because his head would have issues escaping the bush because of all the thorns. How the head could escape at all when not attached to its body is a moot point.

Edmund – and presumably his head – was taken to what is now Bury St Edmunds, the name of which is self-explanatory. He was soon beatified and made the patron saint of England. His shrine was destroyed in 1539 during the dissolution of the monasteries.

Personally, I wish we could have kept him as our patron saint. Much more so than George, who was born in what is now Turkey, died in what is now Israel, was not a knight and never came to England. However, he was a Christian martyr, executed in the fourth century for refusing to worship pagan gods. And, I am really, really sorry, but the dragon bit is an invention.

People in the Middle Ages – and some now – believed in demons, evil spirits and witches. They believed witches could fly on broomsticks, make potions, and cause people to become ill. Witches were usually women – here we go back to Eve being the original temptress luring Adam into sin – and their familiars would be a black (naturally) cat or a raven, sometimes a toad.

Horses were believed to repel witches and thus the 'lucky' horseshoe came into being. However, it had to be a horseshoe that the horse had cast off naturally, and it had to be made of iron.

The other great influence on superstition was driven by the church, who even then had an eye towards profits rather than prophets. The church was very much into intimidating people into obedience whilst preying, and I use the word advisedly, on fears for their immortal souls. If you look at the gargoyles and demons over church doors today, it can be posited that they are there to make sure they take the rain away from the door, but they were called Hellmouths, beasts who would devour sinners at the day of judgement. A kind of 'obey our rules or this will happen to you' warning.[2]

Purgatory was believed to be the halfway house between the earth and heaven. It was where the soul went to expiate sins before being allowed into heaven. But, always with an eye to making money, clerics decreed that people could, for a price, donate money or goods to the church to enable their souls to transit Purgatory more quickly. One way for the very poor to do this would be to attend church regularly so that they could hear doom-laden preaching. Slightly richer people might give livestock or whatever few coins they possessed. The emerging middle classes would give silver or altar cloths, the wealthy would donate ornate altar pieces or a stained-glass window. Monarchs frequently built chantries.[3]

The whole edifice was to equate sin with transgression and crime. And nowhere in the history of England was it a greater mortal sin/crime to go against the rule of the monarch and the teaching of his/her church than in the Tudor era.

Money could also buy forgiveness and, were a person to be considering committing a sin, they could buy a pardon in advance of their action.

Certificates giving dead loved ones a faster route through Purgatory were also a common feature of the mediaeval church.[4]

Inside the church, walls were frequently painted with scenes of sinners being tortured while the 'good' people were seen on their way to heaven.

All these practices were aimed at making a profit as well as saving souls. For those who didn't believe or didn't care, or simply couldn't be bothered to get out of bed, there were fines to pay and if the transgressor persisted, the punishments would escalate.

The phrase 'walk of shame' might easily have originated in the Middle Ages for adulterers and drunkards. The former were forced to walk naked through the streets, the subject of ridicule and shame. Drunkards had to wear the Drunkards Cloak – a barrel with holes cut in it for the arms – and parade themselves through their neighbourhood. And we all know how successful these punishments were at stopping people from reoffending, don't we?

People believed that tolling certain bells would keep thunder and lightning away, that reading the gospel to sick cows would cure them, and that reading the gospels to a woman giving birth would ensure a healthy child. Holy water would be sprinkled on crops to make them grow. In this way, the church made sure its priests were the most important people in the life of the village/town/city and firmly in control of their parishes. If the people were under control, so was the crime rate. Allegedly.

The church was also very strict with its own people. There is a wonderful instance in 1315 of the local abbot who oversaw the nuns at Rosedale Priory in Yorkshire, admonishing them for giving too much money away to the poor and allowing puppies to play in the quire.[5]

Using astronomy and astrology to see portents of doom in the stars, advising when to go on journeys, get married or take medicine were common. One of the 'reasons' given for the allied victory in 1945 was because, although Hitler used astrology in 1940 to tell him when to invade Britain, he forgot to check England's stars, which were then in the ascendent.[6]

Every doctor in mediaeval times had 'charms' to help his patients and medication was usually accompanied by prayers. People believed that anything could happen outside the boundaries of their own parish. Allegedly, some people believed there was a place in Ireland where nobody ever died. The number thirteen was – and still is – thought to be unlucky because twelve was thought to be perfect. Twelve months, twelve apostles, twelve signs of the Zodiac. Conversely seven is thought to be lucky because it is used in the Bible as a symbol of completeness.

The role of superstition in the justice system

Seven years of bad luck for breaking a mirror also stems from the Middle Ages. It was believed that the reflection seen in the mirror was the person's soul. If the mirror was broken, the soul was separated from the body. All these superstitions were used by the church to control the people.

We must remember there were very few prisons at this point, so justice was instantaneous. It was also frequently driven by superstition. One example is trial by ordeal. This could involve the defendant being forced to grasp a red-hot iron bar, after which his hand would be wrapped in silk. If after several days the wound had festered, he was declared guilty. Fire was frequently used as a tool for trial by ordeal. The defendant might be forced to walk through red-hot coals a distance of approximately 9ft (2.7m). The feet would then be wrapped in silk as above and examined after a set period, usually around three days. If the wound was healing, it was believed that God had intervened to declare the innocence of the defendant. If it was festering, he or she faced exile or death.[7]

A famous legend is that Emma of Normandy, mother of Edward the Confessor, who, when accused of adultery with a bishop, walked over three red-hot ploughshares and emerged with no wounds to her feet, her innocence clear for all to witness.

Later on, human intervention ameliorated this type of punishment. The burn was frequently smothered in ointment before being wrapped in silk and if it was still raw the following day, more ointment would be applied so that by the time the silk was removed, the wound would either be healed or be healing. There was also no edict as to how hot the fire or iron bar had to be.

Ordeal by water meant the defendant being thrown into water. Water was thought to repel sin. If the culprit sank, he was declared not guilty. But there was no rule about how deep the water into which the alleged felon was thrown had to be, or how long they had to stay under water to prove their innocence. A quick ten seconds holding their breath and they might be dragged out and declared innocent.

Tavern Talk:
In Victorian times people kept locks of hair in lockets as mementoes. The Tudors put cauls – or birth membranes, rare in live births – in lockets, too. These allegedly gave protection against drowning, which was why sailors liked to get hold of them. Cauls were also supposed to give the holder 'second sight', which must have been a mixed blessing because anybody foretelling the future risked accusations of witchcraft.

The Power of the Press

The press, I hear you ask. What does the press have to do with a book on Tudor crime and punishment?

Today, we are used to the media in all its forms giving us information, disinformation, propaganda, rumours, and downright lies. It was the Tudor rulers and their councils, who realised the dissemination of information to the masses through the power of pamphlets that could be read to families and other gatherings, was a seriously good way of making sure the people were told what the monarchs wanted them to know.

The late, great Sir Terry Pratchett, in his book *The Truth* takes as his target the power of the press in its role of social engineering. Pratchett has as his protagonist William de Worde. One of the first printers in Tudor England was Wynkyn de Worde. At the beginning of the book, William is still using reversed writing to send out monthly newsletters to the other cities on the Disc. He ends up as editor of *The Times*, which uncovers a plot to depose the Patrician. However, by the very end of the book, not only are the paper's readers well versed in newspaperspeak and skilled in sound bites, they are also much more interested in strange-shaped vegetables than government scandals.[1]

Before 1520 there was a trickle of printed ballads and romances. By the end of the century that had turned into a torrent of pamphlets, broadsheets, letters, and dialogues. Demand was not created by the press but by people's insatiable appetite. Put that together with the low cost of these sheets and soon scandal, often stretched to unbelievable limits, was the order of the day.

One of the first current news publications was a pamphlet in 1513 detailing the English victory over the Scots at Flodden and the death of the Scottish king, James IV. This was followed by a much more detailed account, *The True Encounter*. Whilst it provided more details about the battle, it wasn't that accurate. What it did uncover was the human appetite for news, preferably with a human element. Tales of love, hate, trust and jealously had been around for centuries, recounted by troubadours, but at the beginning of the sixteenth century this was transferred to the page where it could be read by anyone to anyone.[2]

Traders and travellers passed on volumes of news via word of mouth. Alehouse keepers relied on that to enhance the quality of their trade: ale and scandal as you relax at the end of a hard day's work. This oral tradition fed demand for printed news.

As early as 1486 William Machlinia printed a broadsheet detailing the Papal bull from Innocent III which supported Henry VII's claim to the throne of England. Suddenly there was a new element for public curiosity – the lives of the royals. Pamphlets on royal events, such as the marriage of Prince Arthur to Katherine of Aragon, a copy of which lies in the Bodleian library, became useful propaganda tools. This particular publication has a woodcut of the royal pair, with attendants, in the act of being married by a bishop. It also has the word 'Remembrance' in the title, rather like today's royal events are usually marked by souvenir supplements slipped within the pages of the newspapers.

Wynkyn de Worde printed the funeral sermon given by Bishop John Fisher at Henry VII's funeral. It is a masterful sermon in that it concentrated, not on Henry's rapacious accumulation of wealth, often to the detriment of the lives of his ordinary citizens, or his determined secular view on life, but on his end-of-life repentance. Henry's will also majors on his fear of Purgatory and contains detailed orders of where and when masses are to be said for his soul.[3] The document printed by de Worde was intended to bolster the reputation of the dynasty Henry created in the hope that everyone would forget his actions of the previous twenty-four years. Henry recognised early the power of the written word disseminated throughout the country and used it to reinforce his right to the crown as much as anything else.

By the mid-1520s printed news was on the verge of thriving. At first books mainly concentrated on histories and religious writings, although printed ballads, broadsheets and pamphlets were becoming more regular. Before the death of Henry VIII in 1547, there was a demonstrable desire for 'newes' and 'tydings'.[4]

Initially, news pamphlets were intended to be read and discarded, but some became part of the historical record. Edward Hall was quick to see the advantages of these publications and historians still rely to a large extent on his chronicles.

Although only some of these ephemeral sheets were written in English, it was not until 1532 that the first report in the vernacular, detailing the visit by Henry VIII and Anne Boleyn to Calais to meet Francis I, was published. The account is meticulous, and, no doubt, because it aggrandised the importance of the king, Henry VIII would be happy for his subjects to read it. It goes into details about the clothes worn, the masques performed and the houses in which entertainments were staged, as well as details on the feasts, pastimes and other entertainments.

So great was the interest that Gough the printer was forced to publish a second edition. However, one part of Henry's plan did not come to fruition. Francis' queen, to whom Anne Boleyn had been a maid, refused to attend. This meant that Anne could not attend the meetings with Francis and was therefore not included in the report, although she is mentioned as the Marchioness of Pembroke attending one of the suppers.

Anne's coronation in 1533 produced another pamphlet and this led to national events being reported as a matter of course. By the 1550s broadsheets, etc. pandered to sensationalism, often accompanied by moralising. As far as Anne was concerned, it fed the public hatred of her for usurping the much-loved Queen Katherine.[5]

By contrast, in 1542 a single sheet pamphlet about an earthquake not far from Florence, describing houses being destroyed and people dying, emphasised God's mercy in sparing those who did not die, and linking the event to the Day of Judgement.

Although printed ballads became popular in Tudor England, only three prior to 1557 survive. The first is about the aforementioned Battle of Flodden in 1513, a second about 'Malicious Slanderers' in 1540, and a ballad about the defeat of the Cornish rebels in 1549.[6]

The arrest and martyrdom of Anne Askew in 1546, published in 1624, has its sources in contemporary ballads. Whilst very few survive, it seems clear that they played their part in raising the cognizance of events throughout England and changed social awareness of what was happening in the higher echelons of government – and not always to the honour of the monarchy. This was especially important because the laws regarding religious observance, for example, changed regularly. Ordinary people needed to know the latest information to ensure they did not accidentally transgress and find themselves – literally – in hot water.

It is as the religious see-saw swung ever faster from 1532 onwards that the press was used to keep everyone informed. The earliest known religious ballad survives in the library at Magdalene College, Cambridge, and deals with Martin Luther's writings vs The Pope's edicts.

Under Mary, the press was very vigorous and a large part of why she was so unpopular. By the time she married Philip of Spain, she had begun to burn heretics and these two events raised the spectre of press censorship, mainly because Mary was a fanatic. The more pragmatic Elizabeth was much more successful at managing the press.[7]

The power of the press came of age when items were published in English, the vernacular that ordinary people understood. Literate people would read 'the news' to their less literate friends and neighbours. Although some in high society considered vernacular English to be 'vulgar', Sir Thomas More opined that the people should have the scriptures translated into English. The 1543 statues forbade these scriptures being read to women, artificers, apprentices, journeymen and labourers among others.

The typical audience, especially for religious material, had no means of judging the veracity of what they read or was read to them. Whereas in the early days of the sixteenth century, the authorities had no clear realisation of how powerful the press could be – seeming to think it was merely a method of education – by the end, censorship was the order of the day.

The first attempt to restrict reading was when Luther's books and Tyndale's *New Testament* were publicly burned. A 1529 proclamation ordered everyone owning such heretical books to 'give them up to the ordinary', a church official.[8] It was largely ignored. The church and royal authorities collaborated to find these books and prosecute not just the owners but the printers. Some were burned for heresy. Tyndale himself fled to Antwerp but was betrayed and burned after being strangled.

Of course, by the time Henry VIII was well into his plan to divorce Katherine of Aragon, the press then became his means of spreading his version of the truth of the 'Great Matter'. Since some European universities supported his view, Henry used that to 'inform his loving subjects of the truth'. And he declared it to be high treason to write or print anything to 'the prejudice of the king, against his marriage with Queen Anne'.[9]

This set a pattern for the Tudor monarchs regarding the press. From the time of Henry's divorce and marriage to Anne Boleyn, he was fighting the press on two fronts, the Lutheran press on the one hand and the Roman Catholic press on the other. Edward VI had the same problem with his religious reforms, as did Mary and Elizabeth.

By 1546 Henry was on his last legs. He published *A Necessary Doctrine and Erudition For A Christian Man* and this was deemed the standard for religious orthodoxy in England. He ordered all banned books to be given up within forty days; the penalties for not doing so were fines and imprisonment. However, it was really a case of bolting the stable door after the horse was long gone. Printing of banned books moved to Europe and illicit imports flourished. Clandestine presses, often mobile, would move from place to place to avoid discovery. The government record of prosecutions was deplorable, their actions ineffectual.[10]

So when Mary came to the throne and tried to push the previous twenty-five years back into the genie bottle, she had already lost the battle. Lampoons about her were rife, especially when her marriage to Philip was in the offing. In preparation for his coming to England, Mary stepped up her attack on heretics – with disastrous results. Even her husband, whom she loved with a passion almost as fervent as her religion, could not persuade her to show mercy. Many Protestants moved to Europe, and once there unleashed masses of material that was smuggled into England.

Just at the time when the marriage negotiations were being discussed, Michael Wood in Rouen printed a 'violently Protestant' translation of Stephen Gardiner's *De Vera Obedientia*, written in 1535 supporting the annulment of Henry VIII's marriage to Mary's beloved mother. It emphasised the obedience of the individual within society, a wife's obedience to her husband and up the social scale to subjects' obedience to the king. This was a real embarrassment because by then the rabid Catholic Gardiner was the fanatical Mary's Lord Chancellor and a key player in the negotiations. This smuggled publication became more embarrassing because it arrived in England in December 1553 at the moment when anti-Spanish feelings about the marriage were at their height.[11]

Seditious writings could quickly morph into treason. Sir John Cheke, a statesman under Edward VI who had fled Mary's England, was arrested on the orders of Philip II. Cheke, not being of the stuff of martyrs, wrote to Mary agreeing to obey her laws. He was then released, but at best it was only a moral victory for the Marian authorities.

Some tracts, of course, were written solely to provoke the government. Anti-Spanish publications enraged Mary, but they were, in the main, published to let off steam and none revealed a solid plan to overthrow the queen. However, this did not appease her, and in 1554 she issued a proclamation that anyone found guilty of speeches or publications that 'slandered' her or Philip were to lose their right hands.

As is frequently the case today, none of these thunderous denunciations and proclamations made the slightest difference. In June 1558, five months before Elizabeth's accession, Mary's Council declared that the publisher/distributor of any heretical book imported or printed in England, would be prosecuted under martial law, the penalty for which was execution. This, too, proved to be a failure. Why? Because catching offenders was difficult and that, once caught, magistrates and juries were reluctant to convict. Many Londoners were sympathetic to the views expressed in such publications.[12]

And the zeitgeist must also be taken into account. News of Mary's false pregnancies and the rumour of an ovarian tumour, plus the fact that Philip had high-tailed it back to the continent, having found his wife 'no good from the point of view of fleshly sensuality' all pointed to the hope that 'their' Elizabeth would soon be queen.[13] Why would the authorities want to prosecute when the political winds of change were blowing?

One example of this reluctance suffices to give an accurate picture. *The Copye of A Letter Sent By John Bradforthe*, which libelled Philip, led to six arrests. The prisoners were held without trial for five months. Three were released upon payment of a £40 fine, one was indicted and pardoned, and the other two appear to have just been released.[14]

Even Elizabeth's Italian tutor, Baptist Castiglione, was arrested, but nothing could be proved against him. Not surprising when we take into account Elizabeth's precautions to avoid being in any way involved with anything that might risk her safety. And, no doubt, helped by the obvious interest shown in her by Philip, who thought he could still rule England by marrying her after Mary was dead. Philip's attraction to his sister-in-law was yet another burden the intensely jealous Mary had to bear.

Mary's only real weapon was to grant royal patents to certain printers who would publish material in support of her and against the heretics. However, that didn't work well either because the people were, almost daily, witnessing the wrath of the Roman Catholic queen against ordinary people and raising the menace of the Spanish Inquisition.

Part of the problem regarding censorship was that the responsibility for discovering and dealing with heretical and seditious writings was down to justices of the peace and constables, both unpaid posts. This led to them ignoring publications with which they agreed, something further aided by cumbersome government machinery.[15]

Many nobles and gentry who had made their fortunes under Henry VIII's Reformation stood to lose everything should Mary bring England back to the state it was in prior to 1530. This, plus the unpopularity of the queen and her Spanish husband, led to a certain indolence in prosecuting offenders against heresy and sedition.

Elizabeth learned much from the unrest during her half-sister's reign. Elizabeth was always sensitive to the mood of 'her people' and that became a self-fulfilling prophecy because she frequently stated that she was married to the people and loved them like her children. Her people, mostly, returned that love.

Censorship and propaganda were handled with care and delicacy under Lord Burghley and Francis Walsingham. By the time of Elizabeth's accession, Protestants could look forward to almost forty-five years in which to print and disseminate their literature mostly free from the threat of losing hands and heads or being burned. That said, John Stubbs and a bookseller called Page both had their hands severed because they had written and published a pamphlet against Elizabeth's proposed marriage to the Duke of Anjou.[16]

The Protestant press, supported by the clergy and able to take advantage of anti-Catholic feeling fed by the excesses of 'Bloody Mary', was little short of virulent, leading to centuries of discrimination against Catholics. Elizabeth was quite happy with this, until the presses began to publish extreme Protestant/Puritan literature and ideals, something with which she strongly disagreed but which was supported by leading figures in her Council, including Burghley, Walsingham and Leicester.

The Puritan press in particular was clever enough to make its publications and the demands contained in them at times when Parliament was called. One particular issue was that of religious vestments in 1566. Elizabeth liked her priests to wear vestments. The Puritans did not.

In the main, by the end of the sixteenth century, the majority of the press toed the established line. Authors now relied on backers rather than patrons to provide financial aid. This, in turn, led to a switch in literary patronage where printers and publishers became much more important to authors than patrons.

Tavern Talk:
We know Shakespeare invented phrases we use every day. Some were not invented by him. The word puking which he uses in As You Like It: Act II; Sc 7 is the first use of the word as a verb, but the word puke was in parlance before the Bard used it. He is also credited with the first use of premeditated. However, this word appears in John Bradford's A Frutefull Treatise in 1564, the year of Shakespeare's birth.

Prisons in England

Whereas in the twenty-first century we ponder the role and efficacy of imprisonment, the ruling classes in mediaeval England believed the system to be more than acceptable. And so did the Tudors.

In thirteenth-century London, sheriffs and mayors were granted discretionary powers regarding punishment. In 1444 a charter extended that power and sheriffs and mayors were made both guardians and justices of the peace, with the power to hear cases.[1]

Although the Tudor dynasty officially began in 1485, it was not until 1487 at the Battle of Stoke that the Wars of the Roses truly ended with the death of Richard III's designated heir. The conflict had affected so many aspects of the lives of citizens, it became an imperative part of government that authorities did all they could to avoid public confrontations. Public skirmishes had the potential to escalate into disorder and rioting.

If feelings were running high, curfews were quickly put into effect and these measures extended to inhibiting armed men from gathering in the streets. The king ordered that no prisoner could be released without the information being passed to the mayor or aldermen.

If any offences concerning assaults or breaches of the peace occurred, the location of the offence became important when trying and punishing the offender. If the offence took place close to anything resembling a site of civic authority, the punishment would be more severe.[2].

Whereas in early mediaeval England trial and punishment took place as soon after the offence as was possible because there were fewer prisons, in Tudor England, especially in Elizabeth's reign, people were usually imprisoned so that they could not abscond before their trial. This is still in force today with the remand system.

In Tudor England, serious cases such as murder, rape, arson, highway robbery, witchcraft and grand larceny (thefts of goods worth more than twelve pence), would have to wait for the next assize session. Judges from the Court of the King's/Queen's Bench or the Court of Common Pleas would arrive to try the cases of those already incarcerated. By Elizabeth's reign, there were only six circuits covering the whole of England and the judge responsible for each circuit had to visit all the counties contained within his remit. This often meant a long wait for prisoners' trials to be heard.

In London, sessions took place every quarter and it was not unusual for twenty or thirty people to be sentenced to death. On 21 February 1561, seventeen men and two women were found guilty, taken to the nearest execution ground and hanged. Three days later, another court session found eighteen men and two women guilty, whereupon they, too, were taken off to be executed.[3]

However, not everyone condemned to death actually suffered that fate. If the offender had friends in high places, those friends could, and did, use their influence to save the culprit. Others claimed Benefit of Clergy. Women, of course, could not claim that since there were no women priests. They were able to 'plead their belly' because pregnant women could not be executed. It was common for imprisoned women to try and get pregnant and hope that by the time the child was born they could slip through the net. Some are known to have had more than one child whilst in gaol.

Loopholes such as these enabled those facing execution to escape the rope. Given the sparsity of accurate records, a rough estimate would be twenty-four per cent of those facing serious offences were hanged, thirty-five per cent were acquitted, twenty-seven per cent claimed Benefit of Clergy, and six per cent claimed that they were pregnant. Claiming Benefit of Clergy meant anyone who could quote the required part of the fifty-first psalm in Latin was considered to be of the clergy and therefore exempt from execution. Usually verse three was chosen and came to be called the 'neck verse'.

Of those hanged, seventy-five per cent were found guilty of theft – either of food, horses, money or livestock – eighteen percent were found guilty of witchcraft and six per cent of murder. The remainder were made up of rapists, buggerers and sodomites, arsonists and housebreakers.[4]

Imprisonment was also the usual fate of debtors and they would stay in gaol until they, or a friend, paid the debt. The Fleet prison in London, built in 1197 close to the Fleet river, was known as a debtors' gaol and the place for those who awaited justice in the Courts of Chancery and the Star Chamber.[5] The Fleet was a horrendous place. There would be fifty men to a room with bare boards, no furniture or blankets and with many of their cellmates suffering from some disease.[6]

Although Bridewell began as a hospital, it soon became part of the justice system, its main purpose being to put an end to vagrancy.[7] Bridewell also bore the brunt of public insults. Bishop Ridley called it a 'truly religious house'. His opinion was not shared by one woman who called the governors 'murtherers'. Another called them 'crooked bawds who pooled picking from whores'.[8] In Bridewell, the master and governors had the power to proceed with punishments without reference to anybody.⁹ Shades of Oliver Twist! The governors took advantage of these powers to hunt for and arrest 'all ydell ruffians and taverne hunters, vagabonds, beggars and all persons of yll name and fame' in an area that covered London and its northern suburbs.

As far as records show, Bridewell became the only institution that was allowed to police, prosecute, and punish offenders without any reference to an outside authority. It was approved by royal seal but never sanctioned by an act of Parliament. As such its validity came increasingly under scrutiny as the sixteenth century progressed and many clerics and lawyers spoke out against it.[10]

The raison d'être for Bridewell was not punishment but redemption through work. Inmates were taught a trade and worked for a wage, which they used to pay for their meals. The whole ethos of Bridewell was to reduce vagrancy and begging. By 1579 inmates were making pins, silk, lace gloves, felts, tennis balls, and nails. The women were trained to spin wool or mend clothing. If they did not learn or refused to obey the rules, they were punished by whipping, dietary restrictions or torture.[11] Bridewell thus became England's first labour camp and its practices spread to Europe.[12]

Outside London was even more lawless. Despite Henry VII's strictures, many nobles still kept armed retinues. Gangs roamed the countryside, duels were fought on the slightest hint of an insult. In prisons, people were 'kept lying in filthy straw, worse than any dog'.

In London, in Shakespeare's time, there were around eighteen prisons, including the Tower of London, but Bridewell was excluded because it was not governed by the legal system. Newgate is probably the best known. It would contain debtors as well as felons and those awaiting execution. It was built in 1188 by Henry II and enlarged in 1236 by Henry III. Although it contained people awaiting execution, it was not that secure (Jack Sheppard, a burglar, escaped three times before he was hanged in 1724).

Southwark had more prisons than the City of London, including the Clink, which housed religious offenders. The Marshalsea also housed religious offenders, pirates, and debtors.

Of course, the Tower of London has a grisly history of being a place for prisoners of state. As late as 1952 it was used for this purpose and its prisoners included the Kray Twins, who failed to report for National Service.

Tavern Talk:
Of course, conditions in Tudor prisons were appalling, especially the sanitation – or lack of it! And it was a long time before that improved. However, Sir John Harington designed the first fully working, flushing loo for his godmother, Elizabeth I.

Population

There is some evidence that may suggest the population of England declined during the Wars of the Roses. But it would also appear that after the Battle of Tewkesbury in 1471, when the last perceived Lancastrian threat, Edward of Westminster, was killed on the battlefield, the population of England began to rise again.

Between about 1520 – eleven years after Henry VIII took the throne – and the year 1600 – three years before Elizabeth I died – the population doubled from about two million to about four million, although statistics are rare, and historians do not agree on the numbers. It is impossible to be specific about population growth, but it is likely that sustained growth in the population of England started in the early years of Henry VIII's reign. There were many factors that affected the accuracy of these statistics.[1]

Changes in how farming was organised and the social structures within villages were factors, as was the increasing urbanisation and number of industrial workers. Sadly, at that time there was no National Price Index and few statistics are available. However, grain markets in Exeter, Cambridge and Westminster indicate prices began to rise around 1515. Also, Exeter's cloth market links to Aquitaine helped the city to expand, while the London-centric trade links to Antwerp meant that former centres of industrial success such as Bristol, Hull and York declined.[2]

The wage rate was another central factor, and it is impossible to use this as an indication of population increase since the statistics that do exist are unreliable. So, for example, it is impossible to quote a wage rate for one particular agricultural occupation over a large enough geographical area to make any statistics meaningful.

Of the two million or so people in England in 1520, six per cent lived in 'urban areas', defined as towns of more than 4,000 people, while three per cent of the population lived in London.[3]

One of the reasons people flocked to the towns to find work was because of the enclosure laws. These became more frequent during the reign of Henry VII, and the main effect of enclosures was that, whereas the previous open-field system had provided work, enclosure meant that once a person could prove they owned the land, they could fence it off and do what they wanted with it. Those who could not prove ownership of land they had worked, possibly going back generations, were frequently evicted.[4]

The advantage of enclosure was that land began to be farmed more scientifically in the hope of feeding an increasing population. The disadvantage was that those people evicted generally moved to the towns in an effort to find work, which was not always available.

We must also take into account that enclosure did not begin with the Tudors. Problems finding workers as a result of plague and the Wars of the Roses had forced farmers to turn to pasture farming because looking after animals required fewer workers than working arable land. Enclosure has been confused with 'engrossing'. This term meant that several farms would be amalgamated for economic growth reasons. Engrossing did lead to more evictions.

One interesting piece of legislation was that the Isle of Wight was protected from enclosure because of fears that depopulation would mean it could not defend itself when it was considered to be of strategic importance because of its geographical location.[5]

According to Julian Cornwall, using figures from Oxfordshire which he regards as having 'been stated with some regard for accuracy', population growth was very slow until the middle of the sixteenth century. His estimate of the population of England by 1545 was around 2.8 million. An epidemic of influenza between 1556 and 1558 suggests a 'substantial reduction of the population'.[6]

And then we come to how statistics data regarding population were collected. In Rutland, for instance, despite 'stringent instructions', the majority of omissions in the data gathered in the 1520s related to the poorest members of society. Accurate data gathering was also made more difficult because some adult males in the same village or adjacent villages had the same name. Take into account that men travelled to find work, even though it might only be to the next parish, and it is impossible to say if the Thomas Watson who appeared in Empingham in 1524 was the same Thomas Watson who disappeared from Ryhall in 1522. There were also discrepancies, such as five out of seven labourers failing to appear on the subsidy rolls in 1525, or the same man appearing in the first and third roll but not the second.[7]

As with many aspects of mediaeval life, it is easier to follow the rich man than his poor neighbour. Another reason the richer inhabitants were included on lists was that they could be persuaded to make forced loans and pay subsidies to the government. Their appearance on later lists can probably be put down to their success in evading being put on the earlier lists.

Why is the foregoing at all important? Between 1455 and 1487 England was riven by the Wars of the Roses. This had resulted in many of the noble houses having armed retainers who would be called upon to fight for whichever side their lord supported. And, when you look at casualty numbers from the battles that made up this war, England lost a great number of men of working age. The battle of Towton in 1461, which was fought on a freezing Palm Sunday with constant snow showers, lasted for about ten hours. Known as the bloodiest battle ever fought on English soil, the number of dead has been posited at about 28,000.[8]

Once the paranoid Henry VII had won the throne of England, the last thing he needed was an aristocracy with the financial clout to raise militias. During the thirty years prior to Bosworth, nobles had used the factional strife to increase their own power and Henry could not allow that to continue.

He wasted no time in putting measures in place that would reduce the power of the nobility, whilst being aware he needed their cooperation in order to rule. To achieve this he did not use Edward IV's solution, which had been to play the 'support me and I will give you land' game. Instead, Henry used the carrot and stick method. He awarded some with positions in government and the Order of the Garter, both of which cost the Crown very little. To consolidate his control, he used acts of attainder, restrictions on livery and seized titles and possessions. His first foray into this was the backdating of his reign by one day so the land and title grab could begin immediately.[9]

Bonds and recognizances were simply another way to make nobles who had offended him pay fines. Similarly, if any noble's actions threatened public order, he would make them agree to pay a specific sum if they broke the conditions laid down. One estimate of noble families affected in this way was around forty-six out of sixty-two families. Thus the nobles were kept very firmly in their place and were treated very harshly if they transgressed.[10]

The result of this was that no member of the nobility could afford to retain an armed militia. This left many ex-retainers and ex-servicemen with no jobs, homes or money. Many of them became beggars and vagrants.

Tavern Talk:
People today often believe everyone in mediaeval and Tudor times was short. However, Edward I (1272-1306), known as Longshanks was approx. 6'2"; Richard II (1377-1399) was approx. 6'; Edward IV (1461-70 & 1471-83) was around 6'4" and his grandson, Henry VIII (1509-1547) was about 6'3". Mary, Queen of Scots was just under 6'. A survey of the skeletons from the Mary Rose indicates an average height of the sailors was 5'8" or 173cm.

Policing in Tudor England

When looking at the vexed subject of policing in Tudor England, the first point that needs making is that no formal police force existed, although in European cities there were paid mercenaries who travelled from city to city plying their own form of justice.

The second is that before you can organise an effective form of policing, a solid definition of what constitutes crime must be considered. Otherwise how can anything else – victims, detection, penalties et al – be determined or organised efficiently? Is the infringement an isolated incident or a series of incidents, such as a spate of burglaries or robberies. Burglaries are defined as entering a property with intent to steal goods, whereas robbery is threatening the person with violence and stealing from them.

In modern times any kind of mental issue is taken into account, as is the circumstance of the crime. For example, in the twenty-first century, stealing food because your children are hungry would incur a lesser sentence than stealing a pallet of lager to sell on. In Tudor times, no such difference was perceived or permitted (and, of course, lager did not exist in England at that time).

The legal system in the Tudor era was a hotch-potch of courts and differing practices, with people being treated differently based upon their location and social status. By the end of Elizabeth's reign, due in part to the efficiency of her Council, the legal system was on a surer footing than when her grandfather ascended the throne.

The highest court was the King's Court, divided into the Star Chamber and the Exchequer. The Star Chamber dealt with law enforcement against powerful people while the Exchequer dealt with financial transgressions against the king.

We know that Henry VII was a miser, interested solely in gathering and maintaining wealth to bolster his dynasty. His main advisors included Edmund Dudley and Richard Empson and he gave them free rein to do whatever they wanted so long as it enriched him. This would not only make it easier to fight any insurrections, but it also make his position as England's king and the Tudor dynasty appear to be extremely stable. One might assume that his courts only dealt with those who had enough social standing and wealth to be a potential threat to him, but this was not so at all. One example suffices to explain not just his underhand practices but also his hypocrisy.

In 1507, Thomas Sunnyff, a wealthy and respectable citizen, was falsely accused, along with his wife, of murdering a newborn child and disposing of the body in the Thames. This rumour started with a servant of Edmund Dudley (father of John Dudley, Duke of Northumberland, executed by Mary in 1553, and grandfather of Robert Dudley, Earl of Leicester). Dudley, along with his cohort Richard Empson, and with the knowing connivance of the king, not only jailed Sunnyff and his wife but fined them and then broke into their house and confiscated items to the worth of the fine, grossly undervaluing each item. Sunnyff, put under intense intimidation whilst in prison, finally caved in and signed the agreement to the fine, but later on, Dudley once more had him carted off to the Tower and incarcerated.[1] Henry was not in the least bothered about finding the truth, only about grabbing more money. Penn points out that the king probably knew Sunnyff was innocent. Which makes his action the year before when he believed himself to be at death's door and insisted on paying the debts of people in prison to guarantee the wellbeing of his soul even more hypocritical.

The second tier of the court system was the ecclesiastical courts. They focused on social control through people's fears for their souls' journey through Purgatory after death. Ecclesiastical courts sat in various dioceses. The London, York and Canterbury courts majored on the belief that sin was everywhere and needed judicial public punishment. Of the 287 cases, twenty-five per cent were related to matrimonial issues. The ecclesiastical court in Bangor also concerned itself with 'moulding behaviour' and many of the cases it heard related to promiscuity. By contrast, the court at Lichfield dealt with many cases of fornication and adultery and concentrated on public punishment that would make the sinner think twice before transgressing again.[2]

The local – or leet – courts, some of which still exist in terms of land permissions, might be held at the local manor house and so were also referred to as manor courts. They controlled social and commercial issues where local citizens could attempt to resolve problems and obtain redress. That said, the rich and influential expected preferential treatment. Town mayors swore an oath to 'do every man right', which did not mean treating every man fairly. The leet courts dealt mostly with public nuisance problems, breaches of the peace, failing to maintain fences, etc.

Before appearing at a leet court, all kinds of measures would have been attempted in an effort to solve the problem. These could include the defendant being bound over, or shunned by the locals, or being 'spoken to' by the priest.[3]

Should these measures fail, an indictment would bring the offender before the court. If convicted, punishments were deliberately designed to maximise public shame and terrify the locals. The convicted person would be paraded through the streets to the accompaniment of music before actually being placed in the pillory. Low-class women or women who gossiped were punished with the scold's bridle, a kind of iron helmet with a metal tongue guard which would pierce the tongue should the unfortunate person wearing it move her tongue. Public punishments were such a humiliating event in an era when a man's social standing was paramount. That said, it is a wonder offenders did not settle their arguments before being brought to court, because many, knowing what lay in store for them, committed suicide rather than settle their dispute. Does this indicate that they would rather die than say they had done something they hadn't?

Until the Puritan element gained a foothold in late Elizabethan England, crimes such as theft and treason were not regarded as equal in terms of criminal behaviour. Petty crimes such as some thefts, drunkenness, fighting etc., were considered by the population as 'real crimes' because they affected the common man more than the higher-class crime of treason. Petty crimes were also more prevalent; for example, there were far more instances of drinking offences, defaulting on working on the highways, and theft, than murder and treason.[4]

A kind of expanded system of law and order, not solely dependent on the church, developed during the sixteenth century. By the time Shakespeare wrote *Much Ado About Nothing*, there was a solid hierarchy, although most posts were unpaid, which left the system open to corruption and people being chosen because they volunteered, not because they were efficient. And because Shakespeare's audiences would understand all the in-jokes, one only has to look at the scenes with Dogberry to understand the disrespect with which the parish constables/beadles/watchmen were regarded.[5]

By 1500 the feudal system was in decline and parishes were used by central government to organise the judicial system in each county. Parishes originated as part of the church, and since the church courts were responsible in the main for the English judicial system, they were the logical starting point for the reorganisation of it. Successive Tudor governments expanded the responsibilities and powers of parishes and the officers appointed in them.

By 1555 parishes were also responsible for the upkeep of roads, and in 1601 the new Elizabethan Poor Law, designed to alleviate poverty from a series of disastrous harvests, gave each parish the duty of looking after its poor. This latter responsibility was administered by overseers appointed by the local JP.[6]

There were several levels of the court system. Petty sessions, quarter sessions and assizes all dealt with different types of crime as the suspects moved up the system dependent upon the crime of which they were accused.

Arguably the most important official in the system was the justice of the peace. JPs originated in the fourteenth century as an experiment. There were many teething problems, but by the end of the fifteenth century the system worked more smoothly, and JPs took their rightful place, not just in a legal sense but also as a person who was responsible for administering other things within their county.[7]

JPs could interrogate witnesses and suspects to discover if there was a case to answer or if it was just an argument that had festered too long. They had the power to bind over felons to keep the peace and mediate in disputes between a master and his servants or apprentices. If a soldier sold his horse and weapons without leave, the JP could imprison him. Ditto with poachers, although many counties specified that poaching was only a felony if carried out at night.

Should county court suits be referred to the JP, he had the power to pronounce on them. He could jail people who were spreading false and malicious rumours. (A Tudor JP would have a field day with the twenty-first century press in that regard.)

The strict definition of a recusant is a person who refuses to submit to an authority or to comply with a regulation. However, between 1570 and 1790 the definition was amended to include a Roman Catholic who refused to attend Church of England services. This also came under the aegis of a JP and could be made subject to a binding order. He had the power to regulate the sale of corn and production of malt when food was scarce, usually because of bad harvests, of which there were many at the end of the sixteenth century.

If two JPs joined forces, their powers were very much greater. Should a felon attempt the intimidation or bribe of a judge or member of a jury, the JPs could investigate, interrogate and, if necessary, detain that person for three days. This also applied to embracery, which is not, as one might imagine, someone running around giving people unwanted hugs, but trying to corrupt a judge or jury. Two JPs working together could regulate beggars, vagrants, weights and measures, pedlars, tax evaders and also grant licences to alehouses. They were empowered to determine paternity cases and order maintenance to be paid as well as assessing fines and dealing with statistics on robbery rates. Any serious crimes were passed upwards to the assizes, but the early parts of the investigation would be carried out by the JPs.

In theory, JPs were appointed by the monarch via the Lord Chancellor. In practice, it was usual for them to be chosen by people who held office in that county. Those nominated were normally charged the sum of £20 for the privilege although the post itself was unpaid. They also had to be freeholders (hold the freehold for a piece of land, which, on their death would usually be passed to their heirs). However, as the sixteenth century progressed, this became an issue because people of local standing, who owned land and had sufficient wealth and influence, could also pose a threat to the throne.

The post of coroner – originally called crowner – dates back to the late twelfth century. The first crowners were tax gatherers and only gradually developed into independent officers whose sole aim, via an inquest, is to determine how a person met their death.

After the Norman Conquest, feelings against the invaders were high. It was not uncommon for bodies to be 'left' where they were killed, and since these victims were assumed to be Normans, communities were made to pay a hefty fine, known as a murdrum, from which we have the term murder. The early inquests were dealt with as 'Presumption of Normanry' and it was up to the community in whose parish the body had been discovered to prove 'Presentment of Englishry' if they wanted to avoid the fine.[8]

High Constables, also known as chief constables, date back to the late thirteenth century. Their responsibilities usually related to maintaining the watch in towns and monitoring the removal of vagabonds. However, their most important function was to act as a link between JPs and the parish constables. They also reported to the quarter session courts and assizes regarding grievances and abuses in the local area.

During the sixteenth century high constables were normally made up of minor gentry or wealthy people. Their employment or dismissal was different from the parish constables in that they were normally appointed by JPs and sacked by the local community. The choice of some JPs was most unwelcome to the recipient. One such, Robert Mote, refused to take up his position and refused to be sworn in, showing 'contempt and obstinacy'.[9]

Although initially there was no statutory limit for the term they served, some counties restricted their time in office. For example, by the end of Elizabeth's reign, high constables in Yorkshire were limited to three years in office.

The role needed an energetic incumbent because it involved a fair bit of travel, and it was time consuming. Although they did not normally involve themselves in what was considered to be the duties of the parish constable, their responsibilities occasionally overlapped. In January 1591 Richard Gosling, a high constable from Essex, accused three men from Stowe of assaulting him, claiming they had hit him on the head with a pitchfork, even though he warned them who and what he was.[10]

They were also responsible for punishing parish constables for refusing to obey orders, one such being Thomas Owghan of Burnham who refused to arrest a vagrant, claiming he didn't have the necessary warrant. A warrant for this offence was unnecessary, and the vagrant eventually spent time in the stocks, whereupon Owghan kept releasing him.[11]

The parish constables, or beadles, whichever the particular parish chose to call them, had a day job. They were usually tradesmen or farmers. The post was, unsurprisingly, unpaid, but was arguably the most onerous of the entire structure because they were at the sharp end of policing and the duties were arduous. If a parish was blessed with a dynamic man who was also efficient – probably why tradesmen were chosen because they had to be efficient to run their own businesses – that parish was indeed fortunate.

Parish constables were responsible for the day-to-day maintenance of order within their remit: making sure alehouses and inns adhered to the rules; returning transgressors, including illegitimate children, to their original parish; impounding stray farm animals; arresting criminals; crime prevention; punishing some transgressors such as vagabonds, and keeping a watchful eye on apprentices who were known to be rowdy were among their many responsibilities.

The role of parish constable could be, as is the job of police officers today, dangerous, life-changing, or even life-threatening. In 1554 a baker in Westminster stabbed and killed Robert Hill who was observing a house thought to be disorderly. If a parish constable thought things were going to become dangerous, he had the power to recruit able-bodied villagers to help him, or, if it became necessary, he could demand help from passers-by. But though failing to assist was an offence under common law, such assistance was not always given.

Watchmen were sometimes called bellmen or waits (street singers) because they either rang bells to denote the night hours or sang them as they patrolled the parish. The Watch was an arm of law enforcement first brought to fruition by Edward I under the Statute of Winchester in 1285. The post was – you guessed it – unpaid. People were expected to volunteer, although wealthier neighbourhoods would pay for the men who patrolled their areas. This meant that the onus was put on households to organise their own security and meant the watchmen had few parish responsibilities. These came later with the constables.

By the beginning of the sixteenth century, watchmen patrolled every night. They would keep a lookout for felons and fires, give a helping hand to the drunks to get home, and wake up people who had an early start to their working day. Imagine the scene. It is pitch dark and you are deep in sleep and suddenly under your window comes the shout or song, 'Three o' clock and all's well'. They also sometimes gave listeners the weather forecast. Imagine the scene: you are trying to sleep and some idiot yells 'Two o' clock and it's chucking it down'.

The Justice of the Peace Act in 1361 ordered that every county should have keepers of the peace with powers to quell rioters and other offenders and jail them. These people morphed into magistrates. Over the next couple of hundred years, magistrates became the first kind of local government administrators. They were responsible for the maintenance of infrastructure and transport, functions that would, in time, be allocated to elected local authorities.[12]

Magistrates were responsible for the implementation of The Statute of Artificers, passed by Parliament in 1563. It sought to fix prices, impose a minimum wage and also restrict the freedom of movement for workers. It was introduced because there were long-term labour shortages due to epidemics as well as poverty and social unrest.

Local magistrates were responsible for regulating wages in rural areas while the guilds did the same for urban areas. The aim of such legislation was to make sure there were enough men – and women – who would think of agriculture as a trade, because poverty was driving people away from the countryside in droves. Because of this, there were fewer and fewer people working the land and that led to shortages and higher prices. Bad harvests and appalling working conditions made people believe moving to the towns would give them a better standard of living.

JPs required any unemployed artificers – skilled craftsmen – to work the land. Any workman wanting to transfer from one employer to another was required to gain official permission and the magistrates could fix wage rates for more or less every class of worker. The wages would be assessed annually, based on 'the plenty or the scarcity of the time'. And if employers and workers mutually agreed a wage above that set by the magistrates, they could be imprisoned.[13]

Punishments

Punishments is the section where the reader winces and turns the page, reads with a pained expression, or rubs their hands and says this is more like it ...

In twenty-first century Britain, we name and shame via Facebook, Twitter, et al. However, in Tudor times the church had as much input regarding punishments for lawbreakers as it had enjoyed in mediaeval times. Although there was an element of 'an eye for an eye' when it came to retribution, this was by no means the whole story.

Which is where we come to marketplaces.[1] It has long been asserted that the marketplace was of the utmost importance in the life of the community, be that a village, town or city. Some scholars have argued that it was second only to the family in forming and spreading social and cultural behaviours and beliefs. If one looks at the size of the mediaeval market places still in use, such as the one in Norwich, one gets the idea of how important it was to the life of the settlement and inhabitants. Often if the catchment area was not big enough to bring in sufficient revenue, the market vanished. At times, the rights of the market replaced those of the church as the central focus of the community.[2]

A trip to the market became a social occasion as well as a necessity. It provided a good place to see and be seen. Henry of Lancaster in his *Le Livre de seyntz medecines* ridiculed women who dressed up to visit the market more than they did to go to church. One bishop of Lincoln, admonishing monks who talked too much, complained that they 'chatter as though they were at market.'[3]

Successive monarchs used market days to issue proclamations to their subjects and spread necessary information. This became especially important during the Wars of the Roses when there was so much unrest. These proclamations also garnered support for whichever side happened to be in the ascendant at the time.

From a distance of some 500 years, the Tudor forms of judicial penalties are perceived as unremittingly harsh and inhumane. However, this is not always the case. It very much depended upon where in England the crime had occurred, who was being tried, and society's view of it.

Punishments

Of course, the most complete records we have are those involving the higher courts and the monarch. And many of those will involve crimes such as treason, heresy or insurrection, all of which garnered truly awful retribution. However, for lesser crimes, there was a degree of mercy.

The Tudor monarchs followed the custom of marketplace proclamations. The antiquarian John Hooker described how proclamations in Exeter were enacted in Elizabeth's reign. The mayor, accompanied by aldermen, four serjeants and the municipal sword bearer holding his sword aloft, would process into the marketplace. One of the serjeants would shout 'Oyez!' four times and wait for silence to fall. When it did, he would recite the proclamation, being prompted by a clerk, if necessary. Similarly, in London in the 1530s, the sheriffs wore their scarlet robes and used trumpet fanfares to initiate their proclamations.[4]

It is not surprising then that the marketplace should also be the hub of some punishments. Although we tend to view sentences for mediaeval and Tudor offenders as usually painful – and some were, of course – it was more usual to humiliate the offender publicly in front of his peers. In most towns and rural centres, offenders singled out for public shame were generally sentenced to perform some kind of humiliating exercise in the marketplace. This was at a time when public respect was an essential part of the Tudor psyche, so anything that mortified and chastened was deeply humbling.[5]

Marketplace punishments frequently utilised restraining devices such as the stocks or the pillory. Thews – a simple form of neck ring attached to a post – were mainly used to punish women. Dung carts, though physically less restrictive but infinitely more malodourous, were also used, and if the offender was being whipped, they might be tied to the back of such a cart.

None of these punishments were meant to cause excessive pain, only shame. The shame was that the offender was exposed and powerless in front of his family, friends and neighbours. However – you knew there would be a however, didn't you? – depending on the public opinion of not just the crime but the perpetrator, there was also the threat of physical retribution. In later centuries when the stocks etc. were used to punish paedophiles and homosexuals, public exposure was not only dangerous but could be deadly.[6]

The crimes for which marketplace restraining devices were imposed included theft, prostitution, defamation, forgery, scolding, faulty goods and sharp trading practices. The latter was mostly related to foodstuffs, usually bread. Since bread was the staple food of most people, this was considered a heinous offence. However, it was not unknown for some Tudor courts to make the punishment fit the crime. A tavern keeper found selling putrid wine would be tied to a stake, surrounded by minstrels to attract a crowd, and have his offensive wine poured over his head. Fishmongers, known for freshening up fish that was way beyond safe eating, or butchers who tried to sell rotten meat, would end up in the stocks with their stinking wares burned beneath their noses, something so unbelievably foul-smelling it would attract the abuse of stall-holders and public alike, not to mention dogs and probably rats.

A gongfarmer, or street cleaner, who dumped filth in the streets could be sentenced to stand knee-deep in a barrel of excrement with a mitre on his head declaring his crime.[7]

In 1552 a man and woman found guilty of smuggling pigs from the countryside into London were sentenced to ride through the city with a carcass around their necks and a garland of pig toes on their heads. A year earlier, a Southwark cardsharp was condemned to ride backwards on a horse to musical accompaniment 'with his coat pricked full of playing cards on every side'.[8]

First the most horrific punishments

Beheading

This is exactly what it says on the tin. The head of the offender is removed. However, the devil being in the detail reveals it is much more. Admittedly quicker than the mediaeval way of hanging, there is a level of butchery and suffering (depending on the skill or otherwise of the executioner). Research also questions whether those whose executions were 'botched' suffered less than those who had a 'clean' beheading, as we will see shortly.[9]

As with all those condemned to death, the worst part of the whole process, whether the victim be innocent or guilty, is the waiting. I make no apology for the following account, mainly because Anne Boleyn captured my interest at the age of fourteen. What was more intriguing for me was that my father – not the most imaginative man on the planet, bless his heart – took one look at Holbein's pencil sketch of Anne and declared that it looked like me.

Anne has always been a heroine of mine: strong, courageous, ambitious and outspoken. That last attribute contributed greatly to her downfall. And although many people see Jane Seymour as pious, malleable and the perfect picture of womanhood, what it took Anne six years to achieve took Jane six weeks. Anne was executed on 19 May and Jane was queen by 30 May.

Punishments

January 1536 was a momentous month for the Tudors. Anne was about three months pregnant. Katherine of Aragon died on 7 January. Henry had a jousting accident that left him unconscious for two hours on 29 January. Anne, always extremely anxious and highly strung, frantic with worry about the king, promptly miscarried her fifteen-week male child. Henry had already been dallying with Jane Seymour, something that Anne, unlike Katherine, could not ignore. It was the beginning of the end for Anne.

Now that Katherine was dead and Anne had yet again failed to birth a live son, Henry felt free to accuse her of seducing him by witchcraft. After all, he could no longer be forced to return to his first wife, could he? Anne's enemies, of which there were many, saw an opportunity for gaining power using Jane, and she, unlike Anne, was more than happy to be used.

In political terms it was also good for Henry. With Anne out of the way, he could once again make Mary his heir – until the new wife delivered a boy, of course – and that would mean he could regain good relations with Emperor Charles V, Katherine of Aragon's nephew. This would result in less reliance on French goodwill. Thomas Cromwell was also working towards a reconciliation with the emperor.[10]

And then the ever-jittery Anne made a fatal mistake. She accused Henry Norris, one of Henry's closest friends. of wanting to marry her after the king's death.[11] Cromwell seized his chance. He knew he would have to gather up several of the gentlemen around Anne to ensure there was no counter-attack. This group included her brother, George. Anne was arrested on 2 May. The rest was a foregone conclusion. She begged for Cranmer to hear her last confession. He was, allegedly busy, but it can be assumed that he found time eventually, and he certainly wrote to Henry in a carefully worded letter that could be read as him believing Anne to be innocent.[12]

Imagine the scene. It is early morning on 18 May 1536. Anne Boleyn has been told she will die that day. However, Thomas Cromwell, fearing that 'strangers' (meaning foreigners) might send back reports to their countries that put Anne in a positive light, orders that the Tower of London should be cleared of them and the execution delayed until this has been done.

Anne must have been distraught, telling Sir William Kingston, the Constable of the Tower, that she was very sorry because she had hoped to be 'dead and past my pain.'

It has recently been discovered in a Tudor Warrant Book how minutely Henry VIII planned the murder of his grandest passion, whose only failure was that she had not given birth to a live son. Five men, including Anne's own brother, had already been executed, accused of being her lovers. Her father had abandoned her, perhaps understandably thinking more about his own skin than of his son and daughter. Henry planned her execution down to the last detail, showing how magnanimous he was because he had been 'moved by pity' but that 'the head of the same Anne ... must be cut off.'[13]

It seems clear from correspondence between Cromwell and Kingston that they wanted to avoid any kind of dissent among spectators at Anne's execution, but they also needed to have enough people present to see that justice was done – and done well.[14]

Kingston told Anne her execution would take place at noon on 18 May. However, this delay allowed news of the execution to leak out. About 1,000 people found out about it and decided to be present.

When noon came and went, Anne's mental torture must have been extreme. Chapuys, the Spanish ambassador, had a spy at the Tower who said that Anne had asked Kingston to beg Henry 'that since she was in a good state and disposed for death, she might be dispatched immediately'. However, Kingston was powerless. The execution was rescheduled for early the next morning, 19 May.

That evening, Henry, obviously in a good mood now one wife was dead and the other about to be, rowed to Chelsea to visit Jane Seymour, who apparently already behaved as if she were queen. Agnes Strickland, the Victorian writer thought Jane's conduct was 'shameless' in that she passively accepted the addresses of her late mistress's husband, seemingly without any conscience, colluded in the trumped-up charges against Anne and witnessed the latter's anguish without a qualm.[15] Which, in all fairness, was exactly what Anne had done a decade earlier.

Obviously, Henry's difficulties in attempting to get the equally strong-minded Katherine to step aside hardened his resolve on a quicker resolution to the problem of his second wife.

However, back to Anne in her cell in the Tower. It is the night of 18/19 May. Anne does not sleep (there's a surprise). I don't think anyone could possibly say how they would react in a similar situation.

There is a story told by the historian John Speed, born around 1552 and allegedly told to him by 'a nobleman', that Anne jested she would be called 'la Royne Anne Sans Tete' – Queen Anne without a head. She also apparently called Lady Kingston into her cell and 'beseeched her as in the presence of God and His angels ... that she would so fall down before the Lady Mary's Grace and ... ask forgiveness for the wrongs she had done her.'[16]

Although we cannot now confirm that story, Speed was known as a respected historian. Perhaps Anne hoped that by saying this she would persuade Mary to take her tiny half-sister, Elizabeth, then not quite three years old, under her wing and look after her. What is known is that Lady Kingston visited Mary at Hunsden about a week after Anne's execution, but that proves nothing, and the story must remain apocryphal.

At around 7am on 19 May, Anne heard Mass and received the sacrament. Kingston came for her at around 8am. Her hair was collected up under a 'netted coif' and over that she wore a gable hood. Descriptions of her gown differ from black damask to grey damask trimmed with fur over a red kirtle with a low neckline. If she wore ermine, as described, she would be demonstrating her royal status and the red of her kirtle was the colour of martyrdom. Mary, Queen of Scots wore the same colour at her execution in Fotheringhay in 1587. Rather like the audiences at Shakespeare's plays some fifty years later, who understood all the in-jokes and references, the colours Anne wore would be understood by all. Even her most ardent enemy, Chapuys, declared that Anne was 'braver than a lion'.[17]

There are other apocryphal tales, one of which is that Anne asked a member of her privy chamber to tell the king he had raised her from a gentlewoman to the crown of a queen and now he was raising her to the crown of martyrdom. Needless to say, were this to be true, nobody would have been reckless enough to say it to Henry.

There is a rather lovely glass monument on Tower Green where people were allegedly executed, but Anne's scaffold was almost certainly constructed between the White Tower and the current Waterloo Barracks. The scaffold was draped with black cloth covered with straw. On it stood the executioner, the swordsman sent for from France. He was not dressed like an executioner and he had hidden his sword.

This last detail is strange, since we know Henry was determined on Anne's destruction, allegedly believing all the tales about her adultery, etc. If he believed she was such a heinous criminal, why would he go out of his way to make sure she suffered as little torment and pain as was feasible? This author believes that of all the people Henry executed, he regretted at least two: one was Anne, the other Thomas Cromwell.

There are various accounts of what Anne said on the scaffold, but it is almost certain she commended the king's grace as being a noble and gentle prince, if only to try and protect her daughter. However, she did not confess her guilt, and since there was no chance of a reprieve, why would she want to go to God with the stain of a lie on her soul? Yet another indication that she was innocent?

She undressed to ensure her neck was uncovered, took off her headdress and put on a linen cap so that her hair was out of the way. She was then blindfolded and knelt down. According to Eric Ives, some spectators were amazed she was not bound in any way. Her final words were to ask God to have pity on her soul and commending it to Christ.[18]

At this point, the executioner seized his sword. It probably had a long, leather-bound handle so that it could be gripped by two hands. The executioner's assistant had been told to distract Anne into looking to one side of her while the executioner wielded the sword from her other side, and with one fast sweep beheaded her.[19]

Witnesses were horrified to see that Anne's lips and eyes were still moving when her head hit the straw. She may even have been able to see her body lying a distance away. A white cloth was thrown over her head and a signal was then given, at which point the Tower Wharf cannons were fired to announce that Anne was dead.

No provision had been made for a coffin. She was wrapped up by her ladies and laid in an elm box that had contained bows. Anne was buried near the altar in St Peter ad Vincula, about 20m or so from where she died. Less than six years later, her cousin, Katherine Howard, would join her.

Tavern Talk:
Everyone knows Henry VIII had six wives. Strictly speaking, he married six times, but three of those marriages were annulled. His first to Katherine of Aragon was annulled because she had been married to Henry's elder brother. His second to Anne Boleyn was annulled because she had seduced him with witchcraft and committed adultery, and his fourth because Henry claimed he had never consummated the marriage. So, speaking pedantically, he actually only had three wives.

Those who don't like gory details might want to stop reading here.

There has been quite a bit of research into how long it takes a decapitated person to actually die. A 2011 study on decapitation in rats, both awake and anaesthetized, showed that in the awake group, brain activity was still apparent after fifty seconds. However older studies carried out on human victims have put the time of death at about thirteen seconds.

During the French Revolution, the executioner held up the head of Charlotte Corday, slapped it, and a look of anger allegedly passed over her face. The cause of death is, of course, the severance of the spinal cord, but that does not stop oxygen from reaching the brain until the massive blood loss stops any further consciousness. Neither do the brain's neurotransmitters stop working immediately.

Punishments

In 1905, French doctor Dr Beaurieux examined the newly decapitated head of Henri Languille. He later said the eyelids and lips moved for five or six seconds. He waited until all movement had ceased and the face had relaxed before shouting Languille's name, at which point, the man's eyelids lifted, his eyes focused on the doctor and glared at him. He shouted again and obtained a similar response. The third time the doctor called Languille's name, there was no response. Beaurieux estimated the time at twenty-five to thirty seconds before all movement ceased.[20] If you take a stop-watch and time thirty seconds, while looking around you and taking note of your surroundings, it is easy to imagine the horror of the victim, knowing they are dead but have not yet died.

In 1989, an army veteran related that a friend who had been decapitated in a car accident had looked at first terrified and shocked, and then stared back at his body, grief-stricken.[21]

The plain truth is that although the head has been smitten from its body, neurotransmitters in the brain will still be firing. Once the spine is severed, it is believed that no pain can be felt, but a 1983 study stated that no matter how efficiently the execution was carried out, there was at least two to three seconds of intense pain.[22]

Now we can return to the efficiency of executioners and whether some victims suffered more than others. Not all decapitated victims showed a reaction to stimuli. Perhaps the blow that severed their heads knocked them unconscious, or, if the execution was 'botched', that too might have induced oblivion. We can only hope so. Sadly, this does not seem to have happened in Anne's case, possibly because of the very swift and efficient action of the headsman and the razor-sharp blade of his sword.

Boiling to Death

Boiling to death was not often used in Tudor England to be fair, although it was the designated punishment for coiners on the continent. The method is self-explanatory. The offender would be put into a large container which might be filled with water, oil, molten lead, wax or sometimes wine, heated to boiling point.

The most famous victim was Richard Roose, cook to the Bishop of Rochester, John Fisher. It was established that Roose had decided to poison his master and guests by serving them pottage for dinner. Fisher was known to be abstemious and did not partake of the pottage, and nobody can blame him since it sounds less than appetising.

Pottage was a kind of thick porridge that peasants relied on for centuries as a staple food. For them, it would consist of grains and vegetables, boiled in a pot and often kept simmering for hours or days to make sure it was safe to eat. If rich households ate it, often meat or fish was added, but if you can imagine a kind of hearty soup full of heaven knows what that has been boiled to extinction, you have an idea of what pottage was like.

This case became something of a political 'hot potato' (even though nobody had yet encountered one in 1531 in England). Sixteen of Fisher's guests became ill, one of them, a man called Curwen, died. The rest of the poisoned pottage was given to the poor, at which point Alice Trypptt also died from eating it.[23]

Bishop Fisher had been Margaret Beaufort's confessor and it was he who had taught the young Henry VIII the tenets of theology. However, and here is the political bit, at the time Roose conducted his 'jest', thinking the powder he had put in the pottage was a laxative that would make his fellow servants ill, Bishop Fisher was a vocal opponent of Henry VIII's marriage to Anne Boleyn. Moreover, there were rumours that the Boleyn family had engineered the poisoning. Obviously they all liked pottage.

The Spanish ambassador, Chapuys, and Thomas More, neither of whom were sympathetic to Anne, told Henry of the rumours accusing her, to which Henry is alleged to have answered that she was blamed for everything.[24]

Henry decided he must act with speed to make sure any such rumour was quashed and that neither his beloved's character nor her family were sullied (a bit of a non-starter since she was already known as the 'goggle-eyed whore' by the majority of the population who adored Katherine of Aragon).

Back to Henry. He immediately told Parliament he wanted a bill passing that any servant found guilty of poisoning or attempting to poison their master or mistress should be attainted for high treason and executed.[25]

Henry was quite clever in some ways. Because he made the crime one of high treason, it meant there was no need for prior judicial process or a jury to determine the guilt or otherwise of the defendant. This was not to be the first time Henry dispensed with the tenets of common law.

The disadvantage of doing this was that because under common law Roose was a felon, Henry raised the status of Bishop Fisher – the alleged victim – to that of royalty just at the time when Fisher was castigating him for consorting with Anne. However, Parliament obeyed, the 'Acte for Poysoning' was passed and the punishment was death by boiling.

This was a largely unknown punishment in England, but probably Henry wanted a symbolic gesture to make sure that nobody ever transgressed this law again.[26] He failed on that one as we shall see later. However, what Henry's action did prove was that he could now use this case as a precedent to quickly get rid of anyone he felt was a threat, without recourse to due process under common law. And Roose's attainder was the first of many in the 1530s.

On 5 April, Roose was tied to a rope and pulley and then dipped in and out of boiling water. His suffering was accompanied by a 'lot of yelling' – not surprisingly – until he died.

It was reported that onlookers were appalled at the spectacle, probably thinking that a good beheading or hanging was much more fun to watch. Poor Roose was not afforded benefit of clergy, which meant his crime was an 'unclergyable' offence. In other words, Roose could not get out of the death penalty by quoting the fifty-first Psalm. By 1533 this escape clause had been expanded to include those who refused to enter a plea. However, in 1575 the benefit of clergy plea was moved to post-conviction so that any who pleaded it could have their punishment commuted to a year's imprisonment instead of probably being hanged.

Moreover, the punishment was so severe because the act of using poison could be, and frequently was, indiscriminate. If a killer stabs his victim, then he is visiting upon that person the death the killer intends. Roose wanted to make his colleagues ill. He actually killed two people he didn't know. The use of poison is against the order of nature in a way other methods are not, probably because the results occur when the perpetrator is absent. It has overtones of being 'sneaky'. I will leave the last word to Sir John Croke: 'Of all murders poisoning is ye worst and most horrible 1. because it is secrett 2 because it is not to be prevented 3 because it is most against nature and therefore most hainous 4 it is alsoe a cowardly thing.'[27]

Thankfully, Edward VI repealed this law in 1547.

So, the gory bit. What actually happens to the body when it is boiled?

As accidents in hot springs and the like have recently shown, being boiled alive is a seriously horrible way to die. If you imagine leaning over the saucepan boiling your potatoes, the steam on its own can give you a very painful burn.

As the boiling water touches your flesh, your limbs and extremities will be the first things to burn and we all know how many nerve endings they have. The pain will be immense. But it will not make you unconscious unless your head goes into the boiling water as well, in which case your brain will cook, and although death will be quicker, it will still be prolonged. This is what probably happened to Richard Roose because, according to witnesses, after being dunked three times, he ceased to yell.

As your outer skin cooks, your stomach, liver, heart et al will rise in temperature. According to Laura Allan, even if your epidermis does not show serious signs of damage, upon examination, your organs will be cooked.[28] Nice chianti, anyone?

What is worse is that for most of the time you will be conscious. People who have fallen into boiling springs have been seen to try and swim out of the water, call for help, and even if rescued and beyond help will ask how bad the burns are.

You may also smell yourself cooking, the odour of which is described as sweet and musky. Sorry if this is putting you off your roast pork Sunday lunch.

You will, however, reach a wonderful point when your nerve endings die off, at which point you will feel no more pain. If you manage to survive this, for example, if it is restricted to one or two limbs, it is unlikely that you will ever regain feeling in them.

Of course, should your entire body be subject to being boiled, by the time you die, your skin may have begun to peel or turn leathery, even though at this point, you won't feel anything anymore.

Branding

Branding was used as a punishment for all types of crime. Inflicting pain and torture was, of course, a cornerstone of the legal system in the Middle Ages and Tudor laws did nothing to alleviate this.

Not merely a form of punishment for offences such as vagrancy or murder when the offender claimed benefit of clergy, branding was a useful tool in the arsenal of the torturers. No law protected prisoners who faced torture because it has never been permitted under English Common Law. It was, nevertheless, seen by all the Tudor monarchs and their forebears as an acceptable form of persuasion to get to whatever truth the monarch and their Council happened to want. It was used to extract confessions, motivate the sufferer to give up names of their associates, or as a penalty for transgressing the law.

Branding devices would be heated to red-hot, whereupon the brand would be waved back and forth in front of the prisoner to encourage them to talk. Often the brand was passed so close to their eyes that they became blind. Red-hot pokers and branding irons would be pressed onto the flesh. The branding iron itself had a long handle to keep the heat away from the torturer. The brand at the other end would frequently be a letter.

Those who had committed murder, and who claimed benefit of clergy, were branded, usually on the thumb with the letter 'M'. Under the law brought in by Henry VII, should they transgress again, they would be executed. Vagabonds were usually branded with the letter 'V' and those caught fighting with the letter 'F'.[29]

Burning to Death

Thankfully, it would appear that no country in the world still executes people by burning them to death. There are still very rare instances of *sati* in India, whereby a widow immolates herself on her husband's death pyre.

Things were not always so and burning was the usual punishment for heretics, women who were convicted of petty treason, and witchcraft. Men convicted of petty treason were usually drawn on a pallet to the execution site and hanged but not quartered. It was regarded as a crime under common law, usually an aggravated form of murder.

Petty treason was the charge levelled at a wife who had killed her husband, a clergyman who had killed his prelate, and a servant killing their master/mistress or the master's wife. A 1531 act abolished three former tenets of the law, those being a wife attempting to kill her husband, a servant forging his master's seal, or a servant committing adultery with his master's wife or daughter.[30] By the time of Elizabeth's reign, convicted female felons were usually hanged, not burned. But not always.

The reasons for women suffering a different fate from men were partly because of the social view of women as nurturers and subordinates to men and partly because of the original sinner, Eve. Petty treason was viewed as worse than ordinary murder because there was an element of betrayal in it. So, for a woman to commit this crime was regarded as the ultimate duplicity.

A basic belief in Tudor England was that each person had a pre-ordained place in the culture and betraying that belief threatened the whole of society. Many people had servants and other people subordinate to them and if the murder of their social superiors was not punished harshly, chaos would follow.[31]

The other reason women were burned and not hanged, was that some men were drawn to the gallows wearing very little, to ensure that, as they were dragged over rough ground, they suffered injuries to their backs. It was deemed unthinkable that a woman should be so scantily clad, and the belief was that by burning women, their nakedness would not be on public display.[32]

Nobody appeared to notice the flaw in this idea. Which was that the first thing the flames would remove was the victim's clothing. So, unless the executioner chose his wood carefully, the victim would be exposed anyway. It became the custom for women who were to be burned that the executioner would first strangle them with a cord or halter, and then burn their body. This was the difference between being 'burned' and being 'burned alive'.

The last victim of this latter penalty was Catherine Hayes in 1726 in the reign of George I. Catherine was sentenced to be burned for murdering her husband. The executioner accidentally set the wood alight before he had strangled her. He then tried to get through the flames to strangle her but burned his hand and retreated. His only recourse was to throw pieces of wood at her until 'her skull was broken and her brains came out'. I do hope, dear reader, you are not eating as you read this.

Norfolk seems to have been a hotbed (sorry) of burning people, especially the town of Kings Lynn. In 1515 a woman was burned in the marketplace for the murder of her husband, and in 1535 a Dutchman was burned, reputedly for heresy. In 1590 Margaret Read was burned for witchcraft, and eight years later another woman for the same offence.[33]

Halifax Gibbet

This was the precursor of the guillotine and used in Halifax for those found guilty of theft. The town officials did not bother to wait for the assize judges. If someone stole anything worth more than thirteen-and-a-half pence, the offender would be beheaded on the next market day – a Tuesday, Thursday or Saturday.

The apparatus itself consisted of two tall pieces of timber about 5yds high, the inner side of each piece being grooved. There was a cross-strut across the bottom that formed the place where the condemned laid their head.

A square block of wood was slotted into the grooves. On the bottom of this block, an axe head was fastened. The block of wood was drawn up between the two upright posts and fixed at the top by a rope and wooden pin.

The offender would be brought to the gibbet, confess his/her crime, and lay his/her head on the block. When they were ready, they would put out their arm to demonstrate that justice was about to be enacted. The pin would be pulled out and the axe fall.

The speed of the fall was such that 'if the neck of the transgressor were as big as a bull, it should be cut asunder at a stroke and roll from the body a huge distance'.[34]

Hanging

The official wording for sentencing is 'to hang by the neck until they are dead'. Hanging was the usual method of capital punishment in England for most crimes and became the sole method of execution after we stopped beheading, boiling and burning people.

Tudor clergyman William Harrison, 1534-93, believed that hanging was a very humane method of execution. This writer wonders why clergymen so frequently made these pronouncements (see John Rogers under Heresy), but in truth, the clergy were seen as the fount of all knowledge, and this does tend to encourage arrogance and certainty. The information in the next few paragraphs might just have tempered their opinions.

How hanging causes death is dependent on the method used. Since it is still used in many countries, all with various methods, here are the main points.[35]

Short-drop – this obstructs the carotid arteries and jugular veins, causing cerebral hypoxia or stopping oxygen from reaching the brain. The weight of the body being hanged forces the base of the tongue against the back of the mouth, blocking the airway. Loss of consciousness occurs between eight and sixty seconds. The brain dies within six minutes and the heart usually stops within ten to fifteen minutes.

Pole hanging – is when a long pole has a hook at the top. The noose is placed around the victim's neck and they are lifted onto the hook and let drop.

Standard drop – if the drop is inadequate to break the neck, this is a very cruel way to die. It can take up to ten minutes and be very messy because of damage to the skin, ligaments and neck muscles.

Long drop – this was the standard method in England from the nineteenth century. The length of drop is calculated by the weight of the prisoner. The noose was placed with the slip-knot under the left ear and when the lever was pulled the body would take around half to three-quarters of a second to drop and the neck to break between the vertebrae C2 and C3. Putting the noose in this position brought the slip-knot around to the chin, breaking the hyoid bone and larynx.

In 1874 executioner William Marwood developed the method of using a brass eyelet to allow the rope to run more easily, which led to a quicker death. Before this the rope had been soaped to make it run. Later, the part of the rope in contact with the prisoner's neck was sheathed in leather.

Albert Pierrepoint, probably the most famous hangman in England, detailed in his autobiography how precise he considered the elements of the execution needed to be. Too long a drop and the result could be decapitation: too short and the victim strangled. The weight of the prisoner determined the drop energy needed to sever the spinal column. However, Pierrepoint also took into account the build of the prisoner, so someone with a thick neck would need a different drop length from someone with a slender neck.[36]

In some cases, hanging can cause the voiding of bladder and bowels due to an adrenaline rush. Some men sustain erections or even ejaculate.

During the reign of Henry VIII, John Stow records that some 72,000 people met their deaths at the end of a rope.[37] Usually, only common criminals were hanged. The crimes for which hanging was the penalty included murder, rape or 'the stealing of women and maidens', arson, witchcraft, and theft of items worth more than a shilling, which in 2017 was around £21. Most felons hanged were deemed guilty of theft.

In London the usual procedure was for the prisoner to be taken in a cart from the prison – many from Newgate – with the noose already around their neck and the rest of the rope wound around their waist. Since Tyburn was a frequent site of such executions and it was geographically west of Newgate, the term 'gone west' was born.

The cart would then be placed under the gallows, the slack part of the rope fixed to the gallows and the cart removed. In some cases, the family and friends of the prisoner were permitted to pull on the dangling legs of the hanging person to hasten death.

Not all hangings in London were at Tyburn. Mary had some of the Wyatt rebellion rebels hanged in St Paul's churchyard.[38] Seamen found guilty of piracy were usually taken to Execution Dock at Wapping, where the noose would be put over their heads and they would be kicked or pushed over the edge of the river. They were left there for three tides.[39]

Hanging in Chains

Hanging in chains will be a familiar visual to anyone who has seen the films *Robin Hood, Prince of Thieves*, in which Robin sees how his father was executed by Alan Rickman as the Sheriff of Nottingham, and *Pirates of the Caribbean*, in which Jack Sparrow walks past executed pirates.

Hanging was the normal mode of punishment for the Saxons and the more gruesome version of this was gibbeting or hanging in chains. This penalty would be carried out close to the site of the crime, and certainly in Derbyshire it became a common method of execution in the fourteenth century.[40]

Punishments

The terms gallows and gibbet have different meanings. Gallous is a variant of the term gallows and is used as an adjective – e.g., 'his gallous conduct will lead him to the gallows one day.' Although a gallows may become a gibbet, the reverse is not true. The main difference could be in the perception of the judgement. A gallows was a thing upon which felons suffered and a gibbet was the thing upon which they were displayed.

Gibbeting was intended to inspire terror, not just for the accused, but also any witnesses and onlookers. The corpse – and in some cases, the live body of the convicted felon – would be hoisted up on a gallows and left there, sometimes for decades until almost nothing would be left, especially after the predations of birds. Crows were particularly partial to the soft flesh of eyes and lips, and, if the winter was harsh, the hanging body would provide sustenance.

As far as the felon was concerned, they would know that their body would never be buried and they would never reach heaven. It would be the object of public scorn as it decayed. It might also be stolen, and some corpses were stolen by family and friends who would then give the man a decent burial. Sometimes the bones would drop to the ground and be carried away by predators such as foxes. In short, there would be no resting in peace and that alone would be emotional and mental torture for the accused.

The most famous instances in the Tudor era of being hanged in chains were those of Robert Aske and Sir Robert Constable, in York and Hull respectively. On 12 July 1537, Aske, one of the leaders of the 1536 Pilgrimage of Grace, was hanged in chains outside Clifford's Tower, the keep of York Castle. In most cases, the convicted felon was hanged first and then put in the person-shaped cage. Not Aske or the unfortunate Constable. They were hanged in chains alive and took several days to die, being slowly suffocated to death. This was after Henry VIII had promised them a pardon.

Henry VIII thought that anybody who did not take the Oath of Supremacy was against him and therefore against God. Monks from Charterhouse in London who refused to take the Oath were chained to posts and left to starve to death.

In the reign of Edward VI, in Jersey, three men were accused of piracy. One of them was an Englishman called John Wyte or White, and the other two, Bernabe Le Quesne and Sebastien Alexandre, were natives of the islands. All three were accused of being 'sea thieves', and of waging 'open war' against any trading vessels they encountered at sea.[41]

They were seized, put on trial, and found guilty. Their sentence was to be hanged and then gibbeted. John Wyte, described as a foreigner, was executed on a high gallows near St Catherine's Bay in St Martin's parish. Le Quesne was also hanged, but at the headland of Noirmont overlooking St Aubin's Bay. Their bodies were then bound in chains and put on public display to act as a deterrent and demonstrate the rigours of the law.

The third man was either found innocent or his sentence was commuted for he did not hang. Or, as de la Croix termed it 'The third prisoner, Sébastien Alexandre was happier, his execution was suspended.' There's a joke in there somewhere.

Hanging, Drawing and Quartering

Hanging, drawing, and quartering has to be one of the most barbaric and tortuous ways to die. Strictly speaking, the term should be 'Drawing, Hanging and Quartering', but that doesn't have the same ring, does it?

This was the sentence visited upon some traitors, depending on how heinous the court perceived their treachery. It was pronounced as follows: 'That the traitor is to be taken from the prison and laid upon a sledge or hurdle, and drawn to the gallows or place of execution, and then hanged by the neck until he be half dead, and then cut down; and his entrails to be cut out of his body and burnt by the executioner; then his head is to be cut off, his body to be divided into quarters, and afterwards his head and quarters to be set up in some open places directed.'[42] Sometimes, the victim's genitals would also be cut off, thereby rendering him less than a man.

It was believed that corruption was seated in the bowels and that by removing them and casting them into the fire, they would be purified and the victim would see that happen.

Either the headsman or the hangman would slice open the chest and cut out the heart before holding it up to show the crowd, saying 'Behold the heart of a traitor'. Sometimes the quarters would be sent to various parts of the country to be displayed. The head was usually put on the end of a pike and displayed on London Bridge.[43]

One would like to think that by the time the poor soul had been half-hanged – and probably tortured beforehand to extract as much intelligence as possible – he would not be much aware of what happened next. Sadly, this was not always so. Executioners were taught how to cauterise the ends of the wounds after the intestines were cut out so that the victim's life was extended even by a few minutes to witness the full horror of his ordeal.[44] I do hope you are not eating liver and onions as you read this. If the disembowelling was limited to the intestines and not other organs, the victim would be conscious and in immense pain, but would finally lose consciousness due to loss of blood.

The intent by enacting this form of punishment was to remove the traitor's status, his identity and ensure that by dismembering his body and sending the parts all over the country, there was absolutely nothing left of the man. The body parts being separated meant he would not go forward to heaven.[45]

When we hear the name Henry VIII, we tend to think of his six wives and multiple executions. He did have a good side: somewhere. He ordered the Bible to be translated into English, he started the English Royal Navy, the wording in his will when bequeathing his crown meant that, after his son, Edward VI, England had the first two queens regnant. This latter was probably because he believed they would both marry, their husbands would take over the realm while they had sons and then the male status quo would be resumed. However, for sheer viciousness in terms of the number of executions, especially as his paranoia grew in his last years, Henry would be hard to beat. He did not burn as many people as his elder daughter, Mary, but he was master of the hanging, drawing and quartering punishment. While some of the Charterhouse monks were hanged in chains, others were hanged, drawn and quartered.[46]

Pressing to Death

These days when we put the words 'history' and 'pressing' together, our first mental image is usually that of eighteenth-century matelots escorting drunken civilians straight from the ale-house to the nearest ship to begin an enforced life at sea.

However, in the Middle Ages there was the punishment of *Peine forte et dure* – hard and forceful punishment. In 1275 Edward I enacted the Standing Mute Act to deter defendants from refusing to enter a plea in court.[47] Probably the nearest thing we have in current legislation is the right of silence and the repeated responses of 'No comment' to any question asked by detectives.

The 1275 act was used to persuade a defendant to enter a plea in court. If they refused they would be 'pressed'. We still use press as a verb when trying to put someone under pressure.

Being pressed in the Middle Ages meant that anyone who stood mute when asked for a plea, would be laid on a stone floor, usually naked except to cover their genitals. Their arms and legs would be splayed in a cross formation and then a board would be laid on their chests. Weights of increasing heaviness would then be placed on the board until the sufferer either agreed to enter a plea and go to trial, or died from suffocation.

Many defendants refused to enter a plea, because if they did and were found guilty, their punishment would generally be execution anyway, but also any property would be forfeit and their heirs and dependents rendered homeless and penniless. If they died without having entered a plea, their property was not forfeit, unless it was a case of high treason. So, in truth, it was frequently a case of how they chose to die.[48]

One of the difficulties encountered by the criminal justice system was that the common law courts did not feel able to proceed if a defendant refused to enter a plea, so they generally delegated the responsibility upwards. Because of this, it became imperative that a workable form of punishment be found that would persuade the defendant to give in and agree to enter a plea. These individuals were frequently tried under Admiralty law.[49]

Initially, those who refused to plead were sent to undergo harsh imprisonment. They would be housed in the worst place in the prison, upon the bare ground, and fed bread made of barley or bran, but they only received bread on days when they were not permitted to drink anything and vice-versa.

Pressing to death might take several days and this did not always mean the weights were increased, so it became a slow, agonising suffocation, and, if they lasted past two days, they were only given 'foul water' to drink.[50]

It was also the Tudor custom to show the defendant what he/she was facing. This was a time when some had second thoughts and entered a plea. A refusal to plead was taken as a demonstration of contempt towards the court, and, on a larger scale, a challenge to the legitimacy of the court and the legal system.

Peine forte et dure was abolished in England in 1772. From then on, refusing to plead was regarded as pleading guilty, until 1827 when pleas of not guilty were allowed.

Ducking Stool[51]

Many parishes had a ducking or cucking stool. Basically, it was a long pole with a seat, situated on the end, on a river bank or the edge of a pond. The woman, probably guilty of scolding her husband or spreading malicious gossip, would be dressed only in a smock and then tied to the seat. Sometimes she would merely be raised into the air and left there. However, it was usual if this was the first time she had offended that she would be made to make a public penance in church, at which point she would be warned against repeating her offence.

Should she reoffend, she would be put in the ducking stool, and if she didn't learn from being hoist in the air to be ridiculed by the local populace, she would probably find herself being dipped in and out of the river. Of course, there were some incidents when this led to the woman's death, especially, one would imagine, if it was extremely cold or if the water in which she was plunged was full of the usual rubbish the locals would deposit in it. Men found guilty of the same offence would be either fined or put in the stocks. It is ironic that very, very few single women were punished for being scolds, only married ladies. Enough said.

Mutilation

In Tudor times it was generally believed that one's face revealed one's character. So if offenders had their ears sliced off or their noses slit or they were branded on the cheek, this became a symbol of what type of people they were.

Several letters were used as brands. 'T' indicated a thief; 'B' a blasphemer; 'F' a 'fraymaker', i.e., a disturber of the peace; 'FA' meant false accuser and sometimes this was an 'F' on one cheek and an 'A' on the other. These were documented by Tudor topographer, John Stow in 1556.[52]

Ears were also the target of mutilation. Authors and printers of seditious books or people who did not attend church could have their ears chopped off.

Cutting off hands was another punishment, thought to be more than reasonable, especially if malice aforethought could be proved. This happened in 1599 when a couple attempted to poison several victims who only survived because an onlooker realised what had happened and made them drink olive oil. The man and woman had both their hands cut off as well as their ears.[53]

Offences committed within the royal court were subject to direct justice from the monarch. Machyn's diary tells of Sir Thomas Knevett, who struck a Master Cleere within the court. Henry VIII ordered that Knevett's hand should be amputated. The king's master cook sharpened his knife ready to carry out the sentence. The serjeant of the scullery had his mallet ready and the irons in the fire ready to cauterise the wound, and the king's Master Surgeon was ready with the searing cloth. When they were ready to carry out the sentence, the king sent a message to delay the amputation until after dinner. After having satisfied his hunger, his ire was considerably lessened and Henry decided to pardon him.[54]

Sanctuary and abjuring the realm

Should felons think themselves likely to be sentenced to death, they had an alternative to claiming benefit of clergy. This was to run to a church that offered sanctuary and after forty days, abjure the realm.

Whilst the rate of claiming these two rights was as it had always been, by the time the last fifty years of the Tudors came around, with Henry VIII's religious restrictions, and those of his daughters, the importance of self-exile increased. By 1624 the law was abolished and people could no longer claim sanctuary.

So what exactly was it? The origins are based on the Christian teaching about forgiveness and mercy. By the fifth century, a formal right to sanctuary existed. It gave a fugitive the right to enter a church consecrated by a bishop and claim protection. Common law gave the fugitive, who usually had to occupy a specific place near the altar, forty days in which to decide if he was going to turn up at court and opt for a trial or leave the realm and never return.[55]

However, this was not the only circumstance in which people could claim sanctuary. During times of strife, those who were worried the 'other side' might win often went into sanctuary. Elizabeth Woodville did this during the six months between autumn 1470 and May 1471 when Henry VI was put back on the throne and her husband, Edward IV, together with Richard of Gloucester, fled abroad. Likewise, when the future Henry VIII was six years old, his mother, Elizabeth of York, took him into sanctuary whilst Henry VII faced the Cornish rebels.

The problem became acute when sanctuaries such as Westminster Abbey had the capacity to house hundreds of fugitives and the amenities for them to stay for a very long time. From time to time, judges attempted to stop this exodus into sanctuaries, but it made no difference. Until Henry VIII, who had benefitted from sanctuary at St John's Priory in 1497, abolished all of them in 1530. However, some still existed and were used.

Quite how the forty-day rule came into being is unclear, but it may link to Jesus' fasting in the wilderness as told in Matthew Ch 4: 1-11. Some argued that the forty-day clock only started ticking when a coroner had gone into the church and attended the fugitive. If the church happened to be locked when the suspect came leaping over the churchyard wall, he could claim sanctuary by grasping the door handle. Some claimants were arrested anyway because they didn't realise that not all church ground is consecrated. In 1518 a man accused of heresy was denied sanctuary because he had rejected the basic doctrines of the church in which he now sought shelter.[56]

Violation of sanctuary was not unknown, one such instance being that of Edward IV, after his victory in the 1471 battle, marching into Tewkesbury Abbey where the highborn Lancastrian leaders had taken refuge. A standoff ensued between the abbey and the Crown. Edward wanted his prisoners but did not want to be seen to violate the sanctuary of the church. The abbot faced a similar dilemma on the other end of the argument. Finally, he agreed he could not hold onto traitors to the Crown. Edward agreed to pardon them. When the Lancastrians left the abbey, Edward had them arrested and Richard of Gloucester tried them the following day and executed them.[57] Although this instance was before the Tudors came to power, it did set a precedent.

In 1486 the issue of sanctuary and high treason was very much debated and limited to specific establishments. So when Thomas and Humphrey Stafford sought protection in Culham church in Oxfordshire after an abortive coup, Henry VII had them forcibly removed and Humphrey was brought before the King's Bench.

The judges were between a rock and a hard place, namely Henry VII, in the early days of his reign, and clerical law that had been in power for centuries. The judges ruled in favour of the king – wouldn't you? – and Humphrey was executed. It is likely that Thomas, the younger brother, was pardoned.

This practice of dragging people from sanctuary was something Henry VII used as and when he needed it in future years. Sometimes, violations were referred to the King's Bench by other courts who were unable to make a decision, one such case being that of a man called Rowland who had been dragged out of the Bray parish church. He demanded to be returned to the church and the case was sent to the King's Bench in November 1507 with an unknown outcome. What is known is that some claimants who returned to their sanctuaries were pardoned.[58]

Scold's Bridle or Brank

This form of punishment has almost attained the status of a fable, mostly because it was, and now is seen, as a brutal form of punishment. In form, it was a metal cage that fitted over the offender's head, but with a metal plate on which was a prong. The plate was forced into the offender's mouth and, should the woman try to speak, the prong pierced her tongue.

Today, we see this as a vicious form of punishment, but right up to the seventeenth century it was regarded as appropriate. The antiquary, Robert Plot, speaking in the late 1600s said: 'I look upon it as much to be preferred to the cucking stool, which not only endangers the health of the party, but also gives the tongue liberty 'twixt every dip to neither of which is this at all liable: it being such a bridle for the tongue, as not only quite deprives them of speech, but brings shame for the transgression, and humility thereupon, before 'tis taken off ... nor is it taken off, till after the party begins to show all external signs imaginable of humiliation and amendment.'[59]

This author would quite like to have seen Mr Plot wearing it!

Stocks and Pillory

The stocks were, together with the pillory, to be found in most parishes. They were a kind of go-to for many offences, especially since they were usually found in the local marketplace. As well as being publicly shamed, the offender's health was at risk, not just from rotten fruit – and worse – being thrown. People were often left there all night. The pillory was where the offender stood with head and hands imprisoned. Sometimes the offender's ears would be nailed to the frame. And, of course, this has led to the term 'being pilloried'. The stocks on the other hand (sorry) imprisoned the feet of the offender. If a man and woman were in the stocks together, they had probably produced an illegitimate child.[60]

Tumbrel

We associate a tumbrel/tumbril with the image of French aristocrats being transported to the guillotine, but it was also used in England.

The tumbrel was a cart that tipped backwards, pulled by a single horse or ox. It was mainly used by farmers to make it easier to tip things, usually manure, onto fields. It was used as an alternative to the ducking stool. The offender would be put in the cart and wheeled around the village or town. Of course, it was, like most of what we might describe as lesser punishments, meant to have a significant shaming factor.[61]

The Tudor diarist Henry Machyn was a London Merchant Tailor. Much of his output described funerals, so there is a possibility he was a funeral furnisher.[62] He tells us of the widow of Master Warner, Serjeant of the Admiralty, who, in 1560, was found guilty of being a bawd to her daughter and her maid. Both the daughter and the maid were unmarried and both were pregnant. The widow was paraded through the streets of London in a tumbrel.

Also in 1560 we are told that a cart containing two men and three women was paraded around the city. One man was a bawd for two of the women, one of them being the wife of the landlord of "The Bell" in Gratious Street, and the other the wife of the landlord of "The Bull's Head" beside London Stone. The other two were brother and sister, who had been 'taken naked together' and were punished for incest.

Christopher Langton was a man educated at Eton and Cambridge and a Fellow of the College of Physicians. He was paraded in his finest clothes – 'a gown of damask lined with velvet, and a coat and a cope made of velvet' – his crime being found with two wenches in a three in a bed situation.[63]

Whipping and Whipping Posts

Whipping was the common punishment for thieves, vagabonds, and those guilty of deceit and sedition.[64] Palliards (low or common rascals) and other rogues looking for money or food were, if possible, apprehended and whipped out of town. This made economic sense because the poor were legally obliged to be supported by the parish. If there were people who did not live in the parish, they still had to be supported, so each night the constables would go around the streets and in the taverns. Anyone who could not prove they had a home appeared before the JP the next morning. If found guilty, they would be put in the stocks or pillory for a day and then whipped out of town. This practice was not restricted to vagrants and beggars, but also strolling players.

Petty thieves who stole goods worth less than a shilling were whipped. Two men who cut off the London water supply in November 1560 by removing lead from the water conduits were whipped.[65]

In 1566 a forger who had 'written' documents allegedly in the hand of Robert Dudley, Elizabeth I's Master of Horse, was whipped through Westminster, the City of London, and then over London Bridge to Southwark. He was probably subject to being 'whipped at the cart's arse'. In other words, he was stripped half naked, tied to the back of the cart and forced to stagger along as he was beaten with leather whips until his back bled profusely.

This latter punishment was also used for couples who had an illegitimate child. They would be tied together and whipped through the parish. Twice.

Some parishes had a whipping post. The post would have iron fastenings for the criminal's hands and legs, which supported his body as he was whipped. One boy, under the age of fourteen, was found guilty of stealing garments, sheets and linen worth 31s and 4d. Had he been older, he would have gone to the gallows. He escaped with a whipping.[66]

PART TWO

Crimes and Cases

Preamble

Whilst punishments for various crimes have been covered as much as is feasible, one cannot get the full understanding of the case studies in this section without a preliminary explanation or definition as to what, precisely, each crime entailed.

Therefore, in this section, I have tried to explain what constituted each crime before giving examples of who transgressed it.

The biggest problem with the case studies is that Tudor records, usually from church courts or county assizes, or, if a more serious crime, the Kings Bench, are patchy. Sometimes we are told what a named person did, but not what happened to them when or if they were found guilty. Sometimes, the records have a mere passing mention of the crime or scant details without naming the offender.

Alchemy

The official definition of alchemy is the medieval forerunner of chemistry, concerned with the transmutation of matter, in particular, with attempts to convert base metals into gold or find a universal elixir.

Alchemy in the Tudor age was akin to splitting the atom in the twentieth century. Both, if presented correctly, could be regarded as beneficial.

In Somerset in the 1550s, one Thomas Charnock was utterly convinced he could manufacture the Philosopher's Stone. Over thirty years he attempted to make elixirs and conducted numerous experiments, some of which went disastrously wrong and resulted in explosions. Someone (his mentor?) told him there was a Philosopher's Stone buried in the wall of Bath Abbey. However, by the time Charnock got there, the wall in question had been dismantled and tipped onto a dung heap. The mix of wall and the contents of the dung heap were then spread over several fields, allegedly proving to be a very effective fertiliser.[1]

In 1574, Thomas finally believed he had made a less effective Philosopher's Stone called a 'white' stone. However, the poor man was unable to replicate his experiment. He died in 1581 still convinced he was on the verge of success.

CASE STUDY

In 1570, John Buckley, an Oxford scholar, was arrested for debasing the coinage. Under interrogation, he admitted using a powder to extract silver from a coin without damaging its surface. Because this would lighten the weight of the coin, he averred, he added water to make up the weight. All this, Buckley said, could be done in the home with just the aid of a small fire.

He persuaded William Bedoe, a stationer, to buy the secret of how to perform this simple feat for the price of a gold tablet worth £4 (about £1,400 in 2021).

Bedoe followed Buckley's instructions and was apparently delighted with the result. When he was arrested, Bedoe admitted he had successfully 'lightened' silver shillings and sixpences, to the value of at least £8, thus doubling his investment. He had extracted about 2oz of silver, which he took to a silversmith, proposing to sell the secret to him.

The authorities were not so much interested in the alchemical techniques used by Buckley and Bedoe as in the criminal intent. There is no further information about what actually happened to Buckley, except that he claimed he had only debased Spanish coins and not English ones, which was a smart move seeing that feelings against the Spanish had been high since Philip of Spain married Elizabeth's Catholic elder sister.[2]

What is clear is that, although alchemy was strictly illegal in England, the instant Elizabeth I heard about it, she expressed a keen interest. Never let it be said that the Crown could not be flexible about such things. In the fifteenth century, more than twenty royal licences were issued, granting the right to practise alchemy.

Animals

Animals were the cause of many deaths in Tudor England.[1] However, it was the theft of animals that proved more problematic for the authorities.

The theft of animals became an increasing problem as the sixteenth century progressed. A large proportion of people's capital was tied up in their animals. Therefore, theoretically, animal theft was regarded as property crime and was dealt with as such in Tudor courts.

Most thefts were petty – stealing a chicken/duck or goose, for example. However, the theft of animals valued at over one shilling, regardless of where they had been stolen from, yard, barn, or field, was considered to be grand larceny, the punishment for which was hanging.[2]

The context of animal theft is not that clear, but that it was more than the classic example of a man stealing a sheep for his hungry children is also obvious from assize records. That said, women were involved in stealing, too – mainly poultry – but numbers suggest they stole to feed the family.[3]

The gains from one theft could be substantial. Thomas Cuddington of Ewell stole seven sheep, following that up one week later with four more sheep and a month after that with two lambs. Henry Denman of Southwark, whose accomplice was a butcher – they feature in animal theft a lot – stole forty-nine sheep in one fell swoop. They were probably being driven to market when they were seized.[4]

Of course, when it came to the court case, some animals would be undervalued to lessen the offence, or rather the legal consequences of the offence. Sheep were generally priced at about 3s (around £81 in 2021). Lambs were not as valuable.

In 1599 William Crowche was accused of stealing twenty ewes, each valued at 3s 4d and six castrated males of the same value. In May 1564 George Marwell of Dartford in Kent stole five sheep at a total value of 24s 6d (about £550 in 2021). A short while later, he stole another five valued at 17s. In theory, he should have hanged for the first offence, but records do not tell what happened to Mr Marwell, as is the case with many of the crimes documented in the Assize records.

Pigs were not considered as valuable as sheep or cattle and were more difficult to steal because they usually lived in close proximity to the family. Edward Slyn was accused at the Dartford Assizes in 1569 of stealing a large red cow worth 33s 4d.

It was the effect of horse theft that caused most economic harm. Stealing a horse was the equivalent of stealing the family car today and became such a problem in the early decades of Tudor England that it was regarded as socially damaging. Horses were not just some people's form of transport, but they also worked the land, so losing them affected the agricultural economy of the parish.

Henry VIII considered horses of such importance that he passed two Acts of Parliament, The Breed of Horses Act 1535 and The Horses Act 1540, to improve the breeding of horses. Horses that would be required should he decide to go to war.

The 1535 Act mentions a marked decay in the quality of horse breeding and requires owners of enclosed parks to keep two mares who had to be over thirteen hands high (a hand is 4in). This was because Henry considered horses less than thirteen hands were too small to be of use.[5]

The 1540 Act decreed that no stallion under fifteen hands or mare under thirteen hands could run free on common land or be permitted to run wild. Furthermore, no two-year-old colt under 11.2 hands was allowed to run out with mares. To enforce this, annual round-ups were conducted and any horses found to be under the height limits were destroyed.[6]

This latter requirement for such draconian culls was partially repealed by Elizabeth I in 1566 because poor land could not support horses the size required by the 1540 Act. This was providential in saving many of the mountain and moorland pony breeds we have today.[7]

As the sixteenth century progressed, horses became more vulnerable to theft because many were left tied up in the street. The levels of horse theft became so great, and horses were such a vital part of everyday life, that the Marquess of Dorset wrote to Cardinal Wolsey to complain about the problem. This led to horse theft becoming a different kind of grand larceny. Although the punishment was hanging, it was still subject to Benefit of Clergy. However, in 1545, Henry VIII removed that from the statute book. The horse was the only animal to achieve this importance and although stealing sheep and cattle was common, it was not until the eighteenth century that Benefit of Clergy was applied to them, too.

In 1555 the Marian government introduced legislation requiring a record of sale of horses. Although it quickly became apparent this law was not fit for purpose, it was not amended until 1589 when even horses stabled and presumably safe were being stolen on a regular basis. Stolen animals could be removed quickly to markets and fairs and sold on. After 1589 every horse seller had to register with a market official in order to sell a horse. Furthermore, he had to produce somebody who could vouch for his identity – his name, occupation and where he lived. Purchasers were given a bill of sale at the cost of 2d. The act also stated that any stolen animal was recoverable from whoever had bought it illegally, provided he was paid back the price originally paid for the horse. This was legitimate up to six months after the original illegal sale.

All these were good ideas but mostly they were either ignored or bypassed: mostly. In 1598 a Staffordshire thief stole a horse and rode to Market Drayton to sell it. When told he needed to prove his identity, he climbed back on the horse and decided to return it to its owner. However, he changed his mind again halfway back, tried to sell it to someone else and was detained.

Butchers were frequently involved in animal theft and had the perfect means to slaughter and sell the stolen meat. Proving the identity of a cow when faced with a joint of beef was impossible. This did not involve horses because the English did not – and still do not – eat horse meat, so, if caught, the punishment was not so severe. That said, if the butcher was caught with enough purloined animals, he could still hang.

Selling on became an industry, but it was not so easy to get rid of the plunder. If the thief tried to sell the animal at the local fair, there was a good chance the real owner would be there on the lookout for his property. Stolen animals were usually taken a long way from the crime scene, and this particularly applied to horses because the thief simply climbed aboard and rode the animal to where he wanted to sell it.

In 1532 Thomas Richardson of Sanctuary Grove in Nottinghamshire had stolen two cows from Kirton-in-Lindsay in Lincolnshire. He drove them to the market in North Clay in Nottinghamshire to sell them but was arrested and convicted. Rather than face the gallows, he chose to abjure the realm.

Poultry was much less valued and therefore ideal for the opportunist thief. According to the Calendar of Assize Records in Hertfordshire, in 1585 Richard Hayward, poulterer of Much Hadham, was accused of stealing twenty-six cocks, hens, capons, and pullets on three separate raids. However, because this was not considered as dire as stealing bigger animals, his thefts were valued at 10d. Hayward was whipped before being discharged.[8]

Begging

The definition of begging is to ask for food or money as charity.

> Hark! Hark! The dogs do bark!
> The beggars are coming to town:
> Some in rags, some in jags*
> And one in a velvet gown
>
> Some gave them white bread,
> And some gave them brown,
> And some gave them a horse-whip,
> And sent them out of town.
>
> *Thirteenth century nursery rhyme*
> (*jags are slits in clothing, a popular fashion in Tudor England.)

Most beggars in the Tudor period were quite passive individuals who were not aggressive but were a nuisance. Tudor lawmakers were very suspicious about the Christian tenet of helping the poor and nowhere was this more evident than when it came to the subject of beggars and begging. Most people regarded them in the same breath as thieves and their treatment by the ordinary person was not dissimilar to the twenty-first century when people either ignore or hassle people who have no money, nowhere to go and, often, no hope.

Many Tudor officials and people in authority believed that giving alms and other help to beggars gave them an easy life.[1] Viewed as individuals, they were clearly vulnerable and in need of assistance. Viewed as a whole, beggars were believed to be a threat to society; dangerous and wilful because they were idle.[2]

As the 2020 Covid pandemic proved, events and regulations can affect plans and lives to an extreme degree. In the Middle Ages and into the Tudor era, this was also true. When pestilence and disaster hit, there was no state aid of any kind until the Elizabethan poor laws at the very end of the sixteenth century.

However, what did happen was a development of social conscience about the poor. Until the late 1530s, the monasteries were dominant in trying to ensure that most people had food. However, most in authority remained judgemental and suspicious, finding ways to deny help to vagrants, labourers, and strangers.

The church maintained that people who did not show charity were sinful; that by withholding alms they were no better than a thief robbing the poor. Churchmen warned that those who had more than they needed and did not share their surplus with those who had nothing were heartless and would die in sin.[3] So we know what happened to Henry VII, who used any means possible, legal and illegal to swell the royal coffers, and his son, Henry VIII, when they died, don't we? While the poor became poorer in Henry VIII's England, Thomas Cromwell ensured that, with the sale of monastery lands and buildings at inflated prices to royal favourites and those who had money to burn, the king became richer.

In truth, the dissolution was a huge social and economic disaster in terms of stability.[4] Sir William Ashley, speaking in 1893, said that monasteries were very much responsible for the increase in beggars because their indiscriminate almsgiving fostered the growth of 'professional begging'.[5]

An unknown writer in 1591 opined: 'Many of them [the monks] whose revenues were sufficient thereunto, made hospitals and lodgings within their own houses besides the great alms they give daily at their gate to everyone that comes to it. Yea, no wayfaring person could depart without a night's lodging, meat, drink, and money, it not being demanded from whence he or she came, and whether he could go.'[6]

This attitude became accepted and repeated until, as late as 1959, it was textbook doctrine on the subject of Tudor almsgiving.[7] However, by the 1980s that view was changing because historians were more rigorous in their research. The Benedictine monks of Westminster Abbey distributed over ten per cent of their gross income to the poor. In 1537 it was estimated that the monasteries provided about £6,500 per annum in alms. And when they disappeared, it left a void that was not financially filled by private philanthropy until around 1580, although records are patchy and it is difficult to be precise.[8]

However, monasteries did not simply give alms. They provided healthcare and end of life care in their infirmaries. They gave the local people a rudimentary education and trained them in farming, brewing and animal husbandry, and the local people helped work the monastery land, look after the animals, and help in the kitchens and brewhouses. All that stopped upon dissolution. The onus was then on the local gentry to step in. Many of the new owners kicked the local people out of their jobs. By introducing enclosure, sheep farming and rack-renting, these new owners increased agrarian discontent.

As Becon stated, these men 'abhor the name of monks, friars, canons, nuns but their goods they greedily gripe. And yet, where the cloisters kept hospitality and let out the farms at a reasonable price, the new owners do none of these things.'[9]

The result was a vast increase in the number of beggars who, unable to find any type of work in their home parish, wandered the country.

The situation was made worse because of former armed retainers who were no longer required by their lords after the Battle of Bosworth. Henry VII ensured that the nobility would not have the financial clout to raise any kind of militia that might be used against the Crown. This left many retainers and ex-servicemen with no job, nowhere to live, and they, too, were reduced to begging and vagrancy.

The former soldiers fell into two categories: those who were ex-retainers from the noble households and an increasing number who had been involved in Henry VIII's forays into battle with the Scots or French.[10]

Most of these ex-servicemen were used to a much higher standard of living than they would have experienced in civilian life. They were used to a dangerous existence because of the job they did. This led many of them to eschew looking for what we would now describe as a normal job in civilian life because it lacked excitement. It was also, as has been the prevailing view in the twenty-first century, often easier to make a good living by begging than by getting a proper job.

Henry VII's laws against delivery and maintenance – in other words being a liveried retainer of a noble household – were not entirely successful. Henry was all about making money for the Crown. His drive to extract money at all costs led to many of the noble families having to make cutbacks. Sir Thomas More is quoted as saying 'in the mean season they that be thus destitute of service either starve for hunger, or manfully play the thieves'. Not many ex-retainers 'starved for hunger' if they could possibly avoid it.[11]

A 1593 act came into being that made general provision for pensions, as well as authorising local magistrates to provide financial aid to ex-military men in need on their way home. However, it was stipulated that any soldier or sailor caught begging would forfeit his pension as a matter of course.

When we take into account all the factors – Dissolution; influx of people from rural areas to the towns and the changes in industrial processes; land enclosures; the number of previous retainers put out of work, and the occurrences of rack-renting – the increase in the incidence of begging is not surprising. Until 1576 there was no distinction between a professional beggar and an unemployed man who wanted to work.[12]

The act of 1531 states: 'if any man or woman being whole and mighty in body and able to labour having no land, master, nor using any lawful merchandise, craft, or can give none reckoning how he doth lawfully get his living, that then it shall be lawful to the constables and all the King's officers, ministers, and subjects of every town, parish and hamlet, to arrest the said vagabonds and idle persons and to bring them to any of the Justices of the Peace of the same shire or liberty.'[13]

Each town or parish dealt with beggars in slightly different ways, and this usually depended on the difference being whether the beggar was operating in a rural or urban environment. Southampton is one such example. The city officials took their own legal traditions into account when drawing up the regulations for beggars within the city boundaries. The legal statute declared that the mayor of a town/city was responsible for handling the legislation. This would include a specified area in which begging could be performed and time limits each day as to when they were permitted to beg. A badge, denoting the beggar had a licence, also had to be worn. Any beggar not displaying a badge was put in the stocks. Furthermore, people who gave unlawful beggars alms whilst they were in the stocks were liable for a 12d fine for each offence[14](roughly £55 in 2021).[15]

Travelling beggars could only stay in Southampton for one night, and since the mayor and his council determined the number of beggars they permitted to be within the city boundaries at any one time, anyone outside this number were required to labour or leave the town.

Where Southampton differed from other towns and cities was that the mayor appointed an officer whose sole responsibility was to control begging and beggars. This officer, called the 'Constable Over All Beggars', was paid 6s 8d, although we do not know if that was an annual fee or not. He also wore a badge weighing 2oz.[16]

Blackmail

The definition of blackmail is the action, treated as a criminal offence, of demanding payment or another benefit from someone in return for not revealing compromising or damaging information about them.

Blackmail, or as an original definition, the payment of a tribute, has been around for centuries. We read of the Danegeld charged to King Aethelred to stop the marauding Vikings attacking England.

One of the most famous Tudor subjects of blackmail was the much to be pitied fifth wife of Henry VIII, Katherine Howard. Brought up after the death of her mother by her lax grandmother, the Dowager Duchess of Norfolk, Katherine slept with the maid-servants. She was Anne Boleyn's cousin, but unlike her illustrious predecessor, Katherine was not educated at all, since the Dowager Duchess did not agree with higher education for women, although Katherine did learn to read and write.[1]

She was voluptuous at an early age and therefore attractive to the opposite sex. Henry Manox, the music tutor employed by the dowager, became obsessed with Katherine, although it is not known for certain if she lost her virginity to him. What is known is that she was certainly in a physical relationship with the dashing and handsome Francis Dereham, a Howard relation. They called each other husband and wife.

Then Katherine's fortunes changed, and not for the better. She was sent to court as lady-in-waiting to Henry's fourth wife, Anne of Cleves. It is more than likely that her uncle, the wily Duke of Norfolk, spotted her as a pretty thing who would catch Henry's eye, especially as he was very unhappy with his 'Flanders Mare'. Katherine danced away from Dereham and into court circles, where she quickly caught the king's eye. From that instant, Henry was besotted with her. The day Thomas Cromwell went to the block for his mistake, not just in forcing Henry into the Cleves marriage but his inability to get him out of it, was the day Henry made Katherine his fifth queen.[2]

And that is where it all really started to go wrong for her. She was in her mid to late teens, a lively, pretty, airhead. Her husband was forty-nine, old, fat and increasingly paranoid. Of course, the upward turn of the Howard family bred disaffection elsewhere in the court. And Katherine, never the sharpest knife in the drawer, did nothing to help herself.

First Manox then Dereham petitioned for places in her household, something she dared not deny in case they told of her previous sexual behaviour. Before long, Joan Bulmer, another of Katherine's former colleagues, was lobbying for a post with the new queen.

At this point, had she been sensible, Katherine, in penitent tears, could have gone on her knees to Henry, still enchanted by his 'rose without a thorn', and confessed that these people were blackmailing her. At worst, she would probably have been sent away from court, but chances are that Henry, in a burst of his youthful 'gentil knight', might just have forgiven her.

What she did instead was to fall in love with Thomas Culpepper, one of Henry's gentlemen. And this time it really was love. The two are known to have met clandestinely in a privy during the royal progress north in 1541. That they became lovers is probable, although Culpepper only confessed to adultery under torture and Katherine maintained that she had not committed adultery to the end, in the full knowledge that if she were lying, she jeopardised her immortal soul.

What really set the royal cat among the pigeons was that Dereham, jealous of being usurped in Katherine's affections by Culpepper, got drunk and blabbed. Archbishop Thomas Cranmer was told her story from Manox to Culpepper. Being an opponent of the Catholic Howards, this was too good an opportunity to miss. Cranmer wrote Henry a letter. From thereon in everything was a foregone conclusion.

Manox, Dereham and Culpepper were executed. Katherine and her main lady-in-waiting, Jane Rochford, widow of George Boleyn, Anne's brother, were beheaded on Tower Green in 1542. What is almost unbelievable is the behaviour of Jane Rochford. She knew exactly how the court worked. She had experienced first-hand the results of faction intrigue in the executions of her husband and sister-in-law. She may not have grieved overmuch for them, but to put herself in the position of a co-conspirator was verging on the insane. Her actions have been a much-debated issue.

CASE STUDY

Blackmail is a crime that relies on the victim staying quiet and it is sad but perhaps understandable that so many victims do stay silent.

John Daniell, obviously born under a less than promising star, aimed high for his blackmail in that he attempted to extort money from the powerful Robert Devereux, Earl of Essex, who, at the time, was high in Queen Elizabeth's favour. However, it all went horribly wrong.

John Daniell Senior was a gentleman from Cheshire with an estate near Runcorn. John Junior was born around 1545 and inherited the estate when his father died, leaving the young John a ward of Queen Elizabeth.

He undertook the usual military activities expected of a gentleman and became captain of a band of foot soldiers put on readiness to meet the expected invasion by the Spanish in 1588. Very conscious of his social position, he quarrelled with Christ Church, Oxford, regarding tithes he believed should come to him. Taking matters into his own hands, he was then accused of 'riotous removal' of corn from the recipient of the tithes, presumably Christ Church.[3]

Daniell joined the household of Thomas Butler, Earl of Ormonde, but this did not bring him the advancement he expected, namely a post in the royal household, following his uncle as Serjeant of the Pantry, a position with perks. Daniell transferred his allegiance to the Earl of Essex.

Robert Devereux, Earl of Essex, had been Elizabeth's favourite since the 1580s and many historians are convinced she was in love with him. He was the son of Lettice Knollys, whom Elizabeth hated and regarded as a rival, but he was the stepson of her beloved Robert Dudley, Earl of Leicester, who died in 1588, a few months after the Spanish failed to conquer England with their great armada.

Essex was handsome, ambitious, courageous and adventurous. He was also a poet. In other words the epitome of Renaissance man. Puffed up with his own importance, like some politicians today, he believed himself to be untouchable.

At the time Daniell joined Essex's household, Lady Essex had a protestant refugee from the Low Countries in her entourage. Jane van Kethulle met John Daniell and they were married in late 1595/early 1596. At this point, Daniell was fifty years old and one has to wonder what his motive was in marrying Jane. Perhaps there is a clue in that her mistress had promised her a handsome dowry.

Once again, it seemed, Daniell had hitched his horse to the wrong tree. The headstrong Essex made two fundamental errors. The first was becoming the enemy of Sir Robert Cecil, son of the late William Cecil, Lord Burghley, Elizabeth's 'spirit'. Cecil was every bit as wily as his illustrious father, and obstructed Essex whenever he was sure of being successful, such as blocking the appointment of Francis Bacon, Essex's choice for Attorney General. Essex also failed to get John Daniell appointed as the Serjeant of the Pantry. Again.[4]

The second and by far the biggest mistake Essex made was thinking his influence over the queen was absolute. He lobbied to be sent to Ireland and succeeded, but when things didn't go his way, he disobeyed a direct order from Elizabeth and returned to London.

Worse still, he barged into her Privy Bedchamber early in the morning to be confronted with an old woman, face wrinkled, scant grey hair and absolutely nothing like the bewigged, bejewelled, painted Gloriana he, and everyone else, was used to seeing. He showed no remorse for invading her privacy, calling her 'an old woman … no less crooked in mind than in carcass.'[5]

By this time, Daniell had spent quite a lot of money for no return except a wife and children, all of whom cost money. To add to his growing anger and frustration, Essex's folly had led to the earl being put under house arrest in October 1599 for disobeying the queen. A few days later, Lady Essex entrusted a casket of letters to Jane Daniell.

Daniell's agile mind concluded that the countess would not have done this unless the contents of the casket would be hazardous to the earl if they fell into the hands of the authorities. When things had calmed down a little, four months later, Lady Essex asked for the return of the casket, but then discovered that some of the letters it had contained were not there. Daniell had sneaked them to a London scrivener called Péter Bales, who had copied them.

Daniell later tried to claim that his intention had been to take these letters to the queen as part of his patriotic duty, since they were damaging to Essex who was already in her bad books. Later, Bales claimed that Daniell had ordered him to imitate Essex's handwriting, presumably so he could pass them off as the originals.

Despite pleas from Jane not to upset the Essex applecart further, Daniell, still feeling aggrieved about his lack of social progress and the mythical dowry, promptly demanded £3,000 (about £1 million in 2021). In the early months of 1600, Lady Essex sold her jewellery and scraped together £1,720 (about £600,000 in 2021). Daniell returned the copies of the letters but held onto the originals, probably as surety for the outstanding £1280.[6]

At this point, the Daniells ceased all contact with the Essex household. They leased Hackney Rectory, and renovated and furnished it, claiming they had moved because of the 'healthy air'. The rectory also held the rights to profits from the local harvest.

However, once more Dame Fortune decided to spit on Daniell. Before he had been at Hackney for twelve months, Essex attempted an uprising, his aim being to seize the person of the queen and force her to dismiss

Robert Cecil. This action, depending on your point of view, comes under the heading of heroic failure or arrogantly suicidal.

The uprising failed. Essex was arrested. Daniell was not, since it was known he had broken with the revolting earl. Unfortunately for him, Peter Bales, the scrivener, was also detained and questioned. He lost no time in buying his freedom by telling the inquisitors all about John Daniell and the letters.

At his trial, Essex fulminated about Daniell's trickery, calling him 'an errant thief, one that broke a standard of mine and stole a casket of my wife's'. It became clear that the earl believed Daniell had been in cahoots with his other great rival, Sir Walter Raleigh, although when questioned Daniell always denied this.

However, Essex's action in inciting a revolt against Elizabeth – or was it because he had seen her without facial or dress adornments of any kind? – led directly to his execution. By this time, of course, through the testimony of Bales and the earl, the authorities knew all about John Daniell. They did not take blackmailing of the ruling classes, disgraced or otherwise, lightly.

Daniell was arrested and put in the Gatehouse prison. He was arraigned by the same man who had led the action against Essex. Sir Edward Coke was infamous for his venom and vitriol as a prosecutor. The fact that so eminent a man undertook Daniell's case shows how seriously the government took it.

Daniell was sentenced to stand with his ears nailed to the pillory. However, it is more than likely that this never happened. He certainly petitioned the queen, saying that to punish him in that way would be 'a stain on gentility'. He was fined the enormous sum of £3000, £2000 of which was to compensate Lady Essex.[7]

Frances, Lady Essex, escaped any criticism in the debacle. This was probably because not only was she the daughter of Francis Walsingham, the man to whom Elizabeth owed much of her safety over the years, but also because Frances' first husband had been Sir Philip Sydney, a national hero, the epitome of a gentleman, who had died fighting the Spanish in The Netherlands.

Back to the plot, or rather, Daniell's fate. All his property was seized. He did not even get the first year's harvest rents. Lady Essex asked Sir Robert Cecil to get her £2000 paid immediately and not permit Daniell to repay it in stages because that would mean he was benefitting from his crimes.

Then Daniell's belongings in Hackney Rectory, doubtless purchased with the blackmail money, were seized and sold off at a loss. The lease of the Rectory was sold for £530. Daniell was furious because he believed it to be worth £2000. He was further enraged when, in subsequent years, Heybourne, the new owner, gained the social position Daniell had himself coveted.

John Daniell was released from the Fleet prison in 1604 after James I took the throne. All his petitions to reclaim his lands and bonds were unsuccessful. By 1607 Frances, Lady Essex, was still waiting for her money. Daniell died, intestate, in his lodgings on 30 April 1610.

Tavern Talk:
Did you know that four of Mary, Queen of Scots' black pearls are in King Charles III's Imperial State Crown? Mary I (Bloody Mary) also loved finery and jewellery. A huge 56ct pearl, la perigrina, given to her by Philip of Spain, was given as a gift to another Elizabeth. No, not Elizabeth Tudor but Taylor, when she was married to Richard Burton.

Blasphemy

The definition of blasphemy is the action or offence of speaking sacrilegiously about God or sacred things; profane talk.

It is easy to confuse blasphemy and heresy. Put simply, heresy is speaking or acting against the official religion of the realm. Blasphemy is insulting God. Sedition, which also has religious overtones, is speaking or acting against the monarch. Glad we've sorted that out!

In Tudor England it had become firmly established that those who did not toe the official line of believing the church's teachings should be burned alive. That said, Henry VII took nine years before, in 1494, he burned Joan Boughton, a woman in her eighties, who followed the teachings of John Wycliffe.[1]

The main cause of heretical denunciations was to claim that the bread and wine were not the body and blood of Christ, but merely bread and wine. Henry VIII, that pious son of the church, until it didn't suit him, was an energetic prosecutor and seeker of anyone who transgressed the code of the church. However, heresy in the sixteenth century came to mean not believing the right religion and had little to do with not believing in God.

A huge part of the problem as the Tudor era progressed was that the poor became poorer and that bred discontent. Discontent then leached into every facet of life.[2] And, of course, one of the facets of daily life was the playhouse. Tudor audiences were very politically astute and would know all the in-jokes and howl with laughter or displeasure depending on their views.

All of which leads us to Christopher Marlowe.

CASE STUDY

Christopher (Kit) Marlowe was born in Canterbury in late February 1564, son of a shoemaker. Two months later, in Stratford-upon-Avon, the wife of a glovemaker, called Shakespeare, also had a son whom they christened William. The path of these two men, both clever and both playwrights, is not a subject for this book, but is interesting. The one became possibly the most famous playwright in history. The other … didn't.

However, back to Kit Marlowe. We catch up with him in his twenties when he seems to have been drawn into the world of Elizabethan spies. He had already obtained his BA degree at the age of twenty, but only a government letter three years later, stating that he had been busy in 'matters touching the benefit of his Countrie' stopped him from being thrown off his MA course. Mantel argues that this fed his need to live on the edge. He appears to have been a shifty and unpleasant character, always pushing the boundaries of societal and legal behaviour.[3]

We next see him around 1589 when he was imprisoned for a short time for being present when another man was stabbed to death. It has also been rumoured that he spent time in Paris infiltrating Catholic exiles.[4] However, his true skill was crafting words.

His writings show enough evidence to posit that he enjoyed confrontation with authority. He demonstrates that he doesn't just want to subvert traditional views but spout opinions that were scurrilous, blasphemous and, possibly, treasonable. By the time he and his plays hit the London scene, he was still a young man, but one who wanted to lead a revolution in terms of theatre and performance.. His play *Dido and Aeneas* sailed dangerously close to comparisons with Elizabeth I's courtship by the Duke of Anjou and the situation with Spain.

The story of *Dido and Aeneas* appears on a column in the Sieve portrait of Elizabeth, but Marlowe portrayed the gods in his play as dysfunctional, wilful and irresponsible, caring nothing for the human beings in their care. This was diametrically opposed to everything Elizabeth believed herself to be.

A double agent and informer called Richard Baines made statements to the authorities that Marlowe was an atheist, who loved tobacco and boys too much. He accused the playwright of saying that religion was invented just 'to keep men in awe', that he had claimed Christ was a bastard, and suggested that Jesus and John the Baptist were in an unnatural relationship.

A poem, signed with the name 'Tamburlaine', the main character in Marlowe's play of the same name, was posted on the wall of a Dutch church in London, decrying immigrants. Thomas Kyd, another playwright, was suspected, arrested and tortured. He told his inquisitors that Marlowe had written the poem.[5]

In the spring of 1593, Elizabeth ordered the suppression of Catholics and atheists. She wanted to punish anyone who demonstrated hostility to Protestant immigrants. The Privy Council instructed another informer, Thomas Drury, to gather evidence against Marlowe and on 18 May 1593 a warrant was issued for his arrest. He was accused of blasphemy and 'vile heretical conceipts'. On 20 May Marlowe was brought into the court to attend upon the Privy Council, but there is no record that the Council met on that day. Marlowe was ordered to return each day until told not to.[6]

What happened next is cloaked in mystery. It is known is that on 30 May 1593 Marlowe arrived at Mrs Bull's lodging house in Deptford for drinks with friends and did not leave it alive.

According to the report in the Public Record Office, when the time came to pay for drinks, an argument ensued, presumably about who was going to open his purse. Two witnesses claim that the argument was between Marlowe and a man called Ingram Frizer. Marlowe seized Frizer's dagger, but then Frizer snatched it back and, allegedly in self-defence, thrust it into Marlowe's head just above his right eye. The wound penetrated his brain and he died instantly. He was twenty-nine-years-old.

So, basically, it appears to have been a brawl in a bar that got out of hand. But was it? There is a school of scholastic thought that believes Elizabeth ordered Marlowe to be murdered. His uncontrollable utterances about atheism, immigrants, and his blaspheming utterances became too much to ignore. One informant said: 'Into every Company he Cometh he persuades men to Atheism, willing them not to be afeared of bugbears and hobgoblins, and utterly scorning both God and his ministers.'[7]

At first glance, this theory appears to be unbelievable, but if so, why did Elizabeth issue a pardon to Frizer four weeks after Marlowe's death?

Marlowe, being the character he was, upset many more people than his monarch. Sir Walter Raleigh was allegedly worried about what Marlowe would say when questioned by the Privy Council. Sir Robert Cecil believed Marlowe's plays were full of Catholic propaganda.

However, there is a theory, which is as plausible as any other. It is certain that because of his vocal outpourings, England was becoming an increasingly dangerous place for Marlowe to live. So, it is possible that he faked his death and fled England to escape an inquisition by the Privy Council, which may well have decided to torture him.

This theory goes on to posit that, once safely abroad and obviously living under another name, he continued to write his plays. He then sent them back to England, but, of course, they could not be performed under the name Christopher Marlowe, so he needed another playwright to take the credit. Guess who? William Shakespeare.[8]

Tavern Talk:
Religion was at the heart of many of England's ills in the sixteenth century. If Katherine of Aragon had gone, dutifully, into a nunnery, her marriage annulled so Henry could marry Anne Boleyn, would England still be a Roman Catholic country?

Coney-Catching

The definition of coney-catching is swindling, cheating, trickery, deception; in modern parlance, a confidence trick.

When looking at victims of these types of crime, we must remember that if people were going to market or to a particular shop, they carried money. Depending on what they were buying, that could sometimes be a lot of money.

There were several names for the co-conspirators in this kind of fraud. The subject of the fraud, what we would nowadays call the mark, was called the 'connie'. The 'setter' was the person who made first contact with the person being defrauded. The man who played out the fraud was called the 'verser'. Anyone who aided the trick was the 'barnackle' and any money they won from the connie was the 'purchase'.[1]

Just as today when offenders frequently target the naïve and those who can least afford to lose money, the targets of Tudor fraudsters were frequently apprentices and serving men who were enticed to gamble and lose everything, or more naïve people who came into town from the country.

CASE STUDY

This is the tale of a Suffolk shoemaker, told by Robert Greene, a London writer who wrote about habitual criminals.

The shoemaker lived in Bury St Edmunds. He had 20 marks, (worth about £3000 in 2021) in his purse and was on his way to market to buy a dicker, (ten hides). By mischance, this poor soul ran foul of some coney-catchers, who fleeced him of every penny. The poor, in both senses of the word, shoemaker returned home.

However, some time later one of his swindlers was apprehended and put in the gaol in Bury St Edmunds. By sheer happenstance, the unfortunate shoemaker was in court when this rogue appeared before the justices. They questioned him and asked what his occupation was. He replied he was a gentleman.

Whereupon the shoemaker spoke up, 'Nay, sir, that is a lie, under correction of the worshipful of the bench, you have a trade, and are, by your art a coney-catcher.'

One of the justices, not quite understanding what the shoemaker meant, asked if he was saying the rogue was a wariner, in other words, did he look after a rabbit warren.

'Nay, sir, your worship mistaketh me,' the shoemaker replied. 'He is not a wariner, but a coney-catcher.'

The bench had never heard this term and thought the shoemaker was wandering in his wits, but he persuaded them of the truth. The Justices then enquired about the defendant's life, realised the shoemaker had been swindled and ordered the offender to be whipped.

The shoemaker asked for his money back, which the Justices granted. Whether he ever got his money back is unknown, but he did get some measure of revenge. Greene says that 'he (the shoemaker) lent him (the rogue) so friendly lashes, that almost he made him pay an ounce of blood for every pound of silver.'[2]

Defamation

The definition of defamation is the action of damaging the good reputation of someone; i.e., slander or libel.

Defamation was important in Tudor England. People were very mindful of their social standing and reputations. Defamation cases were heard by ecclesiastical courts, which were kept very busy, especially with cases involving sexual misconduct. If the defendant was found guilty, it could result in social ostracization.

Today, women are more susceptible to trolling because of their gender and, often, their level of education or outspoken views. Dr Kate Lister is a case in point here. A (female) troll who hacked into her online photo album, sent a photo of Dr Lister dressed in the costume of Roxy Heart from the musical *Chicago*, to her employers demanding that this 'slut' be dismissed immediately.[1]

What we now call 'slutshaming' was also common in Tudor England. People – usually women – frequently appeared in the ecclesiastical courts accused of calling their female neighbours whores and strumpets. Anna Miller's case, cited below, emphasises the importance of defamation cases. Since she was a servant, few people and almost certainly not the judiciary or jurors would have taken her word over that of her mistress.

If a man was summoned to court, it was usually his honesty being brought into question. Being accused of theft was frequent. Or questioning a man's origins, such as calling them a 'False Flemmyng' or 'Skottishe prests whore' or 'Walsche prestes son' are examples found in court records.[2]

If the accused failed to prove their innocence by purgation, i.e., testimony from respected members of the community that the defendant was of good character, the courts would usually order a penance. A procession to church – public humiliation – together with a fine usually signalled that the accused had repented and atoned for whatever their misdemeanour had been. It also showed their active desire to regain their good reputation in the eyes of their community.

If the accusers persisted in their defamations but were unwilling to bring the case to court, the church could put the mediaeval equivalent of a gagging order on them, compelling them to keep quiet. This, however, was rarely done.

CASE STUDIES

In 1502, in the London Commissary court, Anna Miller was cited for defaming her master's wife, by accusing her of trying to poison her master. Six months before this, John Daveley was feeling ill and sent Anna to buy medicines. When she returned with the medicine, she gave her master a dose, but saw his wife, Alianor, putting something into it and assumed it was poison.

The following morning, John again asked for a dose of the medicine but Anna said she preferred to make up a new batch: 'Sir, it hath leyn opyn all night, and I wat never fell yn it, therefore I will rather make you another.'

Alianor, being observant and not stupid cornered Anna, called her a 'strong hore', asking if Anna saw her put something in it. John, hearing this exchange, then threatened to make his wife drink all the medicine. Unfortunately, according to the court records, six months after this event, John was still unwell, and presumably unfit to testify. The court was adjourned and there appears to be no record of how this case ended.[3]

Another case from the Norwich Consistory Court in July 1500 demonstrates that public opinion could also play a large part in the bringing of defamation cases. The authorities had no reason to think that Thomas Banburgh had killed his wife, but his neighbours thought so. One of them, Agnes Baken, was candid enough to say in her deposition that she couldn't prove that Thomas had murdered his wife but she was still certain he had: 'All men know nott how sche dyed, for he was hir deith, for he called her upon a pair of stayer & gave her a bloe on the one eyr & brest and said to hir these words, Wilte thow dye for this? I shall quykyn the again.'

Another witness, Joan Wade, gave a slightly different account in that she accused a man called Simon Warner of defaming Banburgh: 'Thomas Bawburgh [sic] was and is a fals and unkind man with his wiff for [he] bete and threw her down a payer of stayers and set his fote on her brest and toke and pullyd hir by the armys till that the wynd was out of her body and so dyed and then he said "Wilt thow dye for this", and toke his fist and bete hir aboute the hedde.'

Whatever the truth of the matter, it is possible Simon Warner and Agnes Baken ensured that, guilty or innocent, not many women would be prepared to be Banburgh's next wife.[4]

In 1596 John Cowper of Swynnerton in Staffordshire was accused of breaking the law regarding working on the Sabbath. Bear in mind that by this time two acts had been passed three years previously, the first being the Act Against Puritans and the second the Act against Recusants. The Bawdy Courts of Lichfield recount the case. They begin by emphasising that no matter what a person's trade or vocation is, they should not work on the Sabbath or a holy day.

We are next informed about the local opinion of John Cowper, which is not complimentary. We hear that the local church minister and other parishioners consider him to be 'a verie slacke & negligent resorter & comer to the Churche to heare divine service', and who often engages in 'worldelie exercises & buissnesses' on Sundays and holy days, and by so doing sets an 'evil' example to his neighbours.

To make matters worse, not only is Cowper not going to church *and* working on Sundays, he also drives his cattle past the church making a lot of noise and interrupting divine service 'to the greate scandal & offence of the godlie'.

Cowper is specifically accused of absenting himself from divine service and enticing other people to do the same. When a church official tried to serve a warrant on him to appear before the court, he grabbed the papers and kept them so that due process could not be followed. John Cowper was not the first inhabitant of the village to risk the wrath of the law for not conforming to religious requirements. Sadly, the court records do not tell us what happened or even how Cowper came to fall out so badly with the church authorities. Although there may be a clue in the citing of his taking his cattle past the church. Perhaps he was simply a farmer who was far too busy with his cattle on Sundays to adhere to the law.[5]

Embezzlement

The dictionary definition of embezzlement is 'theft or misappropriation of funds placed in one's trust or belonging to one's employer'.

In this section we enter the world of the customs officials in Elizabethan England. Goods coming into the country have always been subject to customs checks and often stored in bonded warehouses. However, these did not exist in Tudor England. The payment of duty on imports had to be made at the time the goods arrived in the country, or a bond that promised payment in due course was given to the authorities.

However, it was not always possible for the person importing the goods to find enough sureties to cover the bond and he had to sell the goods in order to raise the money to pay the duty owed. Of course, if prices were low, that proved an enormous problem, not helped by the fact that the duty had to paid in one lump sum. This raised the price of the goods and together with the fact that heavily taxed goods required a large amount of capital, it stifled competition.[1]

The system used by officials in late Tudor England was flawed because it was very tempting for the customs officials themselves to defraud the government and almost impossible to legislate because it was not centralised.[2]

Administration was almost non-existent and therefore it was extremely difficult to regulate. Allied to that was that officers' wages were very low. Although Marquess Winchester tried to reform the system, by the closing decades of the sixteenth century corruption in the customs system was rampant.

People who tried to blow the whistle on fraudulent practices were usually informers trying to get a payout from the authorities. Two petitioners in particular, Richard Carmarden and Oliver Dewbeney, were assiduous in their petitions to the queen.

Carmarden was a merchant and began to investigate customs fraud around 1565. He wrote 'Caveat to The Quene' describing abuses committed by Williams Byrd and Rivet. Dewbeney wrote further reports to Lord Burghley in the late sixteenth century and named offenders.[3] However,

Embezzlement

Carmarden does not in these petitions request any particular reward. Unlike Dewbeney, in 1572, who wanted the post of surveyor. He was unsuccessful and repeated his petition the following year, but this time with a covering letter to Treasurer Burghley asking him to let Burghley's thanks and reward be appropriate to Dewbeney's service.

When both Carmarden and Dewbeney were investigated to ascertain the true situation, it became clear that the customs officers named were violent in the protection of their illegal dealings. The two men had a difficult relationship with both the customs and merchant fraternity because they kept informing on the officials, and, presumably, any merchants who were complicit in the embezzlement of duties. Indeed, by 1582 Carmarden is still petitioning the queen, saying he is trying to inform her of illegal acts at the risk of his life, and that he was threatened at Windsor when the court was sitting there.

It is certain that the corrupt political elite were at risk of being unveiled. These included one Thomas Smythe, a powerful customs officer who was bribing Burghley, Walsingham and Leicester to the tune of £2,000. They also ordered the queen's grooms not to admit Carwarden to Elizabeth's presence, but she sent for him and heard what he had to say.

Although some have tried to discredit Carwarden's testimony, it is certainly true that violence directed at informers by customs officials was common. Thomas Watkins complained about one officer called John Dowle of Bristol, so it is likely that Carmarden was telling the truth.

Officers – called waiters – were often the first point of contact for merchants since they were supposed to ensure no goods entered the custom house that had not had the required duty paid. The waiters would target merchants who imported fine goods and strike up a friendship, or, if the merchants were too high on the social scale, their servants. They would offer to conceal a portion of the imported goods, saying that the duty required was too high. The waiters would then split the saving 50:50.

There were perhaps eighteen waiters in London alone. If the merchant tried to hide the goods to avoid paying either the duty or the bribe, waiters would be incensed at the merchants breaking of the League of Thievery.

At the other end of the system were the searchers, who were responsible for making sure the certificate of customs – known as a cocket – for goods being exported matched what was actually on the ships. Should merchants want to smuggle goods out that were not on the cocket, the searchers were usually amenable to a bribe. Being paid to look the other way was a lucrative business.[4]

The aforementioned Williams Byrd was a customs officer, Rivet was a controller, and their accomplice, Richard Gray, a searcher. It was alleged that they had fabricated cockets and these would be given to the merchant or the master of the ship before it sailed. Gray would make a false declaration that a certain amount of cloth on the cocket could not be loaded because of unforeseen circumstances and a certificate would then be issued saying that the unloaded cloth would go out on a later sailing without payment of duty.

Ensuring the success of such embezzlement involved many people; meetings with merchants and officers to make sure the records going to the exchequer matched. The searcher would also be charged with ensuring the merchant did not try to double-cross him and his colleagues.[5]

Fraud

The dictionary definition of fraud is 'a person or thing intended to deceive others, typically by unjustifiably claiming or being credited with accomplishments or qualities'.

When detailing a case study, it is usually easy to categorise the crime. However, there was an inveterate conman in late Tudor England whose activities cover alchemy, fraud, magic, and probably more we do not know about. I am indebted to Alec Ryrie's excellent book *The Sorcerer's Tale* for an account of the deeds of one Gregory Wisdom.[1]

Of course, a conman's actions can encompass several crimes, but the fraud case study I want to highlight is that of Henry, Lord Neville, someone who we would today probably say was credulous – if we were being polite.

Greed fuels many crimes, including this one. Sharp practice comes in many packages. Some are legal. Some are witty. One such running only a few years ago involved an advert put in a newspaper which said 'send me £1.50 and I will send you back instructions on how to make a lot of money'. An outlay of £1.50 to make a lot of money? Irresistible. Of course, when the instructions arrived, they said: 'put an advert in the papers saying that for £1.50 you will send instructions on how to make a lot of money'. Amusing. But not illegal.

Henry, Lord Neville belonged to one of the oldest families in England. One of his forebears was Richard Neville, Earl of Warwick, self-styled kingmaker, during the Wars of the Roses. The Neville family was also involved in the Pilgrimage of Grace in 1536.

Henry, Lord Neville was living proof that a fool and his money are soon parted. He was in Henry VIII's favour and became the king's carver in his Privy Chamber. However, he was also a gambler and frequenter of brothels. It is interesting to note that many gambling houses doubled as brothels, so these establishments had a double pull for Henry Neville. Very soon he was deep in debt.

One of his household servants, a man called Ninian Menville, was a favourite of Henry's mother. Indeed, she had once saved him from being hanged after he had committed a violent robbery and he took full advantage of her high regard.

Menville knew all about Lord Henry's debts. And Menville knew Gregory Wisdom. They played the hapless lord like a fish. A greedy and desperate fish.

Menville introduced Neville to a man with the single name, Wisdom. Wisdom told Henry he could create a ring that would affect how the dice fell and that the ring would net Henry £2,000-3,000 very quickly.

For this service, Wisdom asked for a pension for life of £20 per annum. This roughly converts to just under £14,000 in 2021, and by today's standards is not extortionate. Henry, thinking he was being clever, offered £10, but only if the ring worked and only when his father, Sir Ralph Neville, died and he inherited the estate.

Wisdom agreed, but not wanting to submit too easily, haggled for Henry to pay his expenses. Had he agreed quickly to Neville's terms, Henry might have become suspicious. Or perhaps not.

Wisdom moved into the household, but did almost nothing, assuring Henry that the ring was 'being made by angels'. On Christmas morning he presented Henry with the ring and a contract for the £10 annual pension to begin immediately.

Later on Christmas Day, Henry went out with his new 'magic' ring to visit friends and play dice. He won £30 and came home delighted. Wisdom asked for most of the £30 to 'go out and get new supplies'. Wisdom continued to promise things that never materialised, and eventually Henry became irritated and Wisdom 'withdrew'.

To celebrate his freedom, Henry then went out to his favourite gambling den and lost all his money. He sent for Wisdom, who questioned him. Knowing Henry's inclinations, Wisdom opined that Henry must have had 'to do with women'.

Menville and Wisdom's next trick was to tell Henry that there was a great sum of money buried on the Neville estate under a wayside cross. Wisdom assured Henry that he had a spirit, kept in a crystal, who would find out just where the money was. The next day he returned with the good news that the treasure totalled £2,000. Of course, there was no money. Anyone with two brain cells to rub together would think that by this time Henry would realise he was being conned. But no. He really was that stupid.

Menville and Wisdom played on his desperate need for money to pay his debts. Wisdom, having realised Henry did not get on with Lady Anne, his wife, and that he would come into a great deal of money when Sir Ralph died, persuaded Henry that he – Wisdom – could kill his wife and his father and make both deaths look like an act of God.

To give him his due, Henry was appalled and sent both Menville and Wisdom packing. However, three weeks later, they met again and Wisdom assured Henry he had already put a spell on Lady Anne and Sir Ralph. This was presented, no doubt, as what is now called a win-win situation. Lady Anne would go to heaven, Henry would inherit, and he could choose a new and more congenial wife. Naturally, neither Lady Anne nor Sir Ralph died.

Because his debts were colossal, Henry was arrested on 1 October 1546 and sent to the Fleet Prison. Then the story about the fraud came out.

Menville and Wisdom were rounded up and Menville once more appealed to Lady Katherine, Henry's mother, to save him. Menville was imprisoned and not released until 1550. Henry faced execution because the 1542 Act Against Conjurations, Witchcrafts, Sorcery and Enchantments decreed that anyone who consulted a magician had committed a capital crime and the punishment for the offender and the 'magician' was death by hanging.

However, as we find time and again, it isn't what you know, it's who you know. Henry, Lord Neville knew many influential people at court. Lord Paget was Secretary of State and a member of the Privy Council. Neville begged Lord Paget to spare his family the shame of an execution. It was obvious he was no threat to the state and this was, perhaps, the major factor in the decision not to execute him. The fact that Sir Ralph and Lady Anne intervened to save him must also have helped.

Lord Henry spent a few months in prison before being released in March 1547, two months after Henry VIII died. His debts totalled £437, roughly £193,000 in 2021. Sir Ralph paid them.

Henry, Lord Neville went on to live close to the court. He inherited the earldom from Sir Ralph in 1550, and, under the protestant Edward VI, was made a member of the Privy Council and ambassador to Scotland in 1552. In May 1552 he was also made a Knight of the Garter and Lord-Lieutenant of Durham.

After Edward VI died, Henry changed his coat, supported the Catholic Mary Tudor, and participated in her coronation ceremony. When Mary died and Elizabeth became queen, Henry turned his coat again and was made Lieutenant-General of the North. He died in 1563. There is no information on whether he ever conquered his love for gambling and brothels.

Gregory Wisdom is a fascinating character, mostly because, in truth, we know so little about him. He appears to have romped through the sixteenth century employing a startling number of cons so diffuse in character, it is hard to believe they were the brainchild of one man. Probably the last mention of him we can find is his will, made in 1599, shortly before the Tudor era ended.

One cannot help but think he would have made an absolute killing with Elizabeth's successor, James I, who believed utterly in fairies and witchcraft.

Gangs

Although small groups of criminals working in consort have always been with us, in the Norfolk Assizes in 1452, a gang of villains roaming the county terrorising the inhabitants was highlighted. It cited the case of a Mr Paston, who may or may not have been one of the family who wrote the series of letters during the Wars of the Roses. Mr Paston and his servants were attacked at the door of Norwich Cathedral,. Paston was hit on his bare head with a sword thus 'polluting' the sanctuary of the church.[1] It was not until the middle of the sixteenth century that organised crime began to seriously raise its head.[2]

The reality of organised gangs of thieves, cut-purses, pickpockets et al became a real problem in London. The primary cause of the proliferation of these gangs was the expansion of trade with Europe and beyond, and the fact that many out of work people and casual workers flocked to the city to either find work or for more nefarious reasons.

As London became an economic centre for everyday, less exclusive merchandise, this provided an excellent breeding ground for crime. The lower social orders were able to afford the multitude of goods displayed on market stalls. Shoplifters and thieves were attracted to stalls selling these products, and even more to the browsing customers who wore them. Many customers wore scarves or ribbons, or might be wearing silk or metal bracelets. All things that were meat and drink to thieves.

As London became richer, it enticed the ruling classes and gentlemen to relocate. Skilled professionals knew they could find work there. All these people carried valuables and/or money. And some of them were not wily in the way of foists etc. who could, and did, relieve them of everything they had on their persons.

Another factor that helped the increase of criminal gangs was that London was organised so that certain districts were devoted to one trade. Should crowds be in that place, then opportunities for resourceful thieves were plentiful. From around 1550 London gradually became a place of conspicuous consumption. Gardens and parks appeared, as did gambling houses, pleasure gardens, bowling alleys and theatres, all places known for high spending, gaming and prostitution.[3]

With the growth provided by skilled professionals who needed workers, labourers flocked to the city at a time when land enclosures had put many rural people out of work. Rising food prices and disastrous harvests all conspired to drive people to London. The suburbs grew and became the locations for industries like leather-making, glass-making and brewing. Since these industries were in the suburbs, they were not within the purview of city regulations or taxes, or even the rules applied to apprentices.[4]

One estimate stated that in 1602 there were '30,000 idle persons and masterless men' in the city. As homeless, unemployed people moved to London, the authorities began to build hospitals and collect taxes to help the poor. Instead of improving the situation, this meant that people housed in these institutions often formed schools to teach other inmates how to rob houses, pick pockets and cut purses.[5]

Of course, such a profitable industry found opportunities to expand. People were happy to use their skills for felonious purposes. A new industry grew up – informing. Inn keepers would tell pedlars and highwaymen which of their guests were worth robbing and where they were travelling the following day. Ballad singers and street vendors picked up gossip, passing it on to street thieves and blackmailers. Singers drew crowds, the perfect setting for robbery. Servants to the wealthy were not above passing on information about their masters.

And so organised crime became an occupation, helped by the fact that policing and the judiciary were not unified. Another fact helping criminals was that some areas, called liberties, were immune from city legislation because they came under the umbrella of ecclesiastical privilege.

The Reformation eroded the power of the church. The sale of former church lands led to what were termed 'bastard sanctuaries' springing up which gave gangs a relatively safe place in which to carry on business as usual. Powerful families bought or were given previously church-owned property and these became the Tudor equivalent of no-go areas where the authorities had no power to arrest felons.

The physical layout of London also helped the gang culture. Houses overhung the streets making them dark and dangerous at the best of times. Some streets were mere paths with the detritus of previous centuries underfoot. Travel was hazardous. Piles of dung and rotting material, aided by the lack of decent light from lanterns, meant that patrols frequently couldn't provide protection to ordinary citizens.

Fencing shops grew up. These provided a convenient place for ill-gotten gains to be stored. Often thieves lived in the same house as their fence, who provided them with enough stability to enable them to be more effective criminals. Fences also formed schools to teach others how to pilfer and rob houses. Children would be taught how to lift a purse without the owner of it feeling a thing. Parents taught children just as they had been taught by their parents.[6]

Certain public houses or taverns became known as bousing kens, where criminals could share their knowledge and experience; teach other felons new skills and meet their accomplices. Talents taught in these dens of iniquity would include confidence tricks, picking pockets, prostitution, and thieving. There were also 'pennyrents', which were low lodging houses that helped foster the increase of the criminal fraternity.

Officers employed by the authorities to control criminal activities were grossly underpaid and overworked, in addition to the lack of any kind of coordination with other nearby areas. Despite the existence of the watch, constables, urban militias and the Privy Council, there is ample evidence that they did not have the resources to investigate or punish crime, let alone stop it. What happened was that the authorities took to issuing pardons in return for the felon turning informer. In fact what usually happened was that the newly turned informer conspired with the local fence to fine tune their criminal activities.[7]

CASE STUDY

This is not a specific case study, more an example of how gangs took advantage of events wherever they could.

One of the finest opportunities for the criminal fraternity to ply their 'trade' was the annual Bartholomew Fair, held at Smithfield. This fair had been protected by royal charter for centuries. For a day or more, it was the perfect chance for the underworld to make a killing as they mingled with more respectable citizens. Unlike most of the other local fairs, Bartholomew was a national event attracting vendors and customers from all over England.

The formal opening was performed by the mayor, who, on horseback in his robes, read a proclamation: It began: 'The right honourable lord mayor of the City of London, and his right worshipful brethren the aldermen of the said city, streightly charge and command, on the behalf of our sovereign lady the queen, that all manner of persons of whatever estate, degree or condition thy be, having recourse to this fair, keep the peace of our said sovereign lady the queen.'

It further stated that anyone found breaching the peace would be imprisoned and fined; that all food and beverages would be 'wholesome and of true measure'. Only civic officials had the power to arrest anyone.

The fair had its own court of complaints called the Court of Pie-Powder, which was for the hearing of complaints regarding commercial activities. The lawyer Sir Edward Coke opined that justice was enacted in the Court of Pie-Powder as fast as dust fell off the feet. The authorities had spies who went around the fair ensuring that fair play was done and seen to be done.[8]

Heresy

The dictionary definition of heresy is 'belief or opinion contrary to orthodox religious (especially Christian) doctrine'.

Many people believe in karma, or 'what goes around comes around'. This was exemplified in the case of clergyman John Rogers who insisted in 1550 that Joan Bocher should be burned as a heretic. When John Foxe – he of the *Book of Martyrs* – remonstrated and asked that she be spared the fire and another kind of death be chosen, Rogers replied that being burned alive was gentler than many other forms of death. What a shame we cannot ask him if that's true because five years after Joan was burned, Mary I burned Rogers for the same offence.[1] I think the relevant response is hoist with his own petard.

In Tudor England the usual penalty for heresy was to be burned at the stake. We can feel sorry for the ordinary population of England from the time of Henry VIII's Reformation onwards. Religious edicts could change from year to year and the penalty for heresy was harsh. It became the sixteenth-century equivalent of George Orwell's 'Big Brother'. Today, this is the law and will always be the law, except that tomorrow it might be different.

There was also the north/south divide, which was quite as strong then as it is now. Most of the north of England – which seemed to begin north of Essex – was Catholic and although most people complied with reluctance, there were active pockets of resistance.

In the fourteenth century, John Wycliffe came to prominence. Wycliffe, a priest and theologian, challenged the authority of the Pope and the immoral behaviour of clerics and monks. He also believed that the Bible, not the church, was the supreme source of religious authority. He had the Bible translated into English so that 'ordinary' people could read it, although quite how many ordinary people could read is questionable.

The Pope accused him of heresy and he was burned in 1384. Many of his followers, called Lollards, were also burned. They were named thus because they allegedly prayed with a low muttering sound.

The Tudor monarchs were all alert to the threat of heresy, though the numbers of deaths in each reign varied. Henry VII executed twenty-four, his son, Henry VIII, eighty-one. Edward VI only executed two people and Elizabeth four.[2] The most prolific was Mary I, who burned 283 heretics, and in the twenty-first century there are still people who look askance at Catholics because their religion in some quarters is inextricably connected with 'Bloody Mary'. This prejudice was still alive and well in the early twentieth century when the composer Edward Elgar suffered socially and economically because he was a Catholic.[3]

The Glorious Revolution of 1688 brought back horror stories of Bloody Mary and her burning martyrs, so when the Catholic James II was ousted by the Dutch Protestant William III and his English wife (who happened to be James' elder daughter), the Act of Settlement was enshrined in law in 1701. It stated that the monarch 'could not be or marry a Roman Catholic', a tenet of law that forced Prince Michael of Kent to renounce his – admittedly very slim – claim to the British throne when he married Marie Christine. This rule was overturned in 2015.[4]

In Tudor England, heresy did not escalate until Martin Luther's doctrines emerged in the early part of Henry VIII's reign. But the spread of the new religion really took hold in the late 1520s when Henry's attempts to divorce Katherine of Aragon became public. His divorce crisis was one catalyst for the Reformation and the rapid spread of what would become Protestantism.

This is ironic because Henry had won acclaim from Pope Leo X for his treatise against the new doctrines being preached by Luther. The Pope awarded Henry the title of 'Defender of the Faith'. Just ten years later, he repudiated many tenets of Roman Catholicism in order to achieve his divorce.[5]

There then followed years of confusion about what was and was not acceptable. Archbishop Thomas Cranmer, one of Mary's victims, joined with Thomas Cromwell to produce the Bible in English, and in 1538 Henry VIII agreed that every parish must buy and display a copy of the Coverdale Bible in the nave of their church with ready access by anyone in the parish who was literate.[6]

The most famous of Henry's victims accused of heresy, and the one who came closest to his personal life, was Anne Askew. Henry's last wife, Katherine Parr, was an adherent of Askew's and almost came to grief herself because of it. Henry regarded her talking about the new religion as preaching to him. Katherine only realised at the last moment that her sole chance of safety was to throw herself on Henry's mercy and declare she had never been trying to preach to him or teach him but merely take his mind away from the pain of the ulcers on his legs. Henry believed her.[7] Nice catch, girl.

However, when Mary came to the throne, everything reverted to pre-Reformation statutes and England reverted to Roman Catholicism. When it comes to the Marian Persecutions of Mary I's reign, so much has been written that there is little to add to the wealth of literature about the Protestant martyrs, many of whom are celebrated in Foxe's *Book of Martyrs*.

It is all very well looking back almost five centuries and commenting on Mary's behaviour, but this author has real issues about why she could truly believe that the more people she burned, the more the rest of her subjects would come to believe that Roman Catholicism was the true faith. One wonders if she would have gone to the stake for her faith. I think she might. There is no doubt that her husband, Philip of Spain, an advocate of the Spanish Inquisition, thought Mary far too radical.[8]

It would be logical to posit that the reverses and horrors of her youth – being wrenched from the company of her beloved mother, being forced to wait upon her half-sister, Elizabeth, and, worst of all in her eyes, betraying her faith by taking the oath that proclaimed her father head of the church – would be likely to bring on hysteria. She certainly suffered under the latter years of Henry VIII and under her half-brother, Edward VI. 'My health is more unstable than that of any creature and I have all the greater need to rejoice in the testimony of a pure conscience', she wrote to the Council of King Edward VI, in January 1552.[9]

One of the most horrific accounts from Mary's reign dates to Guernsey in 1556 when three women, Perotine Massey, Guillemine Gilbert and Katharine Cawches, were tried for heresy. All three declared that they had been acting according to the policies of Edward VI. Neighbours averred that they had refused to follow the measures set in place by Mary. They were condemned to be burned at the stake. Perotine Massey was 'great with child', and though in times past pregnant women could not be executed, sixteenth-century Catholics apparently thought it was fine and dandy.

The executioner tried to strangle them but the ropes snapped and they fell into the fire. The heat caused Perotine's stomach to burst and her baby was cast out. One of the witnesses, a certain William House, grabbed the newborn and laid it upon the grass. At this point, the bailiff, Helier Gosselin ordered that the child should be picked up and cast back into the fire.[10]

Elizabeth was more measured in her approach to heretics. This was especially difficult for her because, by now, many of her Council, including William Cecil, Lord Burghley, and Robert Dudley, Earl of Leicester, were Puritans. Elizabeth found herself fighting on two fronts: against the Catholics, who had been told to kill her if they could; and against the Puritan element, which she found too extreme the other way. During her reign, the official religion was Protestantism with some traditions of the Catholic mass. The Puritans wanted Elizabeth to change the Religious Settlement to remove anything that pertained to Catholicism. However, as the Puritan element of her Council died out – Burghley, Dudley, Walsingham et al – the Puritan impetus weakened.

Supporters of some martyrs, especially during the Marian Persecutions, made the victims a special garment, called a 'Shirt of Flame'. This was to represent them going to God clean and pure. Sometimes, the shirt would be doused in oil first to reduce the length of the victim's suffering.[11]

CASE STUDIES

Joan Bocher

Edward VI came to the throne at the age of nine. His government, led by the Duke of Somerset, the Lord Protector until his fall and execution in 1552, started out being fairly tolerant where religion was concerned. Somerset was a secret Protestant, something he had kept well hidden while Henry VIII was alive.

Stephen Gardiner, Bishop of Winchester, argued with Somerset about permitting Protestant innovations during a minority rule. Gardiner had complained about Protestant books being circulated and incidents of church images being smashed. Somerset accused Gardiner of scaremongering and warned him to behave himself.

Edward VI, under the tutelage of Somerset and Cranmer, became a Protestant, but he disliked extremists. So when the Anabaptist movement gained momentum, it caused Edward and his ministers a few problems.

Anabaptists not only opposed infant baptism but they also denied that Christ was divine or born of the Virgin Mary. They denounced the ownership of private property, advocating that all things should be owned by the people in common.

Heresy

Joan Bocher had been an Anabaptist for years. After the execution of her friend, Anne Askew, she began circulating pamphlets stating what, to Catholics and Protestants alike, were obnoxious views. She was brought before Bishop Nicholas Ridley and found guilty of heresy. John Rogers, a clergyman and translator of the Bible in English, was brought in to talk to Bocher and persuade her to recant. She refused. Rogers declared she must be burned at the stake.

John Foxe tried to persuade Rogers to spare Joan, even though he disagreed with her views. There is a story, possibly apocryphal, that the then twelve-year-old Edward VI refused to sign her death warrant but was berated by Archbishop Cranmer, another of Mary I's victims, that according to the law of Moses, Joan must go to the fire. Edward is alleged to have replied, 'Cranmer, I will sign the verdict at your risk and responsibility before God's judgement throne.'

Cranmer also tried to convince Joan to recant, but she still refused. She was burned at the stake on 2 May 1550, still upbraiding anyone trying to convert her and saying they would all see in time that she had been right. One of her dying claims was that there were a thousand Anabaptists living in London.[12]

As a result of her final words, a commission was set up in January 1551 to deal with the problem of Anabaptists and any other groups preaching heresy. George van Parris was one of the first people to be arrested. He was examined by Cranmer, Nicholas Ridley and Miles Coverdale, who interpreted because Parris did not speak English. He was particularly asked about his beliefs on 'God the Father is only God', and 'Christ is not very God'.

This meant that, unlike the agreement at the Council of Nicea and the introduction of the Nicene Creed, which refers to God, Christ and the Holy Spirit being equal – the Holy Trinity – Parris believed Christ was not equal because he was born as a man and was therefore inferior to God. This was a view first expressed by the Alexandrian priest, Arius. Parris refused to recant, was condemned as an Arian, and burned alive in April 1551.[13]

Joyce Lewes (or Lewis)[14]

Joyce (or Jocasta) was born a gentlewoman, according to John Foxe and delighted in 'gay apparel and suchlike foolishness'. Sounds a girl after my own heart. She was married twice, first to Sir George Appleby with whom she had two children. Appleby was killed at the Battle of Pinkie in 1547, and in September of that year Joyce married Thomas Lewis of Mancetter, just off the A5 near Tamworth in Warwickshire. She was a good Catholic under Mary I, until she heard of the suffering of the martyr, Laurence Saunders, in Coventry in 1555.

Joyce began to talk to a neighbour, John Glover. Glover's brother, Robert, had also been executed in 1555. Glover told her that the mass was a Papist invention and therefore odious in the sight of God. He also reproved her for delighting in the material things in life and not thinking enough about what would please God.

Joyce began to hate the mass, declaring it evil and abominable – much to the displeasure of her husband – and refusing to go to church. At this point she was accused and brought before the Bishop of Lichfield, Ralph Baines. He sent a citation to her which, according to legend, Thomas Lewis forced the messenger to eat. Joyce told Baines that by refusing holy water, she was not displeasing God nor had she offended against His laws. Baines then ordered her husband to bring Joyce to trial within a month or pay a fine of £100. Despite pleas from her friends, Thomas brought her to trial, but he asked friends, and especially John Glover, to find some way to save her because he would not pay the fine, nor forfeit anything for her sake. True to his word, at the end of the month, Thomas brought her before Baines again. He could not move her and she called his attempts to persuade her to take the sacrament 'ungodly and wicked'.

She was condemned and spent a year in jail in Lichfield. The night before her execution, two priests came to hear her confession, at which point she told them they would be disappointed because she had already made her confession to Christ.

She was, allegedly, very merry and gay all that night, spending it in prayer, reading and talking to those who had come to give her comfort. The sheriff came next morning to tell Joyce that Queen Mary had determined she must die that day. She told him she welcomed the message. One hour later, accompanied by a friend to give her comfort and support, Joyce was taken to the execution site, a fair distance from her prison. Because she had been inside a cell for a year, when she emerged into the December air, a friend asked the sheriff to allow Joyce a drink.

She then prayed, desiring God to abolish the idolatrous mass and deliver the realm from papistry. Several people shouted 'Amen'. She appeared to be very cheerful when chained to the stake and neither struggled nor stirred, probably because the 'drink' had been laced with something powerful. She was seen to hold her hands upwards to heaven and died very quickly.

Heresy

An old priest who had witnessed the execution then tried to discover the names of the people who had shouted 'Amen', but to no avail, or as Foxe terms it, 'God, whose providence sleeps not, did defend them from the hands of these cruel tyrants.'

Tavern Talk:
Mary I had many griefs in her life. Her inability to make Philip of Spain love her or turn England once more into a Roman Catholic country. However, one of her final griefs was the loss of Calais in 1558. England had held the town since 1347 during the 100-years war. Mary said that when she died, they would find 'Philip' and 'Calais' inscribed on her heart.

Insurrection

The difference between rebellion and insurrection is that rebellion is armed resistance to an established government or ruler while insurrection is an organized opposition to an authority. In other words, they are very much the same thing but with a slightly different emphasis. It would appear that a rebellion is an armed uprising and an insurrection … isn't. Like different flavoured sausages!

When Henry VII seized the throne after Bosworth and began to show his true character –like backdating his reign to the day before the battle so that all Yorkists were traitors – England found itself in a state of flux. The system had always been that the nobility ruled their particular demesnes and, within them, the local population. However, while the appetite after thirty odd years of constant conflict and uncertainty was for peace, some of the aforementioned nobles became disgruntled very quickly.

Edward IV had always ruled by promoting those close to him to various earldoms etc., based purely on their support for him. So, when it became expedient to take the earldom of Northumberland away from his close friend and cousin, John Neville, Edward believed their friendship could take the strain. But at that time, it was a political decision to give the Northumberland earldom to Henry Percy in March 1470. Edward made John Neville Marquis of Montagu instead, but John lost all the revenue from the Northumberland earldom. Consequently, and apparently with some reluctance, he turned from Edward, joined his brother at the Battle of Barnet in 1471, and was killed.[1]

So, basically, whoever was king had always promoted the people around him, nobles who were his friends and supporters. Henry VII did not do that. He didn't have friends, and, in truth, at court his supporters were usually in two minds about him. There's a surprise!

Up until the Battle of Stoke in 1487 there was unrest at court caused by Henry's claim to the throne. It was at best tenuous and he was never able to eradicate the taint of illegitimacy surrounding his lineage and, therefore, his claim. After being an exile for fourteen years, always on the lookout for a secret dagger thrust to get rid of him, Henry, understandably, developed a distrustful nature.[2]

Some of his nobles began to wonder if they had made a grave error in supporting him because, to put it in modern parlance, they were getting nothing for their money. Henry did not have one tenth of the charm and allure that had drawn people to Edward IV. Even Richard III, who was disliked in London because he had looked after the north for so long that he had taken on their blunt way of talking, was, at first, reasonably popular. Then, of course, came the spectre of the young sons of Edward IV who had so conveniently disappeared after being declared illegitimate. However, compared to Henry VII, Richard III was Mr Charisma himself.

CASE STUDY

Sir Humphrey Stafford had fought with Richard III at Bosworth Field, as had Francis Lovell, who had been one of Richard's close friends from an early age and one of his most ardent supporters. However, one could not even call their attempt at insurrection in April 1486 anything other than a woeful failure. The two main protagonists of this debacle had, since Bosworth, been in sanctuary in Colchester, but they had escaped and began to prepare to unseat Henry and put a Yorkist back on the throne.

In April 1486 Henry VII left his pregnant queen in London and went on a progress to the north of England. Although some people in later years, Sir Hugh Conway for one, insisted that Henry did not credit Stafford and Lovell with scheming to unseat him, we must remember that displaying an attitude of complete confidence in his own claim to the throne, and his stability on it, would be second nature to Henry, despite any ideas he had to the contrary. Perhaps he already had in place a network of spies to keep him informed.[3]

Nonetheless, by the time Henry reached Pontefract on 20 April, the rumours that Stafford and Lovell were moving from thought to action was becoming clear. For Henry, this must have been something of a jolt. His reign was eight months old, still precarious, but while the nobility might have reservations about him, the north had traditionally been Lancastrian.

This was despite the enormous esteem in which the north of England had held Richard III when he was Duke of Gloucester. He had brought a degree of stability to the area – especially important when it was common for the marauding Scots to come as far south as Newcastle. Furthermore, rumours that Richard had killed or caused to be killed, the princes in the Tower, had shifted popular support to the new regime.

Meanwhile, Francis Lovell had led uprisings at Richard's former home in Middleham Castle and then moved to attack York while the Stafford brothers, Humphrey and Thomas, were planning to capture Worcester. And this is where it all went wrong for the plotters.[4] Mostly because they were incapable of arranging two cakes on a plate.

On 23 April Lovell attempted to seize Henry in York. Needless to say, he failed, whereupon he fled to the court of Margaret of Burgundy, sister of Edward IV and Richard III and unwaveringly anti-Tudor. (As an aside, Lovell was prominent in supporting Lambert Simnel in the Battle of Stoke the following year and may have escaped to Scotland after the battle. At which point, he vanishes from the history books.)

However, back to the plot – literally. After the failure of Lovell to capture and assassinate Henry, the king offered a general pardon to Lovell's troops, at which point they very sensibly deserted him. News of this reached the Stafford brothers in Worcester where they had been trying to raise more troops. According to documents and letters, Humphrey Stafford had contacted a man in Kidderminster called Richard Osenay, and in an attempt to recruit him, told Oseney that Henry had pardoned him and produced forged letters to confirm his assertion. He and his followers said that Henry had been captured in York and that Edward, Earl of Warwick, a simple child, had been set free and was in York with Lovell.

And this is where the whole thing fell apart, mostly because the Staffords were abysmal planners but also because Henry had a lot of support in the Midlands. Two factors were in play here. The first was that everyone was sick and tired of continual civil strife. The people had been going through this for the past thirty years. Henry offered the prospect of peace, and with peace would come stability and economic growth, both of which were desperately needed. The second reason was the spreading rumour that Richard III had killed his nephews, resulting in a general lack of support for the Yorkist cause.

Henry, who made sure to obtain details of who had aided the rebels through the system of letters and documentation that became a hallmark of his reign, soon had indictments flying hither and yon in Worcestershire. The bailiff and people of Worcester were indicted for allowing Stafford to enter the city and not putting an efficient guard on the gates.[5]

Sessions were held in Birmingham and Worcester and Henry took a close interest in them. Some of those on trial cited the production of Stafford's forgeries that the king had pardoned him as the reason for their actions.

Insurrection

These were generally dismissed as *de mandato domini regis viva voce* – at the voice of the king. This became a benchmark of Henry's rule; if it concerned him, he would, and did, interfere in judicial proceedings.[6]

What happened next was to set a precedent. After the Battle of Tewkesbury in 1471, the Lancastrian nobles fled to the abbey for sanctuary, but it was not a designated place of sanctuary and they were dragged out.[7]

In 1486, after the aborted attempt to take Worcester, the Stafford brothers were tracked to some woods near Bewdley, but by the time Thomas Cokesey, who had apparently been ordered by Henry to find them, arrived, the Staffords had already gone. They fled to Culham in Oxfordshire and back into sanctuary.

A man called John Savage, assisted by a band of about sixty followers, went into the church and forcibly removed them. This led to a legal case during which Humphrey argued that his removal from Culham was unlawful and he and his brother should be returned. The judges wanted to consult the church, but it was argued that this was a secular matter; that the king had letters patent saying that he alone had power over the realm and no ecclesiastical authority, not even the Pope, could change that.

Stafford decided to fight this ruling. It soon became clear that Henry was becoming impatient with the judges' delay in making a decision. To add to his woes, there had been small pockets of rioting against him in London. Eventually, the judges in the Stafford case decided that sanctuary could not be pleaded in cases of treason. This was the start not just of Henry interfering in the judicial system if it suited him but developing the habit of generous pardons to followers and brutal treatment of anybody who led an uprising.

The decision regarding the protection of sanctuary led to protests to the Pope. He issued a Papal Bull which excluded suspected traitors from the right to such asylum.[8]

Henry did show a degree of mercy in this case. Although Humphrey Stafford went to the block at Tyburn on 8 July 1486 for his part in the insurrection, the king pardoned Thomas.

Infanticide

The definition of infanticide is 'murder of an infant soon after birth'. English law defined infanticide as 'the killing of the child after the entire body is brought from the womb alive'.[1]

Historically, the most frequent victims of murder within the family were children. Although the strict definition of infanticide is the murder of a newborn, during the sixteenth and seventeenth centuries the term was also used for murders of children up to the age of eight.[2]

The family as an entity has become an area studied in some depth, and, of necessity, this includes family life in the past. Not just the family as an economic unit but family dynamics in terms of power, abuse, and violence.

In mediaeval times, wife and child abuse was both casual and common. Husbands came home drunk and battered their wives. Babies who cried were knocked senseless or killed to quieten them. In mediaeval France customary law condoned wife-beating. The incidence of violence at home was such that John Fletcher (1579–1625) in his book *Wit Without Money*, said 'charity and beating begins at home'. What is true is that infanticide was the commonest form of murder committed by women.[3]

In our current climate, when most marriages are based on love, it is sometimes difficult to accept that up until modern times marriages were made for the gain of the families of the couple – for land, power or money. Affection was certainly not in the top ten list of reasons to marry off one's child.

Most couples jogged along; some high-born couples made sure of an heir and spare and then more or less lived separate lives as best they could within the confines of their particular domestic situation. However, during the course of the sixteenth century there began a small but determined body of opinion that tried to warn of the perils of hasty or ill-considered marriages. Strife within marriage was not an unusual state of affairs, but equally, not as easy to solve as it is today by divorce. The church did not recognise divorce, and only those who could prove some obstacle to the marriage existed, or that it had not been consummated, could gain their freedom.

Just as in our own times, domestic violence was not a one-way street with men battering women. There are many instances of violent wives.

Quarrelsome, assertive, extravagant or scolding wives transgressed the social order, and because of the perception that male dominance was an imperative, few men who suffered a domineering spouse would take their case to court. If it was felt necessary, the community would step in to correct the offending behaviour. Therefore, there is little 'real' evidence of how much of a problem violent wives were because of under-reporting.

This was not a problem when violence turned into murder. In late Tudor England the population was, to a large extent, happy to cooperate with the coroner.[4] Murder was not an easy thing to hide, even if the victim and killer lived within the same family circle. It is true that there was a fair amount of relocating, presumably due to finding work, in preindustrial England. However, the disappearance of a family member would be noticed, especially in a time when the neighbourhood community was actively involved in each other's lives.

We can get an idea of the incidence of domestic violence from the Home Circuit of Assizes which began in the mid-sixteenth century. Sadly, the records that do exist are very hit and miss and by no means form a coherent whole. Also, because official depositions are mostly missing from the archives, the historian must rely on the popular literature of late Elizabethan England to tell the story.[5]

So there is very little qualitative evidence available. What we do get from the popular literature is a contemporary viewpoint of offences and offenders. According to the Essex Assizes 1560–1709, between 1560 and 1609 a total of 132 homicides were recorded. Fifteen of these were familial and nineteen were of servants or apprentices. Considering today's rate of domestic murder, in the last years of Elizabeth's reign, Essex at least had very few.[6]

It is interesting to note the role of the mother during the mid to late Tudor era was partly shaped by the perception of Anne Boleyn, Elizabeth's mother. Relentless political discussions as to the legitimacy of Queen Elizabeth carried on throughout her entire reign. It was not solely the desire of some Catholics that sparked the uprisings to put the 'true heir', the Catholic Mary, Queen of Scots on the throne, but the fact that the Protestant Elizabeth was considered to be illegitimate, although she herself emphasised at every opportunity that she was the 'mother' of her people.

What is an interesting slant on the role of a mother, at least according to Henry VIII, is that Anne's death-knell sounded when she miscarried a fifteen-week foetus in January 1536. The likelihood is that it was deformed, although many historians dispute this and Ambassador Chapuys is reported as saying the foetus was a fully formed male child.

Since Henry VIII never would or could admit paternity of a deformed foetus, had that been the case, the blame would be laid firmly at Anne's door, on the understanding that she must have committed adultery and the child was not the king's.

It was also a perfect opportunity for him to say she had seduced him through witchcraft. This then paved the way for her to be arrested and executed for adultery. And it also hardened society's view of women as inferior and only fit to be submissive wives and mothers.

Most cases of infanticide were committed by spinsters, many of whom flatly denied they were pregnant when quizzed by suspicious neighbours. Occasionally, married women were suspected and some escaped detection either by hiding the corpse successfully or declaring that they had dropped the child.[7]

Sometimes, despite a guilty verdict being declared in the records, there is no clear record of the punishment that followed. This might be because there was an element of doubt as to whether the death was accidental or possibly the jury wanted to show clemency. And, at a time when the coroner required payment, there was a disincentive to report cases. We must not forget compassionate neighbours who would help cover up the death. That said, there are instances where women were convicted and gaoled because they were pregnant at the time of the trial. Some may well have been released since there is no further information about the cases.

One somewhat complex case was that of Margaret Judge. In July 1560 Margaret was convicted of infanticide. However, the punishment was delayed because she declared she was pregnant. Margaret was held on remand. Note the date here: July 1560.

Her claim of pregnancy was not investigated until one year later, in July 1561, by a 'jury of matrons', who examined her and agreed that, yes, Margaret was pregnant. And this is where the reader may begin to smile. Let's face it, we are talking a *Guinness Book of Records*-length pregnancy here! But things became more complicated. After the July 1561 proof that she was pregnant, Margaret was sent back to gaol. In July 1563 she was again declared to be pregnant. Again, in July 1563, she was returned to gaol. In 1565 she was eventually pardoned. But we do not know whether or not she was still pregnant at this point. Or what happened to any children that might have been born in the previous five years.[8]

Most newborns were either drowned or dumped in the privy and asphyxiated. Some were strangled. Unsurprisingly, if injuries were apparent on the body – and coroners were responsible for measuring every mark or injury before the inquest – convictions were more likely. The records mention the baby of an unnamed Essex woman who had cut the baby's throat, weighed it down with stones and thrown it in a stream.

Infanticide

Popular literature in the late Tudor years has proved a godsend to historians. Pamphlets, ballads, news sheets and broadsides were the sixteenth-century equivalent of the British red-top newspapers today. Some historians give them the more accurate name of 'street literature'. Crime was, as it has always been, a juicy topic guaranteed to attract a goodly readership. But these sheets also served a secondary use – that of instructing the reader on correct behaviour and telling him in no uncertain terms the consequences of wickedness.

Of course, from this distance of time we have no clear idea who read the sheets, only that the producers of them would slant the content to a known readership in order to make money. Rather like today, when so many papers print lurid and inaccurate versions of the facts, this does not help the historian present an accurate account.

Terry Pratchett brings this to light with his unique form of spiky humour in *The Truth*, in which the editor of 'The Times' investigates and uncovers treachery in Ankh-Morpork, but his readers are far more interested in amusingly shaped vegetables.

How ironic that little has changed since the broadsheets of the sixteenth century, except that in the twenty-first century, papers make no bones about spreading rumours, true or otherwise, about the royal family. In late Tudor England, the interest would be solely aimed at the lower orders, unless a publisher wished to see the inside of a cell in the Tower of London. Which some did.

It is very frustrating for the historian when it comes to specific case studies. Few are described in any depth. These include:

> Anne Lynstred or Lynsted, in 1594, allegedly threw her newly born daughter into the fire, described in the indictment as a 'seething furnace'; Elizabeth Brown of Lenham, in 1593, according to the report, 'ripped open the stomach of her newly born male child with a knife and tore out its entrails'; Margaret Chaundler or Chandler of Richmond, in 1591, is supposed to have stuffed earth and the leg bone from a goose into the mouth of her newborn son and left the child in a ditch, where it died the following day; Alice, wife of Robert Hilley, in 1588, had an affair with Thomas Freemason, became pregnant by him and was accused of killing the resultant child – she was acquitted; Sibyl Allyot [sic] of Kindford in Sussex, in 1565, was accused along with her clergyman husband, William, of killing her child and burying the body in the vicarage garden. The case was complicated because the Lewes assizes named spinster Christine Grantham as the killer with the Ellyots named as accessories. A year later the case was tried and all three were found guilty.[9]

Infidelity

It was not until 2009 that the Coroners & Justice Act repealed the infidelity defence that had allowed those who killed adulterous spouses to claim that they had been provoked to an intolerable degree whereby they killed their spouse – and sometimes the lover, should the pair be caught *in flagrante delicto* – and should only be charged with manslaughter.[1]

It was during the sixteenth century that the difference between murder and manslaughter became clarified by dint of the intent to kill. That said, some accused of manslaughter in a fit of temper hanged, and some accused of brutal, intended murder did not hang.[2]

The marriage laws in mediaeval times were, to our modern way of thinking, strange to say the least. Marriage had nothing to do with love but with property or money. It was assumed that love was so trivial as to be unimportant, or it might grow. The one tenet of belief that we lost with the Victorians was that it was believed that women could not conceive unless they experienced pleasure during the sexual act itself.[3] The 'lie back and think of England' quotation is often accorded to Queen Victoria, who, allegedly enjoyed the romping in bed bit but not the childbirth that so frequently followed.

In medieval and Tudor England, the sole aim of marriage was to produce children. Custom had changed from the simple saying 'I will marry you' in front of a witness, to the calling of the banns over three weeks before being married by a priest, who would conduct the ceremony in the church porch. After that, everyone went into church to celebrate a nuptial mass.[4]

The space of time between the banns and the marriage gave enough time to ensure that the happy couple were not breaking consanguinity laws, but if they were, a hefty donation to the church and a Papal bull often sorted that out.

What was clear was that no person should be forced into marrying, although this happened because children were taught to obey their parents second only to obeying God. This resulted in many unhappy marriages, especially early on when girls of twelve and boys of fourteen were considered adult enough to marry, but there would frequently be a caveat that if the pair were young the marriage should not be consummated. Margaret Beaufort gave birth to the future Henry VII when she was thirteen years and eight months old. Since there was no appearance or declaration that Henry was premature, Margaret was pregnant before the age of thirteen. The resulting difficult birth meant she was unable to conceive any more children.

Krista Kesselring states:

> in English legal history, the judicial acceptance of adultery as a provocation of the sort that could reduce a charge of murder to manslaughter came late in the development of provocation defences over the seventeenth century. Moreover, when it developed, and for a long time thereafter, it mitigated only a husband's killing of the other man, not of his wife. The adultery defence as we understand it today seems to have emerged in the nineteenth century, not earlier. Only in the nineteenth century do we see mounting evidence of popular beliefs, held by judges as well as jurors, that husbands might be somewhat excused for killing their unfaithful wives, not just their male rivals, with the novelty masked by talk of an "unwritten law" sanctioned by long history.[5]

Therefore, it would appear that Tudor cuckolded husbands were not allowed in law to kill their adulterous wives.

There were two views on marriage – secular and sacred. The secular view was that children married to form political alliances or to gain land and property, but this only happened in the higher echelons. In high society, the ages of the bride and groom would be nearer the twelve and fourteen, as referred to earlier.

Lower down the social scale the two families would get together and agree about the marriage, but often the pair would not marry until their midtwenties to give them time to save enough to put a roof over their heads.[6]

If push came to shove, for either political or financial reasons, should a marriage need to be annulled, there were plenty of ways of getting out of it. A pre-contract was sometimes used where one party would declare the other had promised to marry someone else before marrying the current spouse. One of the parties could claim coercion or, if desperate, that their spouse was insane.

Sometimes, of course, the couple took their fate into their own hands without reference to their parents. One instance of this was from the fifteenth-century Paston family in Norfolk. Nineteen-year-old Margery fell in love with Richard Calle, the family steward, and married him in secret. This, of course, horrified the Pastons, who resorted to forcing Margery to repudiate the marriage by beating her and asking the Bishop of Norwich to berate her. All this failed. Margery refused to give Richard up and the marriage was a very happy one and produced three children.[7]

Despite all the foregoing, most parents tried to ensure that their children would be happy and this was mostly the case. But there were some absolute disasters, one of which was the marriage between William Parr, brother to Queen Katherine Parr, and Anne Bourchier.

William was four years older than his bride and she was ten years old when they were married, but they did not live together. However, when they did finally set up house, Anne grew to hate her husband. He was at court, she preferred the countryside. He was quite sophisticated, she was barely educated. In 1541 she deserted him and set up home with her lover. By 1543 William was petitioning Henry VIII, now his brother-in-law, to execute Anne because her infidelity had produced a bastard child who might one day try to claim his, Parr's, estate. The pair became legally separated but they were not divorced until 1552.

CASE STUDY

These are few and far between in the literature, but there is one strange case where William Nelson obviously wanted to divorce his wife. Frances Nelson was prosecuted for committing adultery with a man called Charles Barnby.[8]

What made the case unusual was that William Nelson had drawn up a legal document which detailed the terms for Barnby's access to Frances' body. William then seconded a woman called Mary Readshaw and together they 'discovered' Frances and Barnby *in flagrante delicto*. This gave William the necessary evidence he needed to divorce Frances, and presumably not have to pay her a penny.

For her help with this scheme, William promised Mary Readshaw 'a tuft taffety gowne and a kirle of figured sattyn for her favor to conceale the said fallt'. In other words, to keep her mouth shut. And this is where William took his eye off the ball, because after twelve days Mary Readshaw had still not received her promised 'sattyn'.

Full of righteous dudgeon, she took herself off to the authorities and told them everything, probably not realising that in dumping William in the legal mire, she, as a co-conspirator would join him.

Both William and Mary were prosecuted for bawdry.[9]

Tavern Talk:

Anne Boleyn was executed for adultery. However, at the time of her execution, her marriage to Henry had been declared invalid. So, legally speaking, she was no longer Henry's wife and therefore could not be executed for the crime of adultery. Thomas Cromwell would have been aware of this but also wise enough to keep his counsel and his head – for another four years. Let's face it, the English king was already becoming a bit of a laughing stock. He had married Anne Boleyn while still officially married to Katherine of Aragon and that had caused mayhem throughout Europe. He obviously didn't want to marry Jane Seymour whilst Anne Boleyn was still alive, even though Tudor propaganda made Anne the scapegoat for everything bad that had happened since 1526.

Juvenile Crime

Most crime committed by minors in Tudor England was regarded as a social problem caused by political and religious upheaval, especially as the rapid changes in religion and required belief of the day became ever more confusing.

When the problem of young people becoming criminals became more prevalent, it was attributed to idle youths or those with no masters. Children figure in very few accounts of murder in the Tudor Era, and usually as victims not perpetrators, although contemporary accounts are very rare. There is one account of a child giving evidence to a court regarding his father 'without any blushing feare' who couldn't be swayed from his testimony, so clear and calm was he in the giving of it.[1]

Most accounts deal with either apprentices, who could be as young as twelve, or child vagrants. Towards the end of the Elizabethan period a fixed age limit for child criminals was put at seven years old. By 1600 this was amended so that prosecutors of children between the ages of seven and fourteen had to prove the child knew right from wrong. Below the age of seven, children were considered to be incapable of guilt. However, even for the seven-to-fourteen age group, the law usually used discretion in deciding whether or what to prosecute.

The youngest felon to be executed in the Tudor era, or since then, was eleven-year-old Alice Glaston, hanged in Much Wenlock in Shropshire, although details of what her crime was have been lost in the mists of time and incomplete records.

More usually, those in the dock were boys and very few were even prosecuted, let alone hanged, if found guilty. In 1592 ten-year-old Richard Goodwyn was found guilty of being a cut-purse, but because of his age, he was remanded without judgement. The same thing happened to Rachel Brackley in July 1602 who, because she was under the age of eleven, was remanded, even though she had stolen goods and cash worth £2.[2]

There is one account of James Brown, aged nine, whose original place of birth was Cambridge. James was whipped out of Norwich after being give a pass to return to his home town. Before his penance, he was taken to the nearest bridewell – a house of correction – and given clothes and shoes for his journey.[3]

While there appears to be no centrally organised crime in London, with a Mr Big/Moriarty figure directing it, there were taverns which had definite gangs associated with them, where pick-pockets were much in evidence as well as card sharps and those who played with loaded dice. It is known that children were part of these gatherings.

CASE STUDY

In 1585, during the London sessions, testimony was given about a man called Wotton, who had tried, and failed, to be a merchant, and who kept an alehouse at Smart's Quay near Billingsgate, He was considered to be a gentleman.

He set up a safe house for pick-pockets and what was described as 'a schoolhouse set up to learn young boys to cut purses.' Rather like Fagin in *Oliver Twist*, Wotton's teachings concentrated on purses and pockets which were hung up with small bells attached to them. The challenge, as graphically shown in the 1968 film *Oliver*, was to pick the pocket or cut the purse without ringing the bell. Any child who could achieve this was adjudged 'a judicial nipper'. A nipper was the term given to those who could pick purses or cut the purses off, whilst those who picked pockets were called foisters.[4]

Kidnapping and Abduction

What's the difference between abduction and kidnapping? Kidnapping is usually accompanied with a ransom for money or other gains, whereas abduction is when a person has been taken away from his or her original location by persuasion or by force.

Kidnapping is not a modern crime. Unmarried women, especially if they had wealthy parents or were in a powerful position, were frequently kidnapped, and possibly raped, in an effort to force them to agree to a profitable marriage. Modern writers frequently gloss over this as a romantic gesture for star-crossed lovers. However, it did give some women a say over what happened to them in an era when they had no power over their bodies. Of course, the attitude towards women as being like Eve and inherently sinful made the whole thing more complicated.[1]

Perhaps the most famous (infamous) example of this in the Tudor era was James Hepburn, Earl of Bothwell, abducting Mary, Queen of Scots and forcing her into marriage before impregnating her with twins that she later miscarried.

Since it suited the English Tudor propagandists to blacken her name as much as possible, this situation was presented as her eloping with Bothwell. We will never learn the truth and much ink has been used to argue the point.

CASE STUDY

The Seymour Brothers and a Case of Desperation!

When Henry VIII died in 1547, despite his very best endeavours, he left a boy to succeed him. The nine-year-old Edward VI was quickly taken over by his uncle, Edward Seymour, who just as quickly began to rake in as much money and power as he could.

There have always been rumours that Edward's formidable wife, Anne Stanhope, was responsible for much of his actions whilst he was regent. It is known that she demanded the return of the royal jewels Katherine Parr wore when she was Henry VIII's last queen, although when Anne planned wearing them was up for debate since she gave Edward ten children, thus being frequently occupied elsewhere.

A month after the death of Henry VIII, Edward Seymour was created Duke of Somerset and Earl Marshall. This latter post was because the Duke of Norfolk, who had escaped being beheaded by a whisker when Henry died, had been stripped of this title.

So here we have the elder Seymour brother a duke, Earl Marshall, *and* regent for the new boy-king. All these honours severely infuriated Edward's younger brother, Thomas Seymour. The younger brother was nothing like his elder sibling. Edward was known to be a canny operator with an eye to the main chance, yes, but his other eye was usually on the lookout for any accompanying hazards. Thomas on the other hand led the life of a louche bachelor. He was made Lord Admiral, but that was not as prestigious a title as duke by a country mile!

In 1543 he had been secretly courting Katherine Parr before Henry VIII's beady eye dropped on the poor woman. Thomas was promptly sent off to France out of the way. However, when Henry died Thomas wasted no time in marrying the dowager queen, to most people's amazement and disgust. It was her third and his first marriage.

Thomas then acted completely within character. He persuaded the Council to allow the thirteen-year-old Princess Elizabeth, known as the Lady Elizabeth, since she was deemed to be illegitimate, to come and live with him and his new wife.

It has always been acknowledged that Katherine and the princess were very close. Then for the first time, at the age of thirty-five, Katherine fell pregnant and Thomas began to flirt – and possibly more – with Elizabeth. Until the heavily pregnant Katherine found them in compromising circumstances.

For this indiscretion by an inexperienced child, Elizabeth was to learn possibly the most important lesson of her life. Her young life was punctuated by the executions of her mother and another stepmother, Katherine Howard, and then the separation from Katherine Parr, whom she loved. Elizabeth learned how powerful men could be if permitted to gain ascendancy. One cannot help but conclude that these childhood experiences were a driving force in her decision not to marry but to rule alone.

Katherine gave birth to a daughter but developed puerperal fever and in her delirium, before she died, babbled about finding her husband and Elizabeth together. Thomas, fortune hunter extraordinaire and brainless twerp, decided to pursue his plan to marry Elizabeth.

He was also secretly visiting Edward VI and undermining his brother as much as he could. On 16 January 1549 he allegedly broke into the young king's apartments to kidnap him. Quite why he would want to do this has never been explained. However, the king's spaniel began to snarl and bark at the intruder. It is further alleged that Seymour shot the dog, which alerted the guards, who then arrested him. Knowing how much all the Tudor monarchs adored their dogs, one can only think Thomas was either drunk, desperate, or, more likely, stupidly arrogant.

The imperial ambassador, Eustace Chapuys reported to Charles V on 27 January: 'Sire, I have heard here that the Admiral of England, with the help of some people about the court, attempted to outrage the person of the young King by night, and has been taken to the Tower. The alarm was given by the gentleman who sleeps in the King's chamber, who, awakened by the barking of the dog that lies before the King's door, cried out "Help! Murder!"'

However, things quickly went from bad to worse for Thomas. Loose tongues had heard what Katherine had said in her final hours. Elizabeth's servants were carted off the Tower of London, shown the instruments of torture and promptly sang like the apocryphal canary. Elizabeth was subjected to a severe interrogation, which she withstood with astounding courage and composure for a fifteen-year-old.

Thomas was accused of treason for trying to abduct the king and proposing to marry the princess. There was no escape for him. His elder brother was reluctant to sign the death warrant, so Edward VI gave the Council permission to proceed. Thomas was beheaded on 20 March 1549.[2]

One would have thought that with the example of his younger brother ever before his eyes, Edward Seymour would not repeat Thomas' stupidity. By October 1549, he, too, was fighting for his position on the Council. He faced a coup d'etat by John Dudley, son of Henry VII's councillor, Edmund, and father of Robert, Elizabeth's later favourite.

In desperation, Seymour issued a proclamation insinuating that the king was in danger.[3] He whisked Edward away to Windsor Castle, a fortress which could be held against attack. The king was furious, claiming that he had been imprisoned.

The Council published details of how Seymour had mismanaged the governing of England. They also stated that the power of his title of Protector came from them and not, as he thought, from Henry VIII's will. They ordered Seymour to bring the king to Richmond, which he did.

The young Edward was incensed. He accused his uncle of 'ambition, vainglory, entering into rash wars in mine youth, negligent looking on

Above left: Philip Halling: Statue of Henry VII: Wikimedia Commons

Above right: Edward VI: Rijksmuseum Wikimedia Commons

Right: Mary Tudor: Wikimedia Commons

Foxes Book of Martyrs: Execution of Latimer and Ridley: Wikimedia Commons

The Burning of Master John Rogers 1555 Public Domain

Trial by Ordeal Wikimedia Commons. Public Domain

Right: Thomas Seymour - Nicolas Denisot, Public domain, via Wikimedia Commons

Below left: Minstrel Condemned to the Gallows Wikimedia Commons

Below right: Gibbet of La Corriveau_(NYPL)_(cropped-1) Wikimedia Commons

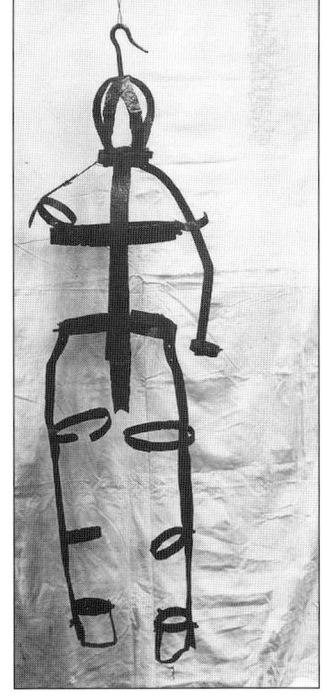

Above left: Fordwitch, Kent GB Ducking Stool: Wikimedia Commons

Above right: A man confined to the Stocks: Wikimedia Commons

Below: Punishment in the Pillory: John Cassell Wikimedia Commons

Margaret Pole execution: Public Domain

The Rack: Pearson Scott Foresman, Public domain, via Wikimedia Commons

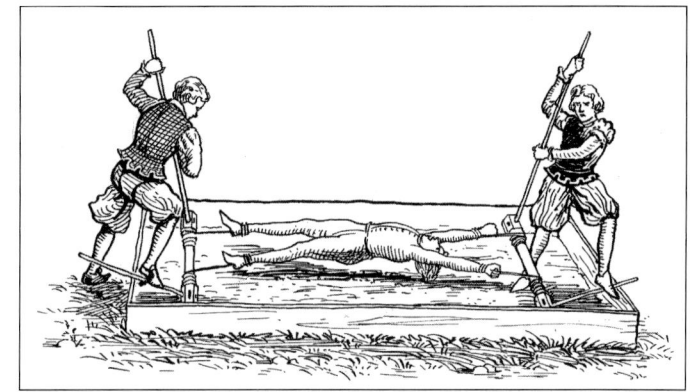

Various forms of torture Wikimedia.org Public Domain

Above: Instruments of Torture via Kozzi

Below left: Anne Boleyn's Execution by Jan Luyken: Wikimedia Commons

Below right: Halifax Gibbet: Tim Green Bradford. Wikimedia Commons

Above left: Pressing to death: Wikipedia Public Domain

Above right: Arden's House, Faversham: Wikimedia Commons

Right: Counterfeit Cranke: Genings-and-Blunt: Permission from Liam R E Quin

Plaque re the last resting place of Christopher Marlowe St. Nicholas' Church, Deptford Green, SE8: Ethan Doyle White

Above left: St. Margaret Clitherow: Public Domain

Above right: Robert Devereux, 2nd Earl of Essex, blackmailed by John Daniell. Unknown author, Public domain, via Wikimedia Commons

Below left: Sir Brian Tuke breaking Sumptuary laws but with possible permission of Henry VIII. Wikimedia Commons

Below right: Holbein sketch of Anne Boleyn: Public Domain: the sketch that began the author's interest in the Tudors.

Newhaven, enriching himself of my treasure, following his own opinion, and doing all by his own authority.'

Seymour was released from the Tower of London in the early months of 1550, but rearrested on a trumped-up charge of treason in October 1551 and put back in the Tower. The Council knew the charge of treason would not convince the people, who believed Seymour was a good man. So they downgraded the charge to felony, in that he sought a change of government by trying to overthrow John Dudley's regime.

In January 1552 the 'good duke' walked down to Tower Hill and was beheaded. He is among the many whose executed bodies were interred at the little church of St Peter ad Vincula within the walls of the Tower.

Larceny

The strict definition of larceny in the UK is 'theft of personal property'. In English law larceny was replaced as a statutory crime by theft in 1968.

Crime in the sixteenth century developed into a broadening of classifications in relation to the victims of crime. The first, and, of course, most important issue as far as the government was concerned, was crimes against the state. The second was crimes against people and this category included any crime where the victim was injured either physically or emotionally.[1]

The final group was crimes against property. It is into this category that larceny was placed, although the line between larceny and theft has always been so fine as to be a case of splitting hairs, which was probably why the crime disappeared from the statute books in the late 1960s.

Thomas Dekker, a dramatist born in 1572, wrote many pamphlets regarding the criminal classes and their misdemeanours. He wrote the *Guls Hornbook*, which advised felons out at night who would be intent on some kind of property crime, and therefore at risk of detention by the Watch, on how to avoid being arrested:

> the Watch will winke at you, onely for the love they beare armes and knighthood: Mary, if the Centinell and his court of Guard stand strictly upon his martial! Law and cry stand, commanding you to give the word, and to shew reason why your Ghost walkes so late, doe it in some Jest (for that will shew you have a desperate wit, and perhaps make him and his halberdiers afraid to lay fowle hands upon you) or, if you read mittimus in the Constables booke, counterfeit to be a French man, a Dutchman, or any other nation whose country is in peace with your owne; and you may passe the Pikes: for being not able to understand you, they cannot by the customes of the Citie take your examination, and so by consequence they have nothing to say to you.[2]

In other words, if the Watchmen catch sight of you as you go about your felonious business, talk in a loud voice about lords and knights, hoping that they will not dare detain someone of an obvious higher social rank. You could also pretend to be a foreigner, but make sure you choose a country that is currently an English ally, and because they will not be able to understand a word you are saying, they will send you on your way.

Larceny as a crime was put in the same category as poaching, fencing, gambling and gaming, usury and other immoral crimes, all of which, depending on circumstances, could be treated as capital crimes. However, when it came to larceny and burglary, the jury would frequently help the defendant to escape execution through 'pious perjury'.[3]

As we see in more cases than common belief would credit, juries did take into account the reason for the offence. If the felon had been forced into crime because of a lack of job or food due to bad harvests, or being turfed out of their home by their lord, the jury would show a high degree of mercy.[4]

Furthermore, juries often undervalued the goods which had been stolen, which then changed the crime from larceny to theft. This was frequently the case with first offenders or a felon who had stolen goods worth more than the monetary limit for theft. When this happened, the felon was punished for trespassing, which was not considered a capital offence.

Should the felon be found guilty and sentenced to execution, the only court of appeal was the Crown as the government body, in the person of the monarch, who could issue pardons. That said, judges could recommend that the guilty person be pardoned.

There was a range of pardons. Some had no strictures applied to them at all. Others demanded that the felon had to meet and maintain behaviours or other requirements in order to ensure that the pardon held.[5]

Murder

Murder is, by most people's definition, the most heinous of crimes. Gathering evidence to identify a suspect and gain justice for victim(s) has always been one of the most actively pursued sciences.

Nowadays, we are fed a constant diet of programmes detailing the often horrific accounts of how some poor unfortunate met their end. Prominent in these programmes is the forensic element of detection, usually referred to as CSI (Crime Scene Investigation). In fact, so prevalent are these programmes that police forces have identified them as a potential problem with juries, which may consist of one or more 'armchair CSI expert'.

A study has been done by Walden University on the effect of the perception of juries on televised portrayals of forensic evidence and the reality of the collection and presentation of forensic evidence in court cases. The author knows several police officers who believe that a jury which cannot make up its mind as to the guilt of the perpetrator will often come back to tell the judge they are undecided and then, when the judge says he will accept a majority verdict of either 11:1 or 10:2, the jury make their decisions very quickly.[1]

Forensic science can be traced back to sixth-century China. Over the following four centuries, advances in medicine and science added weight to evidence given in trials. However, most of the building blocks of our current medical forensic knowledge, upon which many trials depend, began in the eighteenth and nineteenth centuries, especially in the field of toxicology.

Medical detection can be traced back to the Greek School of Medicine in Alexandria in the third century before the common era. One of the biggest influences on medical detection was Claudius Galen, who worked in the School for Gladiators and examined plenty of dead bodies. He determined that arteries carried blood but didn't discover the circulatory system. He also proved that urine was formed in the kidney, not, as had been previously believed, in the bladder.[2]

In 1537 Andreas Vesalius was appalled to discover that his Parisian teachers still espoused Galen but had not sought any further discoveries to move the science forward. They were still happy to dissect dead dogs.

Vesalius was so disgusted, he returned to his native Brussels and stole a body from the gallows so that he could study a complete human skeleton.[3]

Up until 1900 blood could not be identified as human or animal. It was not until 1910 that Edmund Locard posited the most basic principle of forensic science – that every contact leaves a trace. In other words, the murderer/rapist/attacker leaves a trace of himself on the victim and takes away a trace of the victim on himself.

In Tudor England, investigators had no such tools at their disposal. Neither was there a properly organised police force or a consistent method of punishment. There were parish constables and beadles. Shakespeare makes fun of them in *Much Ado about Nothing*. Dogberry is not intelligent and seems to solve crimes by accident. That said, Shakespeare does allow him the honour of making Borachio confess his part in the plot by Don John, the villain of the piece.

There was also the 'hue and cry' or 'cry harrow', both of which dealt with pursuing fleeing criminals with cries and alarms. If any bystander witnessed a criminal escaping, they were legally obliged to sound the alarm and assist in the apprehension of the malefactor. This alarm had to follow the criminal wherever he went until he was caught and taken to the sheriff. The pursuit could extend from town to town and even cross county borders. It could only end when the offender was apprehended, however long that took. The law of hue and cry morphed into the power of any citizen to make an arrest and this dates back to English Common Law in medieval England.[4]

In the sixteenth century it was generally believed to be safest if the suspect confessed on the understanding that he might be tortured if he didn't. And whilst it is a strong part of our psyche to refer to killers as 'he', it is also clear that, during the Tudor era, women malefactors were identified as needing to be brought before the courts because far fewer women than men faced juries.[5] Hence infanticide and witchcraft, which had never been tried before a secular court, became identified as women's crimes.

Witchcraft was not prosecuted until Elizabeth I's reign. One wonders what part the executions of Anne Boleyn and Katherine Howard played in this decision. Henry VIII's propaganda dictated that the whole nation must believe they were traitors. Whatever the truth of it, writers of pamphlets, so frequent in Elizabeth's England they were akin to today's newspapers, found women felons irresistible. Second to them were the crimes of servants.[6]

The corpse of the victim was all important. There was still a strong body of belief that if the killer laid a hand on the victim and the body bled or its eyes opened, that person's guilt was established. Then work could begin to extract a confession.

Tudor law did not decree that all murderers should be executed. In the reign of Henry VII, any murderer who claimed benefit of clergy – i.e., exemption for the English clergy and nuns from the jurisdiction of the ordinary civil courts – would not be executed. If the defendant, irrespective of his social station, could recite a verse or verses of the fifty-first Psalm in Latin, he avoided execution. This led to many felons learning the fifty-first Psalm by heart. Verse three became known as the 'neck verse'. It was a useful way of avoiding the death penalty.[7]

This was later amended to a felon only being able to use the benefit of clergy claim once. Any murderers who escaped by reciting the fifty-first Psalm were branded on their left hand with the letter 'M'. Should these felons then go on to commit another murder, they would be executed. This law was only abolished in England in the Criminal Law Act 1827. One might posit they were branded on their left hand because most people being right-handed would need to be able to use their prominent hand to work or perhaps because of the belief that the left-hand – the sinister – was closest to the Devil. Even as late as the 1950s, children were being forced to write with their right hands, even if they were naturally left-handed, as was the case with the author's brother.

To put this in historical context, from about thirteenth century onwards, the formal law of homicide was split. There existed a narrow category of murders where the defendant was acquitted or given a royal pardon, but the majority of murders, including what today's authorities would class as manslaughter, were prosecuted as capital offences.

From the fourteenth century onwards justifiable homicide, which usually merited an acquittal, was extended to include those who killed someone in the act of burglary, arson, or robbery. Later in the fourteenth century, accidental homicide became recognised as misadventure, and those prosecuted were, more often than not, acquitted.[8]

This led to an attitude in some quarters that the victim was more to blame than the killer. Even today, detectives will say that the victim had a hand in his or her death. Sometimes to get around the law, blame would be apportioned if at all possible to a non-human cause. Horses, carts, ploughs or oxen could be blamed if they played any part in the death of the victim. The belief behind this was that the person riding the horse or in charge of the plough or cart had demonstrated no intent to kill and was, therefore, not guilty of murder.

The biggest instance of almost instant acquittals would be if the victim was killed by a stray arrow. The first Medieval Archery Law was passed in 1252, whereby all Englishmen between the age of fifteen and sixty were ordered, by law, to equip themselves with a bow and arrows.

The second archery Law of 1363 made it obligatory for Englishmen to practise their skills with the longbow every Sunday. This was, of course, during the time when England was frequently at odds with its European neighbours, especially France. And who can forget that glorious scene in the Laurence Olivier film version of *Henry V* where the sky is filled with a rain of arrows all heading for the enemy? However, the Archery Law led to many accidents when people were hit by 'loose' arrows.[9]

The thinking behind the acquittal of defendants where stray arrows had been the cause of death, was that the defendant had set in train the means by which the victim met his or her death, but circumstances beyond his or her control, say, for example, if the arrow was deflected by a tree or off the ground, meant the defendant had demonstrated no intent to kill.

Contributory negligence began to feature in cases because courts concentrated solely on the intent of the defendant. By logical progression, this led to a blurring of the borderline between self-defence and accident. It also led to circumstances where, in the past, the defendant had been acquitted but had to forfeit all his goods and chattels as compensation, but now, not only was he acquitted, he kept all his goods and chattels.[10]

There was a major change in the homicide laws when the Tudors came to power: a distinct tightening to differentiate between murder and manslaughter. The expansion of the benefit of clergy roles allowed juries to convict the defendant but not condemn him to death.

Juries no longer controlled the flow of evidence under Tudor law. Instead witnesses were called to give evidence and the jury then assessed their view of the worth of that evidence in their verdict. And now, for the first time, we see the term *malice aforethought* entering the definition of murder.

At the beginning of the sixteenth century, the crime of murder was associated with underhand, furtive activity, but as the century progressed, the parameters became more clearly defined into intent – malice aforethought – and chance.[11]

In 1553 John Vane Salisbury was tried along with his master and two other men for murder. Salisbury had happened upon a 'fray already under way'. His master and two others had set upon a man called Ellis. Salisbury helped his own master and ended up killing Ellis' servant. The point of law in question was that of malice aforethought as far as Salisbury's case was concerned. The court ruled that if he did not have malice aforethought, his crime would be manslaughter and not murder. And in fact this is how the court ruled. But the punishment for murder and manslaughter was death and Salisbury was condemned to die. However, he was reprieved because the court was unhappy with the verdict when they took the circumstances of the crime into account.[12]

The Marian Statutes in 1554-5 required Justices to formulate depositions – written statements by witnesses to say what had happened. These depositions or statements were then made available to the court. Trial proceedings were also changed. There was a division between the judge and the prosecution. The latter produced its witnesses and their statements. The judge questioned everyone and also controlled the time given to debate. The verdict was still the responsibility of the jury, and, unlike today when the jury can be sent out while sensitive material is debated to rule whether it is admissible or not, at that time the jury heard every word spoken in the court room. The judge's responsibility was to weigh the evidence and this would affect the sentence depending on the decision of the jury.

So the statutes passed during the Tudor era were intended to move from what juries knew or thought they knew, to the emphasis being placed on evidence given by witnesses. This was a significant step forward, by which common law became adapted to be more in line with social views of the time.[13]

CASE STUDIES

Alice Arden

If the Ealing Comedies of the mid-twentieth century had come across the murder of Thomas Arden, it would have made a perfect vehicle along the lines of the 1949 film *Kind Hearts and Coronets*.

We can compare this case to a twenty-first century Netflix drama, driven by marriage and sex. It was actually written as a drama by that prolific author, Anonymous, and called *Arden of Faversham/Feversham* because the case was notorious in Elizabethan society.[14]

Of course, some historians have wondered whether the author was Shakespeare since its publication in 1590 falls in the middle of Will's prolific period. It has been compared to *Henry IV Part II* in its style.

The story goes as follows:[15] Alice Mirfyn, stepdaughter to a certain Edward North, the Clerk of Parliament, was wooed by Thomas Arden, who believed the marriage would gain him an official appointment to the Court of Augmentations, to which North had been transferred, but it didn't.

The married couple moved to Faversham in Kent. There Arden seems to have become a local mover, shaker, and acquirer of various properties, including, in 1545, about twenty houses with yards (messuages) for £117.03.04 (one hundred and seventeen pounds, three shillings and fourpence) in Faversham. He had already bought land and tenements in the north of the county in 1543 for just over £200 – about £173,000 in 2021. These acquisitions made him a very important person in Faversham.

In 1546, he secured the Comptrollership of Sandwich. Although his tenure only lasted three months until the death of Henry VIII in 1547, he was reappointed in 1550.

However, although he may have been the most prominent citizen of Faversham, he was not popular with many of his peers. In 1548 the mayor died and Arden was elected to serve for the remainder of the term. During his tenure he 'infringed the liberties and freedoms of the town' and was banned from serving again. The account in *Holinshed's Chronicles* also indicates that Arden attempted to force the town to hold the St Valentine's Fair on a particular field he owned, thus favouring the weight of his own purse over the town's coffers. That he was not averse to swindling those less fortunate than himself is shown by his having gained possession of that field from the widow Cooke 'most cruelly'. The widow's new husband cursed Arden to his face.

Alice was the granddaughter of Sir Thomas Mirfyn, Mayor of London from 1518-19. When her mother married Sir Edward North, she would have seen at first-hand how the rich and powerful escaped punishment for their misdemeanours. It would appear that North, as Treasurer and Chancellor of Augmentations, had many opportunities for peculation and was summoned from his bed in 1544 to explain to Henry VIII why there was a £3,000 deficit in the court's finances. Hands up who would have liked to be a fly on the wall in that chamber. North slid out of that one by agreeing a land exchange. However Edward VI also accused him of cheating the Crown.

All that must have shown Alice how simple it was to escape the penalty for cheating the monarch. So how difficult could it possibly be to get away with murdering her husband? The marriage had been one of convenience; she was many years younger than him and loathed him. More importantly, she was infatuated by Thomas Mosbye who worked for her stepfather, North.

In truth, Alice did not personally kill Arden. She gathered together a few conspirators including Mosbye and John Greene, a servant of George Bradshaw, a local goldsmith, who was one of Arden's enemies in Faversham. And then we come to a ruffian called Black Will from Calais who had, allegedly, committed many robberies and murders. As we will see, Black Will is almost akin to a pantomime villain.[16]

Alice offered Black Will £10 to kill her husband. Greene went with Will to St Paul's Churchyard, a meeting place for gossips and a hotbed of thieves. Greene identified Arden. Will then decided that Arden's servant, Michael, should also be killed, but was persuaded that Michael was part of the plot. Will's first attempt failed because Arden never seemed to be alone.

Greene, very stupidly, told the servant, Michael, that Black Will had wanted to kill him, too. After that, Michael, understandably, went about in a constant state of terror. This was instrumental in the next attempt to kill Arden. A central part of the second attempt was to force Michael to unlock the doors of the house in which Arden was sleeping. He didn't.

When Arden returned home, he sent a letter to his patron, Sir Thomas Cheyne, the subject of which we do not know. But he used Michael as his messenger. Cheyne wrote a reply and gave it to Michael but Alice took the letter from him, instructing him to tell Arden he had lost it and perhaps it might be better if Arden went to see Cheyne in person.

The plotters then decided to ambush Arden on his way to see Cheyne, and Black Will decided to set a trap for the hapless victim. Which he did, but, unfortunately, he set the trap in the wrong place. One can imagine him waiting. And waiting. And waiting …

Three attempts had been made to kill Arden. Three attempts had failed and both Alice and Mosbye must have been wondering just how Black Will had come by his nickname. At all events, they became impatient. The wretched Arden should have been dead by now!

Mosbye challenged Arden to a dual in an effort to kill him legally. Arden, who knew Alice and Mosbye were lovers, refused. Stalemate. The plotters then held a meeting at the house of Mosbye's sister, Cicely Pounder. It was decided they had to exercise much more control over Black Will – really? By now they must have had serious doubts, not just about his reputation as a heartless killer but also his ability. They finally decided to wait until Arden was out of the house long enough for Alice to send away all the servants not involved in the plot. She hid Will in a closet. Probably the best place for him.

Arden returned and asked if supper was ready. Mosbye, allegedly dressed in a silk nightgown, replied it was not. He invited Arden to a game of backgammon. Arden also changed into a robe of some kind and put slippers on.

At a prearranged signal, Black Will leapt from the closet. From his previous bungling, it is a wonder he didn't fall over his feet. However, he threw a towel around Arden's neck and strangled him. This was actually about as successful as Will's previous attempts had been and it was not until Mosbye seized a 14lb pressing iron and struck Arden on the head that the poor soul appeared to die. Until they carried him downstairs and he showed signs of coming back to life.

Will 'gashed' Arden's face, which probably means he cut his throat before yanking all the rings off Arden's fingers, emptying his victim's purse, and demanding that Alice pay him the agreed £10. Which she did – though heaven knows why. John Greene gave Will a horse and he rode away. They were probably glad to see the back of him.

Of course, the plotters' main problem now was how to dispose of the body. It is alleged that Alice stabbed the corpse several times, possibly to hide any trace of other wounds, but equally possibly because of her hatred for her husband. She then ordered her co-conspirators to dispose of the corpse.[17]

Alice cleaned up the mess, put fresh rushes down and wrapped the knife she had used in the cloth they had cleaned up the blood with, and threw them in a tub at the side of a well that must have been on the property. Perhaps Useless Will's incompetence had rubbed off on her. Any sensible person would have put the knife *in* the well. But she didn't.

Alice, very composed and completely unemotional, then invited two business friends of Arden's to supper. Her lover's sister, Cicely, gave an Oscar-winning performance running back and forth to the window wondering where Thomas could be, especially as snow lay on the ground; he would be getting cold, etc. Yes, well he was.

Arden was very close in fact, in the field adjoining the house. His body was still clad in a robe and slippers, but in their haste to dump the poor man, the conspirators failed to notice a couple of rushes from the floor caught in his slippers. They simply dropped him and scarpered.

Alice sent people out to look for her missing husband, polishing her wailing and weeping skills as she affected extreme distress. Next morning, the Mayor of Faversham gathered a group of townsfolk together to look for Thomas. And then they found his lifeless corpse.

At which point Alice's less-than-carefully laid plans began to unravel. The rushes in the slippers were discovered, and, rather like Hansel and Gretel's trail of white pebbles, the footprints left in the snow by those who had disposed of the body led the mayor right back to Alice's door. Oh, dear. How sad. Never mind.

She, quite naturally, denied any part of the terrible deed – Sarah Bernhardt, eat your heart out. This diva performance did not do her one bit of good, since the search of the house led to the discovery of the murder weapon in the tub, plus some blood and hair. The victim's widow was fairly quick on her feet because she then fell to more wailing and weeping and more or less confessed, no doubt claiming she had been ill-used and it was done in a moment of madness. Mosbye also confessed when the mayor and his assistants found him in bed, his discarded hose covered in blood. Stupidity really is contagious.

In the end all the conspirators confessed. The Arden murder became a *cause célèbre* because it attacked one of the cornerstones of Elizabethan society – the institution of marriage. Wifely obedience was the foremost expectation of a husband. The law was unequivocal in its belief that a wife was subordinate to her husband, the head of the household. A wife's role was to be 'bonny and buxom in bed', one of her marriage vows.[18] She must run the house and make her husband's life easier. When one reads today all the 'wifely advice' so prevalent in 1950s magazines, society didn't come far in 500 years!

However, Alice, in 1551, smashed the perception of an obedient wife. Her deed proved to society that even a prominent citizen like Thomas Arden had no control over his wife and household. Alice had no chance of a divorce to find personal happiness with Mosbye. And because she had flouted such a basic rule of Elizabethan society, she had to be seen to suffer a 'just' punishment.

Those familiar with the plays of William Shakespeare should read Katharina's final speech in *The Taming of the Shrew*. It is generally regarded as the perfect ideal of a tamed virago. However, if you read it with twenty-first century values in mind, spitting the words with venom, the message can be seen as totally different. One hopes Petruchio never found ground glass in his sausages!

> Thy husband is thy lord, thy life, thy keeper,
> Thy head, thy sovereign; one that cares for thee,
> And for thy maintenance commits his body
> To painful labour both by sea and land,
> To watch the night in storms, the day in cold,
> Whilst thou liest warm at home, secure and safe;
> And craves no other tribute at thy hands
> But love, fair looks, and true obedience-
> Too little payment for so great a debt.
> Such duty as the subject owes the prince,
> Even such a woman oweth to her husband;
> … and so on.

Alice was burned at the stake in Canterbury. All her co-conspirators were executed. Most were hanged, including Mosbye and his sister. The servant,

Michael, was hanged in chains –which seems a tad unfair. So was John Greene.

And Black Will? According to Holinshed, he was burned at Flushing in Zealand, but we do not know why. He certainly deserves to go down in history as a heroic failure.

As an ironic end note, the field in which Arden's body was dumped was the same one he had swindled the widow Cooke out of.

Legend has it that she put a curse on him, wishing 'manie and vengeance to light upon him'.[19]

Edward, Earl of Warwick

The case of Alice Arden was a sensation, and by far the most common way in which murder occurred – by malice aforethought. However, malice aforethought had nothing to do with the very sad case of Edward, Earl of Warwick. This can only come under the heading of State Sponsored Murder.

When Henry VII usurped the Crown, or won the crown by right of conquest, depending on your point of view, his most pressing needs were to establish his credentials and his dynasty. He managed the first by marrying the very popular Elizabeth of York, eldest daughter of Edward IV. Elizabeth was sensible enough to allow her formidable mother-in-law, Margaret Beaufort, to rule the roost. Since the new king's accession was a *fait accompli* and nobody with two brain cells to rub together argued with Margaret Beaufort, Elizabeth was very wise in this respect. She and her husband enjoyed a very happy marriage and Henry was devastated when she died.[20]

Establishing his dynasty was by no means straightforward. Contrary to some arguments, Richard III, formerly Duke of Gloucester, did not usurp the throne. There had been fairly recent examples of how disastrous a child-king could be for England, for example Richard II who came to the throne aged nine and Henry VI who was only nine months old when his father died at the siege of Rouen.

When Edward IV died unexpectedly in April 1483, Richard of Gloucester lost no time in riding south from Middleham Castle and taking possession of his twelve-year-old nephew before the Woodvilles could. Elizabeth Woodville was the new young king's mother and there was no love lost between the pushy Woodville family and Richard.[21]

Gloucester was already High Constable of England: shortly after his and the new boy-king's arrival in London, he was made Lord Protector. Before Edward V could be crowned, however, his father's marriage to Elizabeth

Woodville was declared invalid by reason of a pre-contract with Lady Eleanor Butler. Eleanor was dead by this time, but the pre-contract – if it ever existed – rendered all the children of the Edward/Woodville marriage illegitimate.[22]

It is almost impossible to find solid evidence to either confirm or refute this issue. In addition, because Edward IV was extremely tall – around 6ft 4in and his father and brothers were much shorter – a rumour also began to circulate that Edward himself was not Richard of York's son, but the child of a very tall French archer called Blaybourne.

Because of all this controversy, an assembly of lords and commoners begged Richard of Gloucester to take the throne.[23] On the face of it, he did not usurp the throne, and that is very important when we look at the remaining years of the fifteenth century.

After Bosworth Field in 1485, there were many pockets of hatred for the Tudor usurper. Yorkists were attainted and deprived of their lands. Then, as now, land meant money. Henry was forced to defend his throne several times over the next twelve years, but the constant strain and uncertainty resulted in his fixation that anyone remotely linked to the Plantagenets was a direct threat to him and his dynasty. And Edward, Earl of Warwick, a ten-year-old boy at the time of the Battle of Bosworth, was the sole remaining Plantagenet heir. Immediately after Bosworth, Edward was transferred to the Tower of London.

He was the only son of George, Duke of Clarence, brother to Edward IV and Richard III. He had an elder sister, Margaret, of whom more later. Henry was content to confirm that Edward was the Earl of Warwick but he made no move to lessen his restrictions on the boy's movements within the Tower or give him the lands to which he was due.

Edward is thought to have been either uneducated or have a learning disability. In himself, he was no threat to Henry but what he represented – the last of the direct Plantagenet line – *was* a threat. Henry kept him secure in the Tower but the boy became a rallying cry for disaffected Yorkists. One wonders why Henry did not find an excuse to get rid of him. Possibly because the fate of the two princes in the Tower was still very much in people's minds, and since Edward was Elizabeth of York's cousin, it is possible she lobbied him to keep Edward safe and Henry simply kept the boy locked up.

In 1487 Henry decided to begin marriage negotiations with Ferdinand of Aragon and his warlike Queen, Isabella of Castile. He wanted their daughter, Katherine, to marry Arthur, Prince of Wales. The two were betrothed when they were both three years old but, of course, Katherine remained in Spain.

In the interim ten years between the betrothal and the time when Katherine would normally have travelled to England for her wedding, there were several rebellions and uprisings trying to unseat Henry and reinstate the Plantagenet line, the two most famous being those involving Lambert Simnel and Perkin Warbeck. Henry defeated both rebellions. Simnel he put to work in the palace kitchens as a turnspit. Warbeck, whom many believed really was Prince Richard of York, ended up in the Tower of London.[24]

Ferdinand and Isabella were very smooth operators. They had an established background as having not just a marriage as solid as Henry's, but a firm and proven track record as monarchs of a stable dynasty, something that could not be said of the Tudor monarch. The big plus for Ferdinand and Isabella was that the proposed marriage would cement an alliance between England and Spain against their common enemy, France.[25]

All was going swimmingly for Henry's plans, until the lonely earl imprisoned in the Tower of London became a problem for the Spanish monarchs, and a threat to Arthur's marriage. At this time, many Englishmen still believed Edward of Warwick was the true and rightful king, and at this moment, when Katherine could confidently be expected to travel to England, Henry's plans began to fracture.

The marriage negotiations had been signed in 1489 and it was then decided that Katherine would travel to England in 1498 when she was twelve years old. But 1498 came and went and Katherine remained in Spain. This was because her parents both believed that the strength of feeling in England and the rebellions Henry had been forced to crush, to reinstate the Plantagenets, put their youngest child in peril. What would happen if another uprising occurred and Henry lost? They refused to send Katherine until this problem was settled to their satisfaction.

Henry, in true Henry fashion, decided to sever this gordian knot in the simplest way possible. He allowed Warbeck and Warwick to meet and become friends. At which point, he accused them of conspiring against him and had them both executed in 1499. Problem solved! Things went back to normal but it was not until late in 1501 that Katherine arrived and married Arthur. This led to the most hotly debated wedding night in history, and, in 1532, the break with Rome, the Reformation, and years of religious conflict and confusion.

It is strongly believed that Katherine always felt guilty about the executions of Warwick and Warbeck. She felt her marriage had been cursed, originating as it did in the spilling of innocent blood.[26]

To round off the story of State-sponsored murder, let us return to the young Earl of Warwick's elder sister, Margaret, Countess of Salisbury.

She was executed for treason in 1541 by Henry VII's younger son, Henry VIII, who obviously inherited his father's paranoia and carried it to sickeningly savage and brutal levels. It is fairly well established that Margaret was completely innocent. To the last, she declared she was no traitor. The following verse was found carved on the wall of her cell:

> For traitors on the block should die;
> I am no traitor, no, not I!
> My faithfulness stands fast and so,
> Towards the block I shall not go!
> Nor make one step, as you shall see;
> Christ in Thy Mercy, save Thou me!'

She refused to go to the block, declaring that she knew of no crime she had committed, had not been informed of any crime, and was completely innocent. She was forcibly dragged outside to Tower Green. She refused to kneel and put her head on the block repeating she had committed no crime. What makes this event so much worse is that the usual executioner was unavailable.

The imperial ambassador, Chapuys, described the substitute executioner as 'a wretched and blundering youth who literally hacked her head and shoulders to pieces in the most pitiful manner.'

Margaret was beatified by Pope Leo XIII in 1886.[27]

Nuisance

There are, according to Thomson Reuters 'Practical Law' two types of common law nuisance:

> A public nuisance arises from an act that endangers the life, health, property, morals or comfort of the public or obstructs the public in the exercise or enjoyment of rights common to all. A public nuisance is actionable in tort and can also be a criminal offence.
>
> A private nuisance usually is caused by a person doing something on his own land, which he is lawfully entitled to do but which becomes a nuisance when the consequences of his act extend to the land of his neighbour by, for example, causing physical damage. A private nuisance is actionable in tort.

The definition of tort is when someone commits a wrong against another person.

It has always been true that where two or three people are gathered together, there is a high likelihood of disharmony at some point. Quarrelling neighbours are a prime example and probably the most common one today. Disregard for property has been a problem since before the Norman Conquest.

One man might divert a millstream to make his own life easier, without any regard for the miller a few miles downstream. Another might erect a hedge to keep his sheep from escaping, forcing his neighbour's sheep to wander further away looking for new pasture. Neighbours backbite and spread gossip. It all falls under the heading of nuisance.

Of course the response to these issues could be fast or slow: the former if the aggrieved individual took matters into his own hands or the latter if he took his case to law.

When Henry II came to the throne in 1154, thus truly ending the first civil war between Stephen and the Empress Matilda, his intention was to be a strong king. During the previous twenty years of unrest, upheavals like those described above, though intermittent, had caused issues at a local level and were destructive to Henry's idea of a peaceful realm.

Property had to be protected, so he set up the Assize of Novel Disseisin – a court which would decide on the recovery or otherwise of lands that had been seized and the owner dispossessed. In time this court came to be associated with the issue of 'nuisance', since it dealt with property disputes.

Initially, the idea was simple. The injured party applied for a royal writ for the repossession of his land. The writ was sent to the sheriff of the relevant county. It stated that there had been a complaint made to the king, with details of the grievance. The sheriff would then do a superficial investigation and set up a 'site visit' by 'twelve good men and true' to see for themselves how the land lay. If it was decided that there was a case to answer, the twelve good men plus the defendant had to promise to make themselves available for a hearing by the travelling justices.[1]

What frequently happened when the justices arrived, was that some of the twelve good men would absent themselves, with or without the court's permission. However, when the hearing finally took place, there was only one thing to decide. Had X caused the problem for Y because of his action in doing Z?

Technically, there could only one of two answers – yes or no. Sometimes the twelve men explained why they had answered as they had. In theory, it worked well, but, where people are concerned, things are seldom that clear cut. At its simplest, the justices might order the offending hedge to be torn down or the water course to be put back in its original path.

By the time we arrive in Tudor England, nuisance, as a concept, had expanded to include disputes with neighbours.

One such issue drove Goodwife Dannett to write to William Cecil, Lord Burghley about it.

CASE STUDY

The following is taken from an account in the Lansdowne manuscripts, the collection of William Petty, 1st Marquess of Lansdowne, and now held by the British Library. Today, we are used to living with a lot of noise pollution; some people find loud music, be that Mozart or Metallica, disturbing or offensive.

In Elizabeth's England, noise could prove to be a serious issue. Quite what the noise was that drove Goodwife Dannutt almost demented she does not say, sadly. Whatever it was, the poor woman was at last impelled to write directly to William Cecil. She says the disturbance was 'at one of the clocke at an unlawfull time'.[2]

It seems that her neighbour, a man called Johnson, knew about the noise, and she begged Cecil to make Johnson reveal 'the counstables name that dwell next house', and the names of two watchmen, who seemed to play a part in the night-time noise that disturbed her so much.

The poor goodwife is clearly at her wits' end, pleading that Cecil help her 'for godes sake' so that she can see an end to her torment 'for cyste Jesus sake'. It is worth noting that if Dannutt used this language to her neighbours and in her letter to the most powerful man in England, everyone would have been scandalised, considering it to be swearing and breaking the second commandment – the one about not taking the Lord's name in vain.

She also begs Cecil to end her torment without 'gret expense'. Her following sentences appear to intimate that the constable and watchmen make her pay them every night to keep quiet, which, if true, would constitute blackmail.

No 'nightmare neighbour' story is complete without a sense of how powerless law-abiding citizens feel about resolving their desperate situation. Not only was Dannutt complaining about a constable and a pair of watchmen, she also noted that 'the judges of the Kinges Bench ar a kinde' to the offenders, and that they have 'so maney frendes that I coud never reste day nor nighte.' This sounds as if the judges were colluding with her neighbours. Reaching out to Cecil was therefore her last hope for peace, quiet, and a good night's sleep.

The goodwife ended her letter on a strange note. She also claimed that 'moste of the lands that the queen gave he meanes to kepe it from me, and also lamented that every one cossus me & decevses me.'

There are perhaps two conclusions to be drawn. The first is that, like many neighbourly disputes, this one may well have concerned the more serious question of property rights, as well as the nuisance issue of antisocial behaviour. The second is that Dannutt appears to have been socially isolated, and therefore may not have been as innocent a party as she herself claimed.

There is no evidence as to whether Burghley slapped whatever the Elizabethan equivalent of an ASBO was on to the noisy constable, or even whether or not Dannutt ever managed to get a decent forty winks. Even if this incident was resolved amicably, we can at least say with absolute certainty that the problem of noisy neighbours has unquestionably never gone away.

Organised Crime

Just as today, when people – often young women – get off a train at one of the mainline stations, are targeted as prey by some lowlifes and introduced to drugs and prostitution, Tudor London was no different. Except the prey were usually young men come to the capital to make their fortune.[1]

London's fraudsters and felons were organised and ambitious. They had their own jargon and would often use lawyers' terminology to give their honeyed words an air of propriety. Fraudsters called themselves 'escheators', which in mediaeval England meant law officers giving property belonging to someone who had died without legal heirs back to the monarch. The fraudsters termed it as 'conveying goods from one person to another'.

Occasionally, a man they had brought to the brink of destruction would be recruited as a new member of the team.[2] Why not, they would ask him? Everyone does it, from lawyers to merchants.

Loaded dice were common and could be loaded in different ways, which meant it was not unusual for a trickster to carry several pairs of dice in his sleeve. Horse-traders were the Tudor equivalent of the popular urban legend, the used-car salesmen. In 1583, Richard Evans was questioned about horse theft in Warwick. He admitted he 'traded' all over the Midlands.[3]

Playing cards could be marked or pricked. Mirrors were often placed behind the target or, occasionally, a woman would sit quietly sewing in a corner of the room. But a corner where she could see the target's card. Depending on how slowly or quickly she drew the needle through the cloth was a signal to her co-conspirator as to what cards the target held.[4]

Occasionally, a trickster would identify a target (mark) when out walking. He would drop a worthless ring in the street and make sure he bent to pick it up just before the mark could get to it. Whereupon he would pretend to haggle, claiming he deserved half the price of the ring. He would persuade the mark to pay half the value of it.

The long-winded negotiations frequently took place over a few ales in a tavern, at the end of which the trickster would leave a lot richer than when he came in, and the mark had not only parted with a goodly sum of money for half the worthless ring, he would also be left with an equally hefty bar bill.[5]

Occasionally a maidservant would be hailed in the street by a man claiming to be a long-lost relative. He would take his time to get to know her and rejoice that he had found her. But the maidservant would end up with a whipping because her gullibility resulted in her master's house being burgled.[6]

A new game entered the annals in the 1590s. The cheat would defraud the mark in a card game. Then he would pretend penitence and confess what he had done. He would show the mark how he had worked the trick. At which point a 'newcomer' would join them and be invited to play. Needless to say, the 'newcomer' was part of the swindle. They would all play until the mark was utterly confident in his new-found skill and bet every penny he had.[7] And would lose all of them.

In 1585 there was a crackdown against crime in London. A report sent to William Cecil, Lord Burghley, listed a number of 'notorious thieves' and identified forty-five 'harbouringe howses' for criminals, plus a school for pickpockets.

(See also Gangs and Juvenile Crime.)

CASE STUDY[8]

Gilbert Walker tells of the case of a young man identified only as R, who has come to London to seek his fortune. He is wandering around St Paul's churchyard, a centre for people to gather and gossip, especially when new to London. R spies a splendidly dressed man, attended by equally well-dressed servants. The man realises R is a newcomer to the city and invites him home for dinner. After the dinner table is cleared, a silver bowl full of dice and cards is produced.

R is hesitant because he doesn't know these games, but by mid-afternoon he has lost £2 (just under £1,000 in 2021). He leaves the house poorer but no wiser. As is the habit of gamblers, he returns to try and win his money back. By the time he confesses to a more worldly friend what has happened, R has lost £40 (about £21,000 in 2021). His friend tells R he has been targeted – 'hooks were laid to pick your purse'. He further tells him he has been the victim of a well-tuned criminal enterprise that is expert at drawing innocents into its web, whereupon it guts and fillets them and spits them out when they have been picked clean.

Poaching

The definition of poaching in its criminal form is 'illegally hunt or catch (game or fish) on land that is not one's own or in contravention of official protection.'

In a parliamentary act of 1485, soon after Henry VII came to the throne, it was determined that unauthorised hunting in private forests was a felony punishable by death.[1] So far, so good. If the offence was committed during the hours of darkness, or the offenders disguised themselves or wore masks to hide their faces, then the punishment was enacted as a felony and perpetrators were hanged. If the poaching took place during the hours of daylight and the offenders made no attempt to disguise their identity, the penalty was a fine or imprisonment.

In general, game poaching has been a rural pursuit for thousands of years. In the Middle Ages in England vast areas of the countryside were the sole preserve of the king. Anyone caught stealing wood or poaching the monarch's deer was severely punished. The issue was made more confusing because in the thirteenth and fourteenth centuries, Forest Law stated that offences outside the royal forests were common trespass. The view of authorities was that peasants and labourers used the excuse of poaching in order to conspire against their lords.

The Game Code defined killing wild beasts and game as the sole preserve of the aristocracy, and since many of the lords' tenants suffered from the depredations of these animals, feelings soon ran high. Protests ranged from anti-enclosure riots to poaching. The code operated on two illogical assumptions: the first was that all rights regarding hunting should rightly be restricted to the privileged lords; the second was that deer and other game, on which no true value could be consigned, could still be regarded as 'stolen'.

This view persisted into the eighteenth century and was expanded to include anyone found in possession of hunting weapons or nets or hounds. Every parliamentary act endorsed this view so that in time, anybody who hunted and was not part of the ruling elite committed a crime.[2]

Anyone found out at night – termed 'night walking' – was committing a crime in common law. If two or three people were found to be poaching, it was considered a riot.[3]

Poison

The act of poisoning somebody is self-explanatory.

CASE STUDIES

Margaret Davy[1]

An unfortunate maidservant who fell foul of Henry VIII's boiling punishment, as set down in the Acte of Poysoning 1531, was Margaret/ Margret Davy/Davey/Davie/Dawes. And the very fact that so few people regulated the spelling of names, highlights one of the difficulties of searching for information in contemporary sources.

Margaret was convicted of poisoning the inhabitants of three houses in which she had worked, one of the victims being her mistress. Allegedly, the public was not satisfied that she was guilty. The accounts of her horrific death by boiling at Smithfield in March 1542 aroused widespread revulsion. It has been posited by historians that one of the reasons Henry VIII kept this punishment on the statute books was that he had a desperate fear of being poisoned. However, when he died in 1547 and Edward VI ascended the throne, the law was repealed and offenders were either hanged (men) or burned (women). It's the 'Eve Factor' again.

Agnes Cotell[2]

In the earlier years of Henry VIII's reign, in Wiltshire, John and Agnes Cotell were staying with a landowner, Edward Hungerford. On 26 July 1518, John Cotell died. By December of that year, Edward and Agnes were married.

In January 1522 Edward also died. In his will, he left everything to his wife: 'the residue of all ... goodes, detts, catalls, juells, plate, harnesse, and all other moveables whatsover they be'. He left absolutely nothing to his son, Walter, from his first marriage. It was noticed, however, that the will was dated only a month before the unfortunate Edward was in his shroud. Although it isn't stated anywhere for certain, it is more than likely that Walter Hungerford, being dispossessed, did a bit of digging and came up with the convenient death of Agnes' first husband.

However, as events transpired, her servants from the time of John Cotell's death, confessed they had strangled John with a neckerchief and burned his body in the kitchen furnace. No charges were brought against Agnes until the sudden death of her second husband.

It seems likely that she had inveigled the servants, William Mathewe and William Ignes, to kill John so that she could marry Edward, who obviously had a lot more going for him in terms of material goods. It is also possible that Edward connived in John's murder, but this was never investigated let alone proved.

Edward's death so soon after making his will aroused suspicion. Agnes and her two servants were convicted of murder, but William Ignes claimed Benefit of Clergy. Mathewe and Agnes were hanged at Tyburn on 20 February 1523. Ignes lived to sin again and this time he didn't escape. He was hanged for bigamy.

John Brewen

Earlier in this book, the development of the press and its growing power was examined. The public's desire for news of scandals and the like is perfectly illustrated by the murder of John Brewen in January 1590.[3]

A pamphlet was produced, with the less than catchy title of 'The Trueth of the most wicked and secret murthering of John Brewen, Goldsmith of London, committed by his owne wife through the provocation of John Parker whom she loved.'[4]

This lucid and believable account was written by a playwright called Thomas Kyd.[5] Writers are always advised to make sure their titles tell the reader what the book/article/pamphlet is about and nobody can deny that the above does just that. It does not, however, compare with some of its twenty-first century equivalents:

> 'Anti-freeze plot wife guilty', *Manchester Evening News*, 12 January 2013
> 'Life for wife who lured husband's killers with sex', *Daily Express*, 1 August 2012

Or my particular favourite, which does follow the advice:

'Inside the twisted mind of Australia's worst female killer who skinned and decapitated her lover before cooking his head in a pot with veggies and trying to SERVE it to his children', *Daily Mail*, 2 December 2021.

The press has come a long way in 400 years. However, I digress. And not for the first time.

St Paul, in his first letter to the Corinthians, advises that 'it is better to marry than to burn', by which he meant that if you can't be celibate, then marry but stay faithful to your spouse. It is ironic that in the Middle Ages the expected punishment for wives who murdered their husbands was to burn. Any male accomplices were usually hanged.

Burning homicidal wives was considered a just punishment since women, the weaker sex, were going against every rule of society in killing their husbands, who were, naturally, superior to their wives in every way. The punishment was specified in the 1352 Statute of Treasons under Edward III and designated as petty treason. At the beginning of the sixteenth century, victims were usually burned alive but by the end of Elizabeth's reign, unless the crime was considered particularly heinous, the perpetrator would be first strangled by the executioner and then burned.

John Brewen's murder took place in January 1590. As we know from the title of the pamphlet, he was a London goldsmith. What we are not told is that John Parker, his wife's lover, was also a goldsmith.

Anne Welles was described as a 'proper young woman' and a 'comely personage'. Brewen certainly thought so because he became very much attached to her. Unfortunately, she was very much attached to John Parker. She loved Parker far more than Brewen, but Parker refused to marry her.

To spice up the mix, Brewen, seeing how much Anne preferred Parker, demanded the return of all the gifts he had given her in the belief they had had an understanding and she would marry him. Anne refused. Brewen had her arrested.

Faced with a possible prison sentence and the fact that Parker was lukewarm at best regarding their relationship, Anne had second thoughts. Then she discovered she was pregnant by Parker. She immediately agreed to marry John Brewen if he withdrew his legal action. He was happy to oblige and obviously looked forward to a bit of connubial bliss.

Parker now seems to have exhibited classic dog in the manger behaviour. He didn't want Anne but he didn't want anyone else to have her either. Anne and Brewen were married but Parker did not take this defeat well, 'continually urging her to make him [Brewen] away'. To sweeten the deal, he promised that the instant Anne was free, he would marry her.

Although her new husband 'loved her tenderly', she refused to sleep with him after the wedding night, neither would she take his name or live with him until 'he got another house'. Three days after the wedding ceremony, Parker obtained 'sugar sops'; toasted bread that has been soaked in ale, sweetened with sugar and grated nutmeg. Anne played the devoted wife and fed them to her husband. Despite his violent vomiting, she refused to stay with him and decamped back to her lodgings.

When she returned the next morning, Brewen scolded her for leaving him when he was so ill. Anne's response was that she would indeed come and live with him – when he got another house.

Brewen died soon after this, but no suspicion attached itself to Anne. Any marriage difficulties that came to light were put down to her being young and foolish. When she gave birth to Parker's child, it was assumed to be Brewen's.

And had things stopped there, and Anne had used one of her few brain cells, that is the way it would have stayed. However, she soon became embroiled with Parker again. Far from delivering upon his promise to marry her, he developed into the classic controlling bully. For the next two years, she was completely in thrall to him and if she tried to escape his clutches, he threatened her and became abusive.

What really sounded the death knell for this abominable pair was when Anne fell pregnant again. Unmarried, she tried to hide her condition and begged Parker to marry her. He replied he would not marry 'such a strumpet'. She retorted that she had only ever slept with him. His response was that he wouldn't marry her in case she poisoned him, as she had her first husband. She naturally replied with the sixteenth-century equivalent of 'that's rich, you got the poison for me.'

Their argument was so loud, it was overheard, and magistrates were informed of what had been said. The pair were taken before separate aldermen and questioned. Both refused to confess to anything. Then Anne was told Parker had confessed and, believing this, she finally told the truth. There is some doubt as to whether Parker confessed anything. Knowing what we do about Parker's character, and looking at the situation from a twenty-first century perspective with so many documentaries showing interviews of murder suspects, it is likely he went with the Tudor version of 'No Comment'.

The upshot was that Anne and Parker were arrested and convicted of John Brewen's murder. The sentence was ordered to be delayed until Anne's child was born, but after that the punishment stated that Parker was 'to be hanged before her eyes', after which she was to be burned.

On Wednesday 28 June 1592 the sentences were carried out.

Tavern Talk:

Barber Surgeons were formally recognised around 1540, more or less in the middle of the Tudor era. They were separate from physicians because they did not have a university education but served an apprenticeship. They performed procedures like blood-letting, amputations, and cupping, which is where the red and white pole outside their premises originates – denoting blood and bandages. However, they were not allowed to call themselves by the title of 'Doctor'. They remained plain 'Mr'. Fast forward to 1745 when the surgeons split off from the barbers and formed the Company of Surgeons. One wonders if it was a two-fingered salute to doctors and physicians that they insisted on retaining the title of Mr, something that is almost exclusive to the UK.

Prostitution

Known as the oldest profession, the definition of prostitution is 'the practice or occupation of engaging in sexual activity with someone for payment'.

CASE STUDIES

By most of her contemporaries, and in the minds of many people subsequently, Mary Newborough was not a paragon of virtue, although her history is interesting. She was the second wife of George Newborough, a gentleman, who, some time before 1596, was incarcerated for being a highwayman.[1] One wonders what difficulty made a gentleman resort to crime.

When he was convicted, his estate was forfeit and Mary could not support herself. So she turned to the oldest profession in 1597/8. In her first brothel, kept by a certain Eleanor Dethrick aka Mrs Windsor, Mary's clients included Italians according to the deposition taken in Bridewell from one Helen Cootes, of whom more later.

However, in October 1598 Mary was sent to Bridewell, but released after a short period. She is next heard of working for Anne Miller in Chick Lane. But she was soon back in Bridewell and detained from September 1599 to January 1600. The length of her imprisonment is probably because one of her admirers had stolen £70 and showered her with gifts, which she accepted.

At some point, she and another prisoner, were 'carted' through the streets, one of the traditional punishments for prostitutes, which, of course, would result in insults, muck and other horrible things being pelted at her. Once more in prison, in July 1601, she was ordered to wear a blue gown and undertake spinning.

At some point in 1601 her mother was allowed to pay for a special diet for Mary during her confinement. However, in March 1602 the management of Bridewell changed and the innovative business venture of the new owners was to convert the prison to a brothel. There were known abuses to the women during this time and the matter came to the ears of the authorities. By October 1602 the brothel had ceased to exist.

But during the six months the prison was in private hands, Mary really came into her own. She is known to have objected to the treatment of the women thus imprisoned and was, in consequence, beaten very badly by Nicholas Bywater, one of the new owners. She organised a protest and Bywater was arrested. She attempted to escape but failed, and so hit on the idea of convincing the authorities she had turned over a new leaf.

The authorities released her and, with the help of financial aid, Mary was allowed to claim on her now-dead husband's estate. It would appear she managed to keep herself out of trouble, but nothing is known for certain about what happened to her. There is one theory that she is the inspiration for the mention of Mistress Moll by Sir Toby Belch in Shakespeare's *Twelfth Night*, which had its first performance in 1602 while she was still in prison.

Mrs Windsor, referred to above, was known as a notorious bawd. She tailored the activities in her brothel to suit the needs and tastes of her clients, both homegrown and international. And she operated her bawdy house with the connivance and assistance of David English, a clergyman, who gave her establishment the veneer of respectability.[2] Her clients were of the upper-middle class and in a case of what was sauce for the gander reflecting that for the goose, David English gave her a privileged seat in church.

Clergymen in brothels is a well-documented occurrence and English's behaviour was common knowledge. This parish chatter was corroborated by one of Mary Newborough's fellow harlots, the aforementioned Helen Cootes. She deposed that English had attempted to seduce Mrs Windsor's kitchen maid, Jane, and another of her maids, Cecily Gray: 'He laied her on a bed and putt the dore close to and did kysse her.' Quite how Helen could see through a closed door is not explained.

There is no evidence to support her claims, but what is clear is that David English exercised a lot of control over what went on in Mrs Windsor's establishment, down to possibly recruiting the working women and controlling the client list. However, English was never brought to book for helping run a brothel, but Helen did not fare so well.[3] It was, once more, a case of the church looking after its own. Mrs Windsor was fined £5 and that amount seems to confirm that she had a substantial income running an affluent establishment.

Helen Coote was, presumably, sacked from the brothel and began a partnership with a man called George Eden who became her procurer. Then, as now, pimps were the oil that greased the prostitution industry. Eden was a controlling, vicious bully who touted Helen all over the home counties like a piece of property. Their partnership can be likened to the modern-day racketeers smuggling women into the UK, forcing them to become drug addicts and then pimping them out to all and sundry.

Thankfully, when she was sent to Bridewell, Helen confessed all to the prison authorities who realised Eden had lined his own pockets while degrading her. She was not even fined but discharged and told to return to the court each day for a month, at which point she had to eschew London and anywhere else in Middlesex. Her freedom from Eden gave her the courage to face him and accuse him directly of touting her around, something he could not deny. We are, sadly, not told what happened to Helen or Eden.

Quarrels

Tudor England was, perhaps especially because of the reverberations from the Wars of the Roses, an era that set great store on harmony, be that between neighbours, husband and wife, or within the parish. Discord among neighbours was seen as damaging to society. Going so far as to attack somebody in church, something for which Thomas Cuddington stood trial in 1597, was considered much worse than attacking them anywhere else.[1]

Discord between neighbours, often caused by a desire to avenge a perceived wrong, could be construed as sedition, which was much more serious. And again, just like in modern times, many disputes began in the alehouse, especially if a group of people was unhappy with someone in authority within the parish, very often in the person of the priest.

In 1530s Yorkshire, Margaret Fulthorp, who is described as a 'gentilwoman', went to the Chapel of Saint Saviour at Newburgh, near Thirsk, to pay her half-year's rent. The village was on land owned by the Duke of Norfolk.[2]

Margaret appears to have held a grudge against the local prior because after she had paid, she told the prior to 'praye god save my lord of Norfolk'. The duke had, at the bidding of Henry VIII, intervened on Margaret's behalf to end the dispute between her and her husband on the one hand and the prior on the other, over a farm that the latter owned. The dispute had gone on for seven years. Had the good duke not intervened, Margaret said, 'the prior wold have undone and beggared her said husband her and their children'.

The prior, understandably, was a tad miffed when she said this. He allegedly replied that it made no difference to him if one of them, either the king or the duke, were hanged against the other. This would, of course, constitute treason.

Another parishioner, Brian Boye, who was not enamoured of the prior, said he had been deprived of his post as a servant of the prior and keeper of St Saviour's, claiming that the prior had concealed that there were no other worshippers besides him at service and had not been since Lammas, indicating some kind of fraud.

Both these disputes seem to be a case of sour grapes, certainly ill-feeling between the prior and the parishioners. As far as Brian Boye was concerned, the prior said Boye had brought the accusation because he had refused the man's offer of £6 13s 4d (roughly £5,500 in 2021) for the 'convent seal of the kepynge of saynt Saviors chapel'. The prior also said Boye's accusation was made in 'plain malice', something that Boye refuted.

With both the foregoing examples of parish quarrels, the accusations failed to progress because although there were bystanders, including the parish priest, nobody heard the prior say anything amiss. It was put down to wounded pride and a costly suit regarding property.[3]

Sometimes an innocent could get caught up in neighbourly disputes. One such case was that of a pedlar who travelled in June 1537 to the Isle of Wight and announced that 'queen anne was put to deth and boyled in led'. This shows two things: that tellers of tales like to exaggerate, and how slow news was to travel. Anne Boleyn had been dead for thirteen months by the time the pedlar imparted this news.

What happened next depends on which account you choose to believe. One version was that upon hearing the pedlar's news, Sir Nicolas Porter, the parson of Freshwater, who was probably drunk, stated that whilst the king and his Council were busy pulling down abbeys and taking away the right of the holy church, he (the king) was being made a cuckold at home.

A witness, William Welyar, when interrogated, swore on oath that Porter had not said that. Varying versions of the story then abounded, which obscured the original accusation, but it didn't die entirely. Another of the original accusers, William Smyth, wagered Welyar money that he had been present and heard Porter say those words. Welyar asserted the accusation had been made out of malice.

Finally another priest, John Arnold, said he overheard two men – we don't know who – offer to drop the charges against Porter if he 'wold be good unto the clerk ther and leve his sute against hym they wold never speke of the matter'.

It would appear, trying to read between the lines from a distance of 500 years, that the case was probably false and brought against the parson by the community simply to avenge his treatment of his clerk.[4]

Recusancy

Recusants are 'those who refused to obey the religious laws of the land'. In other words, post-Reformation, those who remained staunch Roman Catholics, Anabaptists etc. People found guilty were punished in various ways.

There is a fine line between Henry VIII's post-Reformation laws and those of the European Reformation. The latter was generated from sincere differences in thought and doctrine between the Lutherans and Calvinists on one hand and the Roman Catholics on the other.

Henry VIII's actions have been labelled the 'Tudor Terror' and did not spring from perceived differences in doctrine, but the king's unwavering determination to be acknowledged by everybody as the head of the church in England. That said, the penalties for Roman Catholics, those who refused to sign the Oath of Supremacy, Lutherans etc., were much the same. Death in some form, either by hanging, beheading, or burning.

However, it is in Elizabeth I's statutes that the emphasis changed. When she came to the throne in 1558, she knew the overriding need of the people was for religious persecution to be handled less like the Spanish Inquisition and with a greater sense of mercy. And while she burned a substantial number of people, she did it over forty-odd years instead of five. For Elizabeth, recusancy was nothing to do with religion but everything to do with the politics of being acknowledged as head of the church. In other words that the sole source of power in England was the monarch – of both church and state.

What Elizabeth did in her first Parliament was to repeal all Mary's legislation and replace it with her father's. People still had to take the Oath of Supremacy, but if they refused and kept silent, they were simply barred from any kind of office for life. If, however, they were vocal in their opposition, the punishments rose from fines to imprisonment, and, after the third transgression, to execution for high treason.[1]

As far as Elizabeth was concerned, recusancy was about jurisdiction. The Acts of Supremacy and Uniformity appear to say that the penalty for disagreeing with the doctrine of Elizabeth's government was milder than refusing to accept her as the Supreme Governor of the Church of England instead of the Bishop of Rome (Pope). In other words, the nub was who declared the doctrine, not the doctrine itself.

Repeated attacks on the Book of Common Prayer led to life imprisonment, or a large fine if the offender agreed to become an informer. Speaking or writing against supremacy eventually led to execution. Active opposition was seen as defying the queen's authority and a precursor to the possibility of rebellion or invasion.[2]

For most of the population, just going to church indicated an acceptance that they were obeying the law. During Elizabeth's long reign, Mary's Catholic priests died and most of the others were amalgamated into the Anglican Church, especially when government pressure was applied.

So far, so good. The problem was it didn't work very well in practice. The system of reporting and fining lower down the chain was left to the bishops, and under them, local church wardens. Elizabeth and her Privy Council only regarded recusancy as an element of foreign affairs.[3]

Some bishops did not accept their obligations regarding prosecuting recusancy. Church wardens were often reluctant to report a friend, neighbour, or someone with whom they transacted business.

The city of Chester proved a case in point. Most of the visitations by those supposed to monitor recusants dealt with sexual offences and the behaviour of the clergy. There was no appetite to monitor Catholics or determine if Catholicism was flourishing. The bishops were required to touch base with all recusants once a year and check they were conforming, but this seldom happened.

JPs were obliged to take the Oath of Supremacy, but not all of them did. The system was lax, mainly because Elizabeth believed that if support from continental Europe was cut off, Catholicism in England would die. And, since she relied on the gentry to help her maintain rule, she opted for the slower path of waiting for recusants in office to die and replacing them with Protestants. Early in her reign, therefore, enforcement was sporadic, but a kind of uneasy balance began to be established.

The arrival of Mary, Queen of Scots (Mary Stuart) in her native land after the death of her French husband, in addition to the worsening of Anglo-Spanish relations, began to tilt the recusancy tectonic plates. In 1567 the Spanish Duke of Alva was overthrown in the Spanish Netherlands and England was flooded with refugees, all with horrendous tales to tell. Tensions grew and the north of England, which had always been something of a watched kettle to successive monarchs, began to simmer.

Northern recusants were arrested and questioned. They were forced to post of bond of 300 marks (one mark was 13s and 4d, so that roughly equates to £200 in 2022). They also had to agree to take communion three times a year and hear sermons within three miles of their homes. Again, there was neither the appetite nor the resources to enforce this and the government distrusted local officials to police the policy.[4]

And then three things happened that really put the religious cat among the political pigeons. In 1568 Mary Stuart fled to England after being deposed. This followed the murder of her second husband, Lord Darnley, and what was seen as her outrageous behaviour in marrying James Hepburn, Earl of Bothwell. Once in England, she became a magnet for disaffected Catholics.

In late 1569/early 1570, the powerful northern lords, led by Charles Neville, Earl of Westmoreland, and Thomas Percy, Earl of Northumberland, rode into Durham, took control of the cathedral and destroyed first the English Bible, and then the Protestant communion table. After which they celebrated an illegal Catholic Mass. Elizabeth acted rapidly and the revolt was soon put down. Westmoreland escaped but Northumberland was executed.[5]

In February 1570 the Pope excommunicated Elizabeth and declared that any Catholic who assassinated her would be pardoned. And if that was not enough, in 1571 international banker Ridolfi plotted to assassinate Elizabeth and replace her with Mary Stuart. In 1572 the Duke of Norfolk also plotted with the imprisoned ex-Queen of Scots to kill Elizabeth and reign jointly. Norfolk was executed.

The Puritans were also causing problems for the queen. Both they and the Catholics refused to acknowledge her as the Supreme Governor of the Church of England. Both parties believed that authority was vested in the church.[6]

CASE STUDY

By 1586 the problem of the Catholics, centred in the threat posed by Mary Stuart, had become acute. Recusancy became a political bone of contention for the government. So when Margaret Clitherow/Clitheroe decided to break the law, those in authority decided an example must be made.

Margaret was born in York in 1556, her maiden name being Margaret Middleton. Her father was a wax chandler and Margaret was brought up as a Protestant. She was married at the age of fifteen to John Clitherow, a widower, in 1571. He was a butcher and their shop and house – which now has a plaque on it – was in The Shambles. This street is extremely narrow and full of interesting shops today, making it a tourist magnet. In Elizabethan times, it was a row of butchers shops and abbatoirs.[7]

John Clitherow was a constable and, as such, responsible for finding Catholic priests, and the people who hid them and celebrated private masses in their homes. This was at a time when many houses were built to provide priests' holes. This secrecy/hole in the corner activity by Catholics became more than ironic when Margaret converted to Roman Catholicism around 1574, hired Catholic tutors for her children and sent her eldest son to study at the Catholic college in Douai in France.

Her husband, although remaining a Protestant, was supportive of her and paid heavy fines because of his wife's activities. By the mid to late 1570s, Margaret was a leader of the York Catholics. She sheltered priests and was imprisoned several times in York Castle, beginning in 1577. Whilst in prison she learned to read.[8]

When two priests were put to death on the York equivalent of Tyburn at Knavesmire, Margaret visited the gallows at night as a pilgrimage. Eventually, in 1586, her home was raided and Margaret was arrested. Priests' vestments were found, as was communion bread. Allegedly, a small boy was also found, one so frightened by the inquisitors, he told them everything they wanted to know. Margaret was hauled off to prison and never saw any of her children again.

At her trial in York Guildhall, she refused to enter a plea. When confronted, she said that she knew of nothing she had done wrong and could not, therefore, enter a plea. Since refusal meant the offender would be pressed, the local dignitaries, including the mayor, who happened to be her stepfather, protested at the barbarity of the sentence. The protest fell on deaf ears.

On 25 March 1586 Margaret was stripped naked and made to lie on the stone floor of the toll booth on the Ouse bridge. She was permitted to cover herself with a shift she had made, but not allowed to wear it. She was pressed to death under weights of around 7-8 hundredweights (between 355 and 400kg). Despite pleas from her stepfather to not commit suicide and others who declared she was mad, Margaret was steadfast and took around fifteen minutes to die.

The authorities did not wish her grave to become a shrine. It is possible she was buried secretly in a rubbish dump. However, legend has it that six weeks after her death, friends exhumed her body and reburied her in secret with appropriate reverence. Nobody knows where she is buried, but a hand purporting to be hers is kept at the Bar Convent in York.[9]

Plaques have been put up around the city, including on the wall of the house in which she lived in The Shambles. However, in the eighteenth century the houses were renumbered and so there is some dispute as to which house was the Clitherow one. Margaret was canonised by Pope Paul VI in October 1970.

The poet Gerard Manley Hopkins was made a Jesuit priest and worked among the poor in Liverpool. He wrote of the punishment Margaret had to bear:

> She was a woman, upright, outright;
> Her will was bent at God. For that
> Word went she should be crushed out flat ...
> She held her hands to, like in prayer;
> They had them out and laid them wide
> (Just like Jesus crucified);
> They brought their hundredweights to bear.

The final tragedy was, that, at the time, Margaret was known to be pregnant and should not have been executed until her child was born, but her punishment went ahead nonetheless.

Tavern Talk:

The nursery rhyme Mary, Mary, quite contrary has long been thought to refer to Bloody Mary, but there is no proof of this. In C J Roberts' book Heavy Words Lightly Thrown: The Reason Behind the Rhyme, he posits that it might refer to either Bloody Mary or Mary, Queen of Scots. If the former, the term quite contrary refers to her obsession with returning England to the Roman Catholic fold. 'How does your garden grow?' refers to her lack of heirs, or possibly a snide dig at her chief minister, Stephen Gardiner. 'Pretty maids' is thought to signify Lady Jane Grey and 'all in a row' her executions of Protestants. However, Mary, Queen of Scots, another Catholic, was very much disliked by her Scottish Puritan lords, so the rhyme could refer to her. In which case, 'silver bells' might be a jibe at her love of finery and 'cockle shells' her love of decorative gardens. The 'pretty maids all in a row' are thought to signify her four chief attendants, all called Mary.

Riots

The incidence of riots in Tudor England was, in the main, restricted to enclosure riots. Before enclosures, land was farmed according to the open field system. This system worked well, especially after the introduction of a large-wheeled plough called a caruca, which tilled the heavy English clay soil easily. However, it sometimes needed up to eight oxen to pull it. Peasants would work a strip of land, the size of which was influenced by how much each individual could afford in terms of oxen. The strips were farmed in either a two or three-year rotation with one year being fallow. Most peasants could not afford an ox team, so sometimes it had to be a joint enterprise.[1] This now happens today when groups of farmers collaborate to buy and share expensive farm equipment.

The only open field example remaining in England is at Laxton in Nottinghamshire. It demonstrates that one man with very little capital or land could gradually build up a larger holding within the communal system.

The open field method was not restricted to societal structure. It had evolved under the Saxons and continued through the Norman era. It was only after the Black Death in the mid-fourteenth century that leasehold became customary.

Then, in the 1530s and 1540s, enclosure – another term for privatisation of land – began to have an impact on the social life of the country. Although historically enclosures had not previously caused unrest, the increase in population and the resulting need for food meant that land was enclosed at a faster rate. Supplies of grain and meat became more difficult to farm without access to common and waste land.

The dissolution of the monasteries also produced increased fluidity in the land market. This coincided with new and more scientific ways to farm the land and affected the balance of relationships between landlords, smallholders, and tenant farmers.

The resulting imbalance led to a series of enclosure riots as a means of social protest. Enclosure riots must not be confused with the series of rebellions such as the Pilgrimage of Grace in 1536. Neither must it be assumed that enclosure riots were perpetrated by enraged peasants venting their anger and frustration on a rapacious gentry.[2]

The Star Chamber examined the issue of seventy-five enclosure riots during the reigns of Henry VIII and Edward VI. It concluded peasants and tenants were less to blame than peers and the gentry, who were much more proactive in destroying enclosures. Twenty-nine cases of 'casting down hedges' at the instigation of 'peers' or 'gentlemen' were included in the seventy-five. Four cases of destruction were at the order of a manorial court or municipal officials, and three cases of riot were because a Crown order commanding the removal of enclosures was ignored. In four more cases, the destruction was assigned to townsmen and three further cases to clerics. Only in twelve of the seventy-five Star Chamber cases was it determined that the destruction was at the behest of 'yeomen, husbandmen, labourers or craftsmen'. In other words, only a few of these riots were the direct fault of the peasants.[3]

Frequently, the reason for the destruction was rivalry between gentry. This often included organised poaching parties to the rival's domain. Occasionally these 'visits' were accompanied by violence and threats. The gentry harassed their rivals in the law courts. It is interesting that most enclosure riots were contained within one village or sometimes rival villages where common land between them was under dispute.

Early Tudor enclosure riots were definitely a primitive form of social protest. However, in 1548-49 probably about one quarter of all English counties suffered the issue of enclosure rights. One must also take into consideration that rioters were defending their traditional way of life and protesting against agrarian innovation. And, of course, riots were a perfect vehicle for pursuing feuds.

Some writers were influenced by propagandists like John Hale, who lied about the extent to which enclosures had led to rural depopulation. There was always bloodthirsty talk about ridding England of gentlemen, echoing the Peasants' Revolt of 1381, but in the Tudor era this was enacted by the destruction of hedges, not the gentlemen.[4]

CASE STUDY[5]

Manorial courts had the authority to oversee the implementation of regulations concerning enclosures. However, the 'royal manor and borough of Bakewell' in Derbyshire had to deal with a number of complicated disputes.

One such concerned John Sharp of Derby, a gentleman who was anxious to expand his leaseholdings in the area covered by the Bakewell court. He was brought before the court in 1542 and accused of wrongfully enclosing two common fields, plus other specified plots of land, some of which belonged to Sir George Vernon. Sir George happened to be the chief tenant of the manor.

Sharp was accused of 'keeping [the fields] to himself in severalty, contrary to all laws and customs of the said manor'. He was also accused of enclosing part of the king's highway that ran between the Castle of the Peak (Peveril Castle) and Derby.

The court ordered Sharp to remove the illegal enclosures. He refused, so the tenants of Bakewell Manor, and Sir George as the presiding judge, ordered the jurors to personally level the enclosures and reopen the king's highway. Sharp took those jurors who obeyed Vernon to the Court of Star Chamber at Westminster. Vernon paid their legal fees.

Two months later, Sharp, who had leased some land from a chantry priest in Bakewell, once more suffered the annoyance of having his enclosure hedges removed. Again he took his case to the Star Chamber but the defendants maintained that the hedges Sharp had put up denied them the right of shack, which basically meant that the rights they all had over a portion of common land had been violated because Sharp had enclosed it.

Sharp remained persistent. We hear of him again in 1545 being accused of enclosing land he did not own by 'force of arms'. This area of around thirty acres was, again, deemed common land and by seizing it he denied the right of common pasture to the other tenants of Bakewell Manor.

Scolding

If physical violence has, as a general rule, been associated with men, verbal violence has always been regarded as the preserve of women. This is possibly another reason why the vast majority of those accused of being witches were women.

However, there was a serious aspect to this. Which was that breaches in domestic harmony threatened the perceived social harmony of the neighbourhood and, of course the wider world: the world where men were superior to women in all aspects and therefore permitted to chastise their spouses so long as they didn't kill them.

A post-Reformation homily, which most of the population will have heard, stated: 'He that hath an evil tongue, troubleth all the town where he dwelleth, and sometime the whole country. And a railing tongue is a pestilence so full of contagiousness that Saint Paul willeth Christian men to forbear the company of such ... he forbiddeth us to eat or drink with a scolder or quarrel picker.'[1]

In 1486, the year after Henry VII came to the throne, verbal abuse was tackled as a serious issue by the authorities in Hereford. They had obviously been driven to the point of action because they ordered that anyone found guilty of quarrelling, coming to blows, defamation, disturbing people's rest at night, neighbours at war, resisting or abusing the borough's officers, and breaching the king's peace would be punished by the 'cucking stool' – also known as the ducking stool.[2]

If they were found guilty and refused to accept this punishment, they were to be cast out of the city. Furthermore, any associates and accomplices would be treated as perjurers. Hereford seldom actually ducked anyone. Scolds were put in the ducking stool, with bare feet and their hair down, and presented to public ridicule as objects of shame.

Although at this very early point in the Tudor dynasty, the term 'scold' referred to men or women, by the end of the sixteenth century it became the norm for a scold to be a woman. Since most of the women prosecuted were in dispute with another woman, the issue cannot be regarded as being one concerned solely with male oppression.

The term also became synonymous with anyone who spread malicious gossip – sometimes called back-biting. Scolding became a criminal offence, with offenders prosecuted in the ecclesiastical, borough or manorial courts. That said, surviving accounts are few.

CASE STUDY[3]

The borough of Acomb, to the west of York, seems to have been the epitome of record keeping where scolds are concerned. In 1582 George Gill and two other men, who had obviously failed massively in their social duty to keep their wives in order, were fined because the aforementioned wives kept provoking disturbances with neighbours.

In the same borough, in 1584, Margaret Gill was prosecuted 'for scolding with Mrs Newarke', who happened to be of a higher social status.

Also in 1584, George Gill – yes, him again – and a fellow juror, Robert Spacye, were prosecuted for arguing in court.

As a rule, those found guilty were fined one shilling. Persistent offenders would be fined more. There are further accounts of disturbances in Acomb in the early seventeenth century, which is outside the Tudor era.

Some cases do deserve a modicum of sympathy. One such was that of Mary Stracke of Hempnall in Norfolk in 1597. She was prosecuted for being a common drunkard and sower of neighbourly discord, in other words 'a breaker of the Christian charity'. However, she claimed in court that she was very poor, had three children to feed and had only been asking for alms. Instead of which she was accused of scolding. One wonders how she paid for the alcohol that made her drunk!

Evidence from the Acomb records indicate that the commonest punishment was a fine. The general perception that the ducking-stool or brank (scold's bridle) were used extensively is not true. By the end of the sixteenth century it was easier and less messy to fine someone than dunking them in refuse-strewn, rat-infested water, which could end up with the defendant dead. But also, the stools had fallen into disrepair, were unusable, and not every borough had one.

Tavern Talk:
Most of the people found guilty of scolding were women, but among them were very, very few unmarried women. I'm saying nothing.

Sedition

The definition of sedition is 'the incitement by conduct or speech to rebel against the authority of a state or monarch'.

Although regarded as a political crime, it was not precisely defined legally until the early seventeenth century. In the Tudor era it was mainly understood to mean treasonable words or writings against the monarch.[1]

It was regarded as a threat to both public order and societal values, but some officials didn't seem to grasp that governmental policies could lead to discontent, which after all the evidence to the contrary, was short-sighted of them.

During the 1549 rebellions – Kett's rebellion in Norfolk and the Western or Prayerbook uprising in Devon – officials blamed the spread of rumours and dissatisfaction on vagrants and the towns' watchmen. This assumption was based on the fact that neither vagrants nor watchmen owned property. They would, therefore, always be unhappy with their lot. Other officials blamed drunkenness by soldiers returning from the wars in the Netherlands. Few, if any, government official laid the blame on the social living conditions of the vast majority of the population.[2]

The biggest hiatus of sixteenth-century England was not the tyrannical actions of the much-married Henry VIII but the first shot in his fight to have a living male heir – the Reformation. Many scholars have presented this event over subsequent centuries as being a wonderful path out of the Dark Ages. However, more recent scholars have posited that the change in the religion of England, even though it was initially from Roman Catholicism to English Catholicism 'dug a deep ditch, deep and dividing, between people and their religious past, and in its rejection of purgatory and of the cult of the saints, of prayer to and for the holy dead, it reduced Christianity to the mere company of the living. Overnight, a millennium of Christian splendour ... became alien territory, the dark ages of popery'.[3]

How could the ordinary people of England, not to mention many of the nobles, simply accept this change as one would a change of clothes?

Instead of Henry's desperate action to achieve his divorce, introducing a new modern epoch to his realm, it left England in religious turmoil for the next three centuries. And his successors had to deal with the backlash and the consequences.

The other chain of events that ensured England was in constant religious turmoil was the action of Henry's son, Edward VI, an ardent, bigoted, priggish Protestant, his elder daughter, Mary, an even more ardent, bigoted, Roman Catholic, and then Elizabeth who strove so mightily to tiptoe through her reign trying to please and appease both sides. By 1581, despite Elizabeth I's declaration that it was not her role to look into mens' souls, treason and sedition were almost a part of her daily life.

By the time she had been on the throne for twenty years and was 'beyond the ways of women', in other words, she had gone through the menopause, the attitude of Catholic countries in Europe had hardened against her.

Spain was desperate to depose Elizabeth and put her Roman Catholic cousin, Mary Stuart on the throne. This would return England to the Vatican fold. But the Spanish, indeed all of Europe, believed Elizabeth was illegitimate, because the divorce between Henry VIII and Katherine of Aragon had been unlawful. Since a known bastard was ineligible from taking the throne, this meant that Elizabeth was not the rightful monarch, Henry VIII's will notwithstanding.

'Good Queen Bess' also encouraged pirates to plunder Spanish ships. Whilst overtly decrying this practise, she covertly filled her coffers with the spoils. This infuriated Philip II because much of the purloined money was destined to help him fight his Dutch rebels.

By 1585 Philip had begun to amass an armada of ships to invade England, but it was the execution of Mary, Queen of Scots in 1587 that caused tensions between England and Spain to soar.

The penalties for 'seditious words and rumours' against Elizabeth were put onto the statute book in 1581. The act stated that anyone writing seditious material or spreading seditious rumours would be punished, as a first offence, by being put in the pillory, or losing both ears, or a fine of £200 accompanied by a stay in jail of six months.

Should anyone who had already been convicted and punished transgress a second time, the offence was one of felony. The punishment for this was death and forfeiting property and possessions.[4]

Tavern Talk:

Henry's wish to divorce Katherine of Aragon and marry Anne Boleyn was not the cause of the Reformation. There is another theory held by many historians that says Henry became disillusioned with the vast amounts of money he had wasted in the first twenty years of his reign on futile European wars. He needed to recoup that money and where better than from the immensely rich Roman Catholic church in England – aided by Thomas Cromwell, who was so very efficient in matters like this.

Sexual Offences

In Middlesex, between 1558-1603, according to surviving records, eleven cases of a sexual nature involved girls aged between three and twelve. The men who carried out these assaults were usually hanged.[1]

In Tudor England any sexual activity outside the bonds of matrimony was a crime. Fornication, adultery, homosexuality and prostitution were all punishable offences. In London and Bristol, for example, prostitutes and 'lecherous clergymen' were publicly exhibited in cages. Punishments ranged from being forced to parade in church, usually dressed in white to enact a public penance, to being whipped or put in the pillory for lesser sexual offences.

Sex also reared its ugly head when, post-Reformation, priests and monks who had hitherto been required to be celibate – although many had mistresses – were allowed to marry.[2]

When Mary came to the throne in 1553 and tried to turn the clock back twenty years, making England a Roman Catholic country again, these marriages were declared null and void. Married priests were deprived of their sees where possible, sending them, homeless and jobless, with their wives and children into penury. How ironic that Mary made these laws and declarations whilst being, legally, the head of the Church of England.

Most towns prohibited prostitution, but few took any steps to eradicate it. The regularity of fines for brothels became such that they almost represented a licensing fee.[3] The sexual offences that constituted felonies were usually dealt with as misdemeanours. These included, actual or attempted, rape, sodomy and bestiality.

Rape

Rape has always been a complicated issue, not to mention contentious, with the blame still frequently put upon the victim. One only has to read reports from some parts of the world to realise that women are still paying for Eve's alleged crime in tempting Adam to eat the apple from the sacred Tree of Knowledge.

Part of the complication is that our history is full of instances of heiresses being abducted, raped and forced into marriage to gain land and money. This was prevalent in Saxon England and all through the Middle Ages.

Appeals regarding rape following abduction are vague in Tudor accounts. Most use the word 'ravish', a term this author refuses to use since, by dint of some twentieth-century romantic fiction, the force used and fear generated in the execution of this offence is so much lessened, not to mention rendered imaginary, by the 'happy ever after' ending.

The Middle Ages did use the term 'ravishment', but according to one estimate, between the years 1100 and 1500, of 1213 cases, only nine per cent were defined as 'intercourse by force'. This led to rape being mixed in with lesser transgressions. And to make things worse, a common belief was that without the element of consent, no conception could occur. So, naturally, any woman who was impregnated by rape, was automatically considered to be a liar.[4]

At the beginning of the Tudor era, abduction and rape began to be treated as separate crimes. At that point, rape was defined as forced intercourse: 'Rape is where a man rauyssheth or taketh a mans wyfe, wydowe, or mayde agaynst her will, and hath to do with her agaynst her wyll.'[5]

In 1557 abduction became a specific crime, defined as taking an unmarried female under the age of sixteen out of the custody of her parents or guardians and marrying them in order to have sexual intercourse.

In 1575 a weaver called Thomas Lee, from Effingham, contracted a marriage, with the collusion of the vicar and the vicar's daughter, with a thirteen-year-old girl called Isabel Mace. He was indicted but the verdict is unknown.

As is the case today, convictions were sometimes difficult to accomplish. Evidence was, of necessity, usually non-existent – a perfect case of 'he said, she said'. Juries were reluctant to convict because the offence carried the death penalty. Because of this, cases were frequently brought before the church courts and this continued after the Reformation.

That said, rape continued, despite all the legal difficulties, to be regarded as serious and unpardonable by the authorities, but there were ways around it on occasion. In 1515 Joan Clerke and her husband attacked and killed a man who had raped her. The jury convicted the couple of killing the man in self-defence, which ensured they would be pardoned.

Benefit of Clergy was still used by some offenders. In 1565 Anne Sellett, a six-year-old girl, was raped by John Beamond in his house in

Westminster. He was granted Benefit of Clergy. However, in 1575 this loophole was blocked by the Benefit of Clergy Act, which excluded it being used in cases of rape. So when Henry Cherry was convicted of raping Martha Phippes in the Catherine Wheel tavern in Shenfield, Essex, he was sentenced to hang. In 1590, in the parish of St Magnus the Martyr, London, five-year-old Sara Tumor was assaulted and raped by a man called George Bushnell. The child lingered for six weeks before succumbing to her injuries. The resulting inquest indicted Bushnell for murder but he fled before he could be arrested.

Children under the age of ten were excluded from the act because they were not of an age to give any kind of consent. Rape against young girls was regarded as a misdemeanour until the Benefit of Clergy Act, which stated that it was unlawful to 'carnally know any woman child under the age of 10 years', which made the offence one of statutory rape and the notion of consent did not apply. However, this did not help children between the ages of ten and sixteen who often complied through fear or inducement.[6]

CASE STUDY[7]

Earth Bickley, the wife of Richard Bickley, a weaver of Crediton in Devon, was taken before George Gale on 13 March 1598 to be questioned about her claim that she had been raped by Robert Aileston.

She stated that about two weeks before the Feast of John the Baptist (24 June) the previous year, her husband had sent her to Aileston's house to sell him some yarn. Aileston told her he stored his yarn and materials in his bedchamber and she should go there with him. Immediately she was though the door, Aileston locked the door, threw his arms around her and pushed her 'against the edge of a certain coffer'. Earth was so astonished that she could not remember whether or not she cried out, but stated that 'he did immediately thereupon forcibly and against her will ravish her and had carnal knowledge of her body without any consent yielded by her'.

When she arrived home, Earth, not unnaturally, told her husband what had happened and said Aileston had been so violent in his assault that she was 'very sore therewithal'. When Richard examined her back, he discovered it was very bruised. Earth declared that she 'did feel herself to be much grieved and hurt otherwise by that means'.

Richard Bickley appears to have thought this situation over for a couple of days and then he went to Aileston's brother, Gilbert, and told him that

Robert had 'greatly abused and spoiled' Earth. After a bit of toing and froing, the Ailestons went to Bickley's house because Aileston's wife had entreated them to come to some arrangement.

At this point, Earth was still in bed because of injuries sustained during the rape. She faced Aileston whilst lying in her bed and accused him to his face of having spoiled her and that 'he had to do with her against her will'.

Aileston could not deny the charge but promised that he would get help and medical assistance for her. She described experiencing a burning sensation, which probably meant that Aileston gave her a venereal disease. Bickley spoke to the wife of Ellis Basse, who witnessed Earth's distress. She stated that Earth had been very badly used, but Bickley could not afford her fees and instead appointed a fourteen-year-old called Joane Browning to help Earth. Joane stayed helping Earth to recover but it took almost six months for her to regain her health.

Aileston paid money to Richard Bicknell to pay for Earth's care. At this point George Gale, the examiner, asked why she had taken so long to come forward and Earth replied that her husband had entreated her to keep silent and she dared not make the rape public. However, by the early part of the following year, she told her father about what had happened. He advised her to take the matter to the Exeter Assizes, but the matter does not appear to have been presented to the JP.

Earth also stated that the day following the rape, she had met Aileston at the west end of Crediton by the Green and told him she had told her husband what had happened. Aileston warned her to be careful because if she made it public, he would deny it.

Richard Bickley then gave his statement to George Gale. He confirmed everything his wife had said, adding that she had come home weeping after the offence. He further verified Earth's deposition by saying that it was only because of the entreaties from Aileston's friends and especially his wife, Elizabeth Aileston, that he finally agreed not to sue the man, saying 'that it was no matter for the Queen', by which we might assume it was not a matter to be brought before the queen's justices.

Sodomy[8]

Sodomy does not appear to have been of much concern in Europe until the late mediaeval period. It was, in common with witchcraft, usually regarded as something the church courts should administer and deal with.

With wondrous but unsurprising xenophobia, sodomy was, without any foundation at all, associated with the Italians, especially the citizens of Florence. In 1575 Thomas Wilson declared sodomy to be rife in Florence, but breathtakingly backtracked by admitting 'that some haynous filthynesse is not onelye used there'. Big of him!

The very early Protestants, especially those in Germany, associated sodomy with Catholicism and accused the senior ranks of the Roman Church of the offence. Protestant pamphleteer, Simon Fish accused clerics of the same offence in Reformation England. Fish was accused of heresy but died of bubonic plague before he could be brought to trial.

England was very late to the legal table regarding legislation. It was not until 1516, seven years into the reign of Henry VIII, that a man was accused of sodomy before the Bishop of London's Commissary Court. It is therefore logical to assume that while sodomy cannot have been a rare occurrence, it was either ignored or dealt with via the confessional.

The first statute that formally declared sodomy to be a felony was not passed until 1533. It declared that anal penetration between men, or between a man and a woman, or a man or woman and an animal was a crime that was not covered by Benefit of Clergy.[9] Bear in mind that men could still claim Benefit of Clergy for murder.

The 1533 act was a huge leap forward for Henry VIII, because hitherto ecclesiastical courts had dealt with so many offences, including his divorce from Katherine of Aragon. However, this act demonstrated that real power lay with the state, i.e., him, and not the church.

By contrast, lesbianism was not and never has been a secular crime in England.[10] And for those who have read that a horrified Queen Victoria took her pen and struck it from the 1885 act, this is probably apocryphal, although some have argued that she believed sexual intercourse could not happen without a penis being involved.

Back to the Tudors. Edward VI's government repealed the 1533 act and then reinstated it with amendments, saying that goods and lands could not be forfeit. Mary, bless her, repealed all her brother's legislation, so for much of the 1550s practising homosexuality was not illegal. Elizabeth reinstated parts of the 1533 act in 1563. She probably agreed to this because of the rise in sodomy since the 1553 Marian repeal.

Her amendments, of course, reinforced the supremacy of secular law over sacred law. This is a logical assumption. She was an astute politician and had the history of her father, brother and sister to look back on. Elizabeth was in some ways much more relaxed about religion than her forebears and it is not unreasonable to assume that she realised how difficult a path she would have to tread between the differing religious factions. The few people who were convicted after the 1563 Act were mostly prosecuted for homosexuality with very few for bestiality.

Of the few cases that were prosecuted, the main crimes were men having sexual intercourse with boys. The only conviction for buggery on the Elizabethan Home Circuit was in July 1569 when Roland Dyer from Margate was hanged for sodomising five-year-old Barnaby Wright.[11]

Bestiality

Also called Zoophilia if it develops into a fetish.

Bestiality was regarded as something akin to masturbation, especially if the offender was unmarried. It was considered to be much more serious if the offender was married.

The great fear surrounding bestiality was that of species-jumping, and the possible production of grotesque offspring. Accusations and hoaxes did occur, including Agnes Bowker, who reportedly gave birth to a cat in 1569 in Leicestershire.[12]

Of course, the passage in Leviticus stating that if a man lay with a beast he should be put to death was used to strengthen the 1533 act, although it, along with many other biblical passages, had been ignored when it was convenient to do so prior to 1530.

Post 1533, bestiality was regarded in the same light as homosexuality in that the terminology for both stated that it was an 'unnatural penetration of another being'.

Bestiality certainly seems to have been a feature of rural life, usually reported as men consorting with farm animals. Accounts concerning female offenders are extremely rare, but the few that do exist were mostly concerned with dogs.

Cases that were prosecuted usually involved animals owned by somebody else. Because it was regarded as a particularly filthy practice, it left the legal door wide open to false accusations, with a view for the accuser to gain money or land or whatever the accused owned that he wanted.

Edward VI's amendment to the 1533 act shut this door. It stated: 'No person be received for witness or to lay or give evidence against the said offender ... or take any profit or commodity by the death of the said offender if he were attained or convicted of the said crime and offence.'[13]

Buggery offences were occasionally heard at quarter sessions. George Dawson of Dedham was tried before the Essex quarter-sessions in 1595 for buggering a bitch, 'while not having God before his eyes nor considering the dignity of human nature, but seduced by diabolical instigation'.[14]

Again in Essex, after 1563, eight men were indicted for bestiality. Of those, five were convicted, two acquitted and one died in prison whilst awaiting trial.[15]

CASE STUDIES

Walter Hungerford[16]

Walter, Lord Hungerford inherited Hungerford Castle in 1523, when he was twenty years old. He became an attendant in Henry VIII's household and overtook his royal master regarding the number of his marriages because before Henry had officially married his second wife, Anne Boleyn, Walter was on his third, to Elizabeth Hussey, in 1532.

Elizabeth was the daughter of Lord Hussey of Sleaford, who recommended his new son-in-law to Thomas Cromwell. Cromwell became an important part of Walter's life. In 1533 Cromwell made Hungerford sheriff of Wiltshire and in 1536 Cromwell made sure his protégé was made Lord Hungerford of Heytesbury.

All was looking rosy. However, whilst Walter had gained power and influence under Cromwell's patronage, he also proved to be an abusive husband to poor Elizabeth. He locked her away, starved her and, allegedly, also attempted to poison her. In desperation, Elizabeth wrote to Cromwell detailing that because of her husband's cruelty, she had been forced to drink her own urine in order to stay alive.

Cromwell ignored her plea to bring proceedings against Walter for divorce although her letter alluded to his homosexual activities. Hungerford was present at Prince Edward's baptism and the funeral of the baby prince's mother, Jane Seymour. A few years later, he attended the reception held for Anne of Cleves, Henry's fourth wife.

Karma was soon to strike and it, too, involved Thomas Cromwell. The latter was arrested for treason in the summer of 1540, and at the same time rumours began to circulate about Walter's treatment of his wife. The Privy Council launched an investigation – and not before time.

Just to make sure any mud thrown at him stuck, Walter was also accused of employing a priest who had publicly declared Henry VIII to be a heretic and another priest – is there a pattern here? – to predict when Henry would die.

However, just to add spice to the pot of indictments, Walter was accused of committing unnatural acts which, under the 1533 act, were outlawed. According to the court records, Walter was indicted as being 'Replete with innumerable, detestable and abominable vices and wretchedness of living ... and hath accustomably exercised, frequented, and used the abominable and detestable vice and sin of buggery with William Master, Thomas Smith and other of his servants'.

There was one further irony. On 25th July 1540, Thomas Cromwell did not go to the block alone. Hungerford was alongside. The latter's behaviour was described as 'so unquiet as to be a frenzy'. Nevertheless, his head joined that of his late patron on a spike on London Bridge.

It is doubtful whether the king gave Walter Hungerford a second thought – unlike Thomas Cromwell. Less than six months after the execution of his chief minister, Henry is reported to have told the French ambassador, de Marillac, that he blamed his closest councillors for bringing false accusations against Cromwell and thus forcing him to 'put to death the most faithful servant I ever had'. This is probably the closest Henry VIII ever came to admitting an error.

William Underwood

On Christmas Eve 1575 William Underwood, servant to Francis Hunt, was observed by his master to steal into his stable, pull up a basket behind one of Hunt's mares, drop his hose and bugger her.

Hunt, having caught Underwood *in flagrante delicto*, hauled his servant before the Colchester magistrates. Under questioning, Underwood confessed that he had 'filthily abused himself'. He didn't seem – and neither did anyone else – to have a modicum of sympathy for the poor horse.

Underwood apologised, saying that he was 'sorry, trusting that he shall never do the like again'. Very true because he was convicted of buggery and sentenced to hang.[17]

Tavern Talk:
Apples – the biblical 'forbidden fruit' – were the Tudor symbol of love, sexuality and pregnancy. Which is why when Anne Boleyn publicly declared a craving for apples, it was generally believed that she had finally allowed Henry VIII to bed her and was pregnant.

Spying

The term spy is defined as 'a person employed by a government or other organisation to secretly obtain information on an enemy or competitor'.

When we think of the Tudors and spying, Sir Francis Walsingham, one of Elizabeth's Privy Council, an ardent Puritan and protector of his royal mistress and her throne, comes to mind.

Espionage is known as the second oldest profession. It is mentioned in the Old Testament, when Moses sent out spies to find the Promised Land for the Israelites. The Greeks and Romans were known to use spies. So when Walsingham, aided by Burghley, set up his incredible spying apparatus to keep Elizabeth free from assassination, he was following in centuries-old footsteps.

One of the least-known Tudor spies was Isabella Hoppringle – sometimes called Pringle – who was the Prioress of the Cistercian abbey in Coldstream on the Scottish border.[1] Coldstream, sits on the banks of the Tweed, a rivers-width away from Scotland. When the Scottish James IV married Henry VIII's sister, Margaret Tudor, in 1513, the two countries signed a Treaty of Perpetual Peace. It lasted about as long as a soap bubble.

Isabella managed to play the sides against the middle with Scotland and England when it suited the security of her abbey. She was also a close friend of Queen Margaret Tudor. Later in 1513 Henry VIII declared war on France, and, full of bluster, rode across the channel to conquer the enemy. Since France and Scotland enjoyed the Auld Alliance, the Scottish king immediately caused trouble on the northern border and led his army across the Tweed to Coldstream.

What must have galled Henry somewhat was that a possibly pregnant Katherine of Aragon, daughter of two warlike monarchs and left by Henry as regent in his absence, played an effective role in the planning of the English response. The English army destroyed the Scots at Flodden Field, wiping out not only James IV but more or less the whole of the Scottish nobility. In triumph, Katherine sent part of James' surcoat to France to show her husband proof that the battle had been won, regretful only that she couldn't send the dead king's body with it.

In the aftermath, Isabella and her nuns helped tend the wounded and bury the dead. It is claimed that her convent was left largely unscathed because she was an active English spy. Moreover, it is also claimed that when she died in 1538, a relative called Janet Pringle not only became the new prioress but also an English spy.

CASE STUDIES

William Parry is another spy who tried, like Isabella, to play the sides against the middle.[2] Except that he really wasn't very good at it.

Parry was a serving member of the House of Commons. However, reliable information about his life is not easy to obtain. He wrote a letter to Lord Burghley, and the Elizabethan government issued propaganda about him after his execution, but neither of these documents are dependable.

Parry claimed he was descended from the Conway family of Flintshire, and Sir John Conway offered £1,000 surety for Parry's good behaviour, so perhaps this was true. Apprenticed to a Cheshire lawyer, who sent him to grammar school, he wasn't happy and after a few attempts to abscond, finally succeeded and reached London around 1560.

His way of life was self-indulgent. With an eye to the main chance, he married a wealthy widow. Her money was soon consumed with his dissolute and wasteful manner of life. Parry then went into service with the Earl of Pembroke, William Herbert and stayed there until the earl died in 1570.

It was at this time he entered Elizabeth's service. At this time, he also met his second wife, another wealthy widow, whose husband had been a King's Bench official. Rumours said she was old enough to be his mother and that he slept with her daughter. That is just as likely to be propaganda as it is to be true, but leopards and spots come to mind.

In the early 1570s Parry was sent abroad and began his career as an English spy, reporting back about English Catholics in Paris, Rome and Siena. What was strange was that in his letters to Burghley he urged clemency on English exiles, an attitude he justified by citing political pragmatism, and saying that making them suffer by forcing them into exile and grabbing their lands only made them more dangerous.

Of course, later on, when he was outed as a double-spy, these letters were produced in court to prove he had always been a closet Catholic. However, at the time, Burghley, as ardent a Puritan as Walsingham and possibly the most astute of Elizabeth's Privy Council, does not seem to have thought anything was amiss with Parry's views.

His lifestyle proved his undoing. Living way beyond his means, he returned to England to petition Burghley to pay his expenses, but then fled to France to escape his creditors. In 1580 he began his inevitable path to the scaffold.

It all seems to have begun with a debt of £600 (about £273,000 in 2021) he owed another MP, Hugh Hare. Parry had no means of repaying this debt. Contemporary reports are unclear, but he was charged with breaking into Hare's lodgings in the Inner Temple on 2 November 1580 and attempting to murder him. Parry was found guilty, but, strangely, he was pardoned by Queen Elizabeth. His explanation for this was that his trial had been unfair because he could prove the foreman of the jury was drunk. He also hinted at the interference of influential men, but we are not told who.

What seems to have happened was that the pardon was a political contrivance – one can see Burghley's brain at work here – but Parry did spend time in prison until some leading members of court offered Hare bonds of £100 each as surety that Parry would repay his debt. Parry was bound over to keep the peace with Hare in two sureties worth £1000 each. It is this that makes the modern historian's nose twitch and is ephemeral confirmation that Burghley and/or Walsingham still had plans for Parry as a spy.

Whatever the truth of the situation, Parry was given a licence to travel abroad for three years. He left England in 1582 with doubtful mind to return. Once on the continent, he returned to his spying duties. Although he was working, as before, for Burghley, he became one of Walsingham's agents.

Parry tried to infiltrate himself back into the Catholic community in Paris, but they, not unnaturally, distrusted him, so he took himself off to Italy. He there made an open display of his Catholicism, going so far as to say he had important news of Catholics in England that he wished to impart to the Pope. Discussions regarding safe conduct to Rome proved fruitless, so Parry returned to France.

There is some evidence to show he was sounding out disaffected Catholics and Jesuits about assassinating Elizabeth, going so far as to ask Father Crighton, a Scottish Jesuit in Lyon, if assassinating the queen would be a sin. He also discussed this with Thomas Morgan, a known agent of Mary, Queen of Scots, who sent a letter from Parry to Cardinal Como in Rome.

In 1584 Parry travelled back to England, taking with him two letters from Edward Stafford, England's envoy to France and a double agent. Parry had an audience with Elizabeth and revealed his dealings with the Catholics in exile, and that he had been sent back to England by Thomas Morgan to assassinate her. He said a confirmatory letter would arrive from Rome, which it did.

Later in 1584, through Burghley's influence, Parry was returned to Parliament. One would think that even someone with the brain of a peahen would have learned his lesson, heaved a sigh of relief, and tried to make the best of what, to many, was the prospect of smooth water after rapids.

But no. Parry could not resist putting his fingers in the fire to see if it was still hot, because he then secretly conspired with Edward Neville, a man at odds with Burghley, over a new conspiracy to kill Elizabeth. Parry denounced Neville to the queen. Possibly, he missed the buzz of being an agent provocateur. More likely his two brain cells were not communicating.

Parry's next action was nothing short of preposterous. In December 1584, he spoke against the Jesuits Act, *ex abrupto*, which literally means 'out of suddenness' or 'without preparation'. He said that the bill carried nothing with it but blood, danger, terror and despair, and was not for the queen's safety, but to satisfy the greed of men.

The biggest problem was that Elizabeth's Council had discussed and approved the bill, and by speaking against it Parry was implying that not only did he know better than her advisors, but they had approved the bill solely for their own greedy desires. Despite protesting that he was free to say what he thought, he was removed from the chamber by the serjeant.

Later he was brought back in, made to kneel before the Speaker and asked to justify why he had said what he had. Parry replied he would tell nobody but the queen what he had meant by his words. His plan to see Elizabeth backfired and he was, once more, brought to kneel before the bar in the House of Commons where he made a grovelling apology, saying he was a new MP and was unfamiliar with the customs of the House. Although he had probably informed the Council about Neville, his outburst did him no good at all and his actions labelled him a loose cannon.

Up to this point, we know what happened to Parry because of parliamentary records and his exchange of letters with Burghley. However, after this point, the only sources we have about what happened next are Parry's own words. We do know that in February 1585 Neville denounced Parry. Elizabeth ordered Walsingham to question him and give him a chance to clear his name.

According to a government tract, Parry denied all knowledge of any plots to assassinate the queen, and also denied any conversations about doing so. When he was confronted with Neville, Parry replied that it was Neville's word against his and not enough to convict a man of treason.

However, he was put in the Tower. We do not know where in the Tower, but a few days later he made a full confession. At his trial, he seemed to be confident he would be pardoned, but as the trial progressed he rescinded his confession and said it had been made under duress.

Parliament had no qualms about his guilt. Sir Christopher Hatton, one of Elizabeth's favourites, spoke out against Parry, producing the letter from Cardinal Como as proof. His audiences with the queen were portrayed as Parry's deviousness at trying to lull Elizabeth into a false sense of security.

When he was inevitably found guilty of treason, Parry said, 'I here summon Queen Elizabeth to answer for my blood.' On the scaffold on 2 March 1585, he declared his innocence, saying he was a true servant to the queen, that Elizabeth knew he was, and her conscience would tell her what he said was true.

Parry was hanged, drawn and quartered.

William Herle

Herle was a strange man with an interesting career – envoy, pirate, spy. His linguistic skills were excellent and this may have helped his advancement as well as his expertise at writing very full reports, some of which are held in archives.[3] He worked with the merchant Sir William Garrard, which allowed him enough freedom of movement to gather information at home and abroad. This information covered local gossip and evidence about suspicious individuals. He also worked undercover while working for Garrard and refined his abilities.

Like Parry above, Herle was perpetually short of money and forced to make it where he could. He often borrowed money from friends and moneylenders to cover his debts, and because he couldn't pay back the loans, frequently landed in a debtors' prison.

One such spell in gaol occurred between November 1570 and the summer of 1571. Herle, ever alert for an opportunity to make money by trading information, was drawn into a conspiracy, created by the Council, who ordered him to be sent to the Marshalsea prison and kept in solitary confinement, accused of piracy on the Isle of Wight. Herle wrote protesting his innocence, declaring the accusation was based on malice and gossip. He also enclosed with his letter an account of his movements for the previous six months and made a guarded offer to help the state. This was, eventually, accepted, but as he said in a letter to Burghley, he could not help the state whilst in solitary confinement.

Spying

It seems clear from a distance of 400-odd years that his offer to monitor political prisoners was what Burghley and the Council had been after all along. And by being obviously taken for interrogation, he could allay prisoners' suspicions as to his motives.

The political situation in early 1571 encompassed the discovery of the Ridolfi plot. Ridolfi was a Florentine merchant to whom the Papal Bull excommunicating Elizabeth had first been sent. He became involved in a plot to oust Elizabeth, allow Spanish troops to join English Catholics, and put Mary, Queen of Scots on the throne with the Duke of Norfolk as her husband.

A man called Charles Bailly, servant to John Lesley, the Bishop of Ross, was one of the conspirators. Bailly was intercepted at Dover with letters and books in his luggage and eventually put in the Marshalsea where Herle was sitting waiting for him.

In a plan probably instigated by Burghley, Herle offered to pass letters from Bailly to Lesley, whilst diverting them to Burghley first. The letters were in cipher, of course, and Herle was told to discover the key to the cipher, not just so that Burghley could read them, but also make additions should he so desire.

Herle, anxious to get out of gaol and knowing that his only hope lay with Burghley, now began to collect and collate information to help him devise the best way to obtain the information the latter required. However, the wily Burghley ensured that no written word of his involvement was made, or, if it existed, was destroyed.

Through a series of letters, Herle details his progress. Lesley and Bailly were, understandably, unwilling to accept him at first. So he caused unflattering rumours, purportedly of his activities as an agitator, to reach Lesley. It also helped Lesley's independent enquiries that Herle's impecunious lifestyle supported the rumours. To make Bailly feel more secure, Herle wrote to Burghley to ask for illegal Catholic material to be sent to him; material he could give Bailly. Although it is not certain – what espionage activities are? – it is likely that some people in authority within the Marshalsea were in on the secret.

Whatever and however it came about, Bailly was convinced enough of Herle's reliability to use him as a messenger. Although Lesley remained suspicious of Herle, he disarmed both men by saying they could push their letters through the hole into the attic of the neighbouring cell and they would then be taken to Lesley by a 'selected messenger'. In other words, Herle did not even have to touch the correspondence.

Herle then suggested that Bailly be kept in close confinement and that he, Herle, would bribe one of the keepers to give him access to Bailly's cell. Burghley was adamant the letters must come to Herle first so that they could be copied before being forwarded to the intended recipient.

It all became a tad complicated about who should do what and who was to be trusted. However, with the insouciance of an adventurer, Herle seems to have enjoyed it. He probably enjoyed the frequent, engineered searches of his cell, the intelligence of which would quickly reach his fellow prisoners and further confirm his cover story.

However, despite all this subterfuge, the cipher for the letters remained concealed. One of Herle's fellow pirates, arrested with him, told Herle that Bailly had memorised four ciphers and that the codes could not be cracked.

Herle failed to discover this information and Burghley had Bailly taken to the Tower, tortured on the rack and put in a small cell, possibly the Scrivener's Daughter or Little Ease. Contrary to popular belief, there was only one rack in England; at the Tower. The victim was laid flat on the bed, restrained, semi-naked, with ropes on ankles and upstretched arms. Handles were then turned at either end of the rack to stretch and break ligaments and tendons. Victims would frequently be taken later to the scaffold seated because they could not stand. By contrast Little Ease was a tiny confining device, sometimes a cage or very small room, that did not allow the prisoner to stretch out any limbs, but remain curled up. It was equally excruciating.

It is also clear that Lesley remained suspicious of Herle and that the latter probably used the excuse of frequent cell searches as the reason for the correspondence being delayed: the delay, of course, being caused by the letters being copied with extreme precision because the authorities still did not have the cipher. However, Herle probably used the searches to leave letters in his cell to be forwarded to Burghley.

Herle also knew the importance of verbal communication and often requested meetings so that his status as a client of Burghley's could be maintained. On being released from prison, Herle continued his activities for Burghley on the continent, although his reports were not always accurate.

He clearly disliked the Duke of Anjou, whose proposal was, after Robert Dudley's, the nearest Elizabeth ever came to marriage. In 1582, for example, he wrote to Burghley and Walsingham saying that the Prince of Orange had been assassinated by a Frenchman.[4] The truth was the would-be assassin was Spanish and Orange recovered. Herle tried to cover his letter by saying that he had not known if Orange would recover but thought it better for Elizabeth to be prepared for the worst.

Possibly because of his error regarding Orange, Herle was recalled to England and at once set about sniffing out new conspiracies. He informed the Council about the Throckmorton plot, and, comparing his letter to

Walsingham with later government accounts, it is clear Herle was involved in uncovering the plot, although his involvement may have been played down for political reasons.

After this, he monitored events in the Low Countries, but whilst he kept up his connection with Burghley, began to work more and more for Walsingham. In 1584 Elizabeth sent Herle to East Friesland as a diplomat. At around the same time, a Catholic adherent of Philip II of Spain made another attempt on the life of William of Orange and this time succeeded.

Herle, with his ear, as usual, to the ground, wrote to Elizabeth to tell her that the overwhelming desire of the locals was to throw off the tyranny of Philip of Spain and ask her to be their monarch. Elizabeth hated the idea but it became clear that England could no longer ignore the plight of the Dutch. She ordered Herle to be the intermediary, but the enterprise was underfunded. Herle, as usual, was penniless and unable to obtain payment of his expenses from either side.[5] As late as 1588 he was still writing to Elizabeth, known for her miserly qualities, to beg for his expenses to be paid.

How ironic that the apex of his career – the volatile situation in the Spanish Netherlands – led directly to him remaining penniless. He died around May 1588 in the Low Countries, a few months before Elizabeth's favourite, Robert Dudley, died. A packet of his letters is in the National Archives.

The administration of his goods was made in February 1589.[6] A final irony, since he had so little to leave to anybody.

Sumptuary Laws

Just as in India, where you are born into a caste, dependent upon which caste your parents are in, Sumptuary Laws, much like those for Hindus, were designed to keep you in your designated station in life.

They limited the private citizen to what they could wear, in terms of colours and fabrics, and included most material goods, such as furniture and even horses.

Laws limiting an individual's rights in this matter have been around since the Grecian Empire. All inhabitants of Laconia, for example, were forbidden a house or furniture that was more decorative than that which could be manufactured by an axe and a saw.

Julius Caesar had officers posted in marketplaces, specifically to confiscate goods and materials forbidden by law. Tiberius limited expenditure regarding banquets – though probably not his own.[1]

In England, the reign of Edward III saw sumptuary laws gaining legal force. The Parliament of 1363 legislated to limit ostentatious spending. The 1363 law was repealed in 1364 but reinstated later in Edward's reign.

As the fourteenth and fifteenth centuries progressed, sumptuary legislation was seen as a governmental weapon to control the population, and conflict on the part of the upper classes trying to hold back the rising tide of citizens who became wealthy, and wanted to ape their betters.[2]

During the Tudor era, sumptuary laws were particularly active during Elizabeth's reign. The first statute set down by Henry VIII in 1510 stated that no man below the rank of knight could use more than three ells of fabric – an ell is about 1.5m – in their gown. This also applied to the amount of permitted fabric in monks' habits, but the prior of Durham Cathedral, being of superior rank, was allowed six ells for his gown.

Laws covered not just the fabric of people's clothes but where they bought it.[3] The major difference between English laws and those in Europe was that the English statutes covered the whole country, whereas European ones were usually confined to individual towns and cities.

Despite the difficulty in enforcing these laws, there were five enacted between 1510 and 1553, but Elizabeth's reign produced nine. Some were simply tweaks in current legislation. In 1562, for example, the hierarchy of dress regarding the wearing of the colour purple was reinforced to emphasise that only members of the royal family could wear it.

Mary's 1553 statute specified who could wear silk and succeeding statutes echoed this so that no reference was made as to particular garments, although headgear was sometimes itemised. And, of course, when the English wool industry went through a tough time, Elizabeth declared that all men should wear a hat made of English wool.

Henry VIII's 1533 statute declared that only the royal family could wear cloth of purple silk or cloth made of gold tissue, but dukes and marquises could wear the latter 'in their Dublettes and Sleveless Cootes, Clothe of Gold of Tissue and in none other [of] their garments'.[4]

Some of the restrictions are confusing, not to say illogical. For example, only dukes, marquises and their children, barons and knights of the garter could wear crimson, scarlet or blue velvet. In fact, in the English Sumptuary Law Chart women are not specifically mentioned until we are told that wives of a son or heir of a knight were permitted to wear silk in their hats, bonnets, nightcaps and girdles.

Most of the commons – labourers, servants, shepherds and farmers – were not permitted to wear short gowns or coats using more than 2.5 broad yards of fabric or long gowns using more than 3 broad yards. They were also prohibited from wearing fur of any kind. Only gentlemen who had an income in excess of £100 per annum could wear velvet or fur that originated outside 'the Quene's dominions'.

One of the major sources we have for the adherence or otherwise to the law regarding apparel comes through portraits, especially those of Hans Holbein. His portrait of Sir Brian Tuke, Henry VIII's Treasurer and Secretary of the royal household, shows Sir Brian wearing a doublet made from cloth of gold.[5] His gown is trimmed with dark fur and he wears a gold chain. The fabric of the doublet certainly broke the sumptuary law, although it is more than likely that Henry VIII gave him permission to wear it for this portrait.

Geographical issues and prices were also relevant to adherence issues. London was the biggest city in England, followed by Norwich and Lincoln, but significant towns were Bristol (a huge centre of trade due to its links to the sea and via the river network), Kings Lynn (easy access to the sea and continental Europe and within easy reach of Norwich), Cambridge and Oxford (centres of learning), Canterbury and York (the two most important sees), and Winchester, the old capital of England. All of these towns and cities attracted wealth in terms of merchants, imports and other material goods.[6]

Prices were relatively stable until 1513 when they began to rise, until in 1530 they began a gallop up to 1547, mainly due to debasement of the coinage. At the same time, between 1500 and 1540, wages declined. So the sumptuary laws were one way of stopping people falling into debt because of conspicuous consumption, especially regarding clothing.

It is logical then to conclude that the sumptuary laws were designed initially to preserve class distinctions, so that anybody could recognise the social position of somebody purely by looking at what they were wearing. They also checked extravagance, imbuing it with moral overtones of wickedness.[7]

However, it made economic sense that people did not get into debt. They were also encouraged to buy homegrown materials and discouraged from buying foreign goods. And, of course, it was logical for the monarch to encourage his/her subjects to save their money because it meant that when he/she needed it for wars etc., the people could afford to pay extra taxes. It also helped maintain a healthy balance of payments.[8]

Despite the wealth of statutes, enforcement was very patchy because, to put it bluntly, public officials had better things to do with their time, especially when they didn't have the resources they needed to do their jobs, without the added burden of checking what people spent their money on. They regarded it as a waste of time to go around chasing people wearing the wrong clothes.

The sixteenth century marked the zenith of the regulation of clothing.[9] It was a time when richer materials were imported and fashions became ostentatious, with slashed sleeves and enormous ruffs. Gradually those textiles the aristocracy regarded as being their prerogative became available to those of lower social classes – the burgeoning nouveau-riche.

The whole legislation became complicated in Elizabeth's reign, during which she always tried to tiptoe between the sensibilities of Catholics, Protestants and Puritans, encompassed by her alleged quotation, 'I have no desire to make windows into men's souls'.[10]

Catholics regarded luxury as a sin of personal pride: Protestants thought it the path to moral and societal decay. Puritans believed luxury to be wasteful and uncharitable, but then they tended to regard anything fun as sinful.

Luxury was also believed to encourage crime in order for the perpetrator to support his lifestyle. Henry VIII's 1510 statute states that luxuries impoverished those who couldn't afford them and provoked 'meny of them to robbe and to doo extorcion and other unlawfull Dedes to mayntayne therby costeley arraye'.

In 1574 Elizabeth issued a proclamation that possibly reflects her views on the subject: 'The excess of apparel and the superfluity of unnecessary foreign wares ... is grown by sufferance to such an extremity that the manifest decay not only of a great part of the wealth of the whole realm generally is like to follow ... but also particularly the wasting and undoing of a great number of young gentlemen.'[11]

CASE STUDY

As previously stated, sumptuary laws were seldom enforced. However, if a man really went over the top he would be prosecuted. In 1565 Richard Walweyn was arrested for wearing a 'very monstrous and outraygous greate payre of hose'.[12] We have to remember that to keep her subjects in line, one of Elizabeth's ploys was to remind them that she was Henry VIII's daughter. And the most famous portrait that we know of Henry, the one by Holbein, shows his very-well-formed calves. Shapely calves remained an Elizabethan fashion. Although the official records do not state Walweyn's precise offence, we can probably surmise that he had padded out his calves to a ridiculous degree.

He was described as one of the meaner sort of the servant class. As such, along with apprentices and students, he was not permitted to wear stockings stuffed with more than a yard and three quarters of material. To the modern view, a mental image of someone with almost two yards of fabric stuffed down their hose is more than a little disturbing, so trying to imagine how much Richard Walweyn had used is perhaps better not contemplated by those with delicate sensibilities.

In another case, an unnamed Fellow of King's College was imprisoned when it was found he was wearing a cut taffeta doublet ... and a great pair of galligastion (baggy) hose under his gown.[13] Galligastion: what a fabulous word. It should come back into the language. The word was usually rendered as galligaskins, meaning in the Greek style, or loose, wide breeches.

Another unnamed attorney in the late 1570s/early 1580s found himself out of a job when he presented himself before the Privy Council 'in an apparel unfit for his calling, with a guilt rapier, extreme greate ruffes and lyke unseemelie apparel'.[14]

For all Elizabeth's many edicts, she could not hold back the tide against keeping people in their defined social stratum. When James (I and VI) came to the throne, he waited for a year and in 1604 repealed all the laws of apparel. Occasional attempts were made in the seventeenth century to resurrect them, especially with reference to hats and footwear, but none were successful.

Just as we in the twenty-first century have many people who love the clothing styles of the 1940s and 1950s, clothes for the Tudors had significance because they held a kind of cultural memory.

Shakespeare writes in *Henry IV Pt 2*, as he responds to the news that his father has died, 'I will deeply put the fashion on. And wear it in my heart.'

In modern times, we have a proverb often ascribed to Mark Twain that clothes do not make the man, but Shakespeare and Erasmus believed the opposite. And so did the Tudors.

Tavern Talk:
It was the fashion, especially for unmarried Tudor women, to wear clothes that exposed a breast and sometimes both breasts. Elizabeth was known to have given the French ambassador an audience with her breasts exposed. She also used this device to reinforce her claim as the virgin queen. Apparently, she also exposed her stomach on occasions. Hopefully not at dinner.

Theft

Thieves, beggars and vagabonds are inextricably linked in terms of Tudor sensibilities. All were concerned with extracting money, alms or property from those who owned it. So entrenched and blurred did the boundaries between these crimes become, they shared a common argot, called Cant Speak.[1] Examples of Cant Speak include:

Bob ken – a house that can easily be robbed
Stauling ken – a house that will receive stolen goods
Patrico – a priest
Autem – a church
Mort – a woman
Cove – a man
Cully – a victim
Bung – a purse
Fence – a person who buys stolen goods
Fencing cully – a person who receives stolen goods
Bite – to cheat or cozen
Cuttle-bung – a knife with a curved blade
Foin – someone who uses conversation to steal purses or pick pockets
Knuckle – a young pickpocket
Stall – someone who identifies a victim and moves them to make stealing their purse easier
Bulk the cull to the right – an instruction by a pickpocket to a stall to distract a cully by striking them on their right breast so their purse can be stolen.

Since the crime is self-explanatory, we will go onto one case study. *A Caveat or Warning for Common Cursitors, vulgarly called vagabonds* was first published in 1566 by Thomas Harman.

CASE STUDY

Nicholas Jennings[2]

Harman details the story of Nicholas Blunt/Jennings/Genings, who was known as a 'counterfeit crank' or someone who would feign illness, sometimes frothing at the mouth to gain alms.

In 1566 Jennings, as Blunt, appeared in his lodgings in Whitefriars seeking alms. He was naked from the waist upwards and dressed in rags. His face was smeared with blood and he pretended to have the 'falling sickness' or what we would now call epilepsy.

He was questioned, whereupon he claimed he had suffered from epilepsy for eight years, had been an inmate at the Bedlam asylum for two years, and had only left there recently. However, when his story was checked, the keeper at Bedlam knew nothing about him, so Harman had him followed by two boys who witnessed Blunt refreshing his blood from a bladder and covering himself with more mud in order to gain sympathy. He crossed to the south of the Thames and was apprehended by a constable.

Upon being searched, Blunt had 13s 4d, at a time when a labourer earned 6d a day. He was stripped and found to be fit and well. However, he managed to escape, still naked, over some fields in the dark, and then carried on begging disguised as a sailor whose ship had lost its cargo.

Calling himself Jennings and having managed to obtain some decent clothes, he next appeared as a hatter who had come to London to seek work. Unfortunately, he was accosted by Harman's printer, who recognised him and had him arrested. When the case was investigated, it was discovered that Blunt/Jennings had a well-furnished 'pretty house', complete with a wife, in Newington.

His sentence was physical punishment augmented by public shame. Blunt/Jennings was whipped 'at a cart's tail' through London and put in the pillory at Cheapside.

We know he was whipped because there is a record in the Court of Aldermen for January 1567.

Treason

The official definition is 'the crime of betraying one's country, especially by attempting to kill or overthrow the sovereign or government'. The Tudor treason laws covered many misdemeanours.

By the time Henry VIII wanted to marry Anne Boleyn and was happy to take England into schism to achieve his aim, treason became a catch-all crime. If anyone refused to sign the Oath of Supremacy, stating that the monarch was head of the church, it was classed as treason.

In 1485 when Henry VII ascended the throne, treason was still defined by the statute of Edward III in 1352. This divided the crime into petty treason – if a servant killed his master, or a wife her husband or a prelate was murdered by a cleric of a lower order – or high treason, which was a little more complicated and dealt mainly with crime against the king and his regality. Included in these were:

- To compass or imagine the death of the king, his queen, his heir, his eldest daughter or the wife of his eldest son;
- To levy war against the king in his realm or consort with his enemies;
- To counterfeit the Great or Privy Seal, or the king's coin or to counterfeit money into England, knowing that it was forged;
- To kill the chancellor, treasurer or a JP whilst in the execution of his duty.

During the Wars of the Roses, it was *imagining* the king's death that held most sway.[1]

Between 1485 and 1603 there were roughly sixty-eight new treason statutes enacted. Most of these dealt with the succession and the monarch's supremacy. As has been stated elsewhere in this book, Elizabeth did not really care what religion people practised so long as they recognised her as the supreme head of the church. These two factors were the major impetus for new laws because the Tudor monarchs from Henry VIII onwards did not trust the effectiveness of the existing 1352 law.

One opinion states that Henry VIII's treason legislation abandoned any kind of logic but converted anything the king found heinous into treason, especially if the opinion stated was also disagreeable to the government.[2]

It was actions such as these that gave rise to many scholars' opinion that Henry VIII, Mary and Elizabeth were tyrants. In 1571 an MP called Snagg declared that the 1352 statute was sufficient.[3]

CASE STUDIES

Edward Arden[4]

Arden, second cousin to Mary Arden, Shakespeare's wife, was the High Sheriff of Warwickshire in 1575. From an old family that had held lands in Warwickshire for six centuries, he was wealthy. He was also a Catholic and kept Hugh Hall, a priest, at Park Hall masquerading as a gardener.

His son-in-law, John Somerville, considered by some to be mentally unbalanced, was very vocal in calling Elizabeth I a viper and serpent and insisting that he was going to London to shoot her. The fact that he had neither the means nor, probably, the inclination to kill the queen was irrelevant. He was arrested, put on the rack and confessed. But he told his inquisitors that his father-in-law, mother-in-law and the priest were all part of the plot. Somerville said he had heard Hugh Hall speak about the queen.

Somerville was sentenced to death but committed suicide possibly by hanging himself in his cell before the sentence could be carried out. Arden, his wife, and the priest were all arrested. The priest and Arden's wife were spared and later pardoned, but Arden was hanged, drawn and quartered. He declared his innocence to the last, saying that his only crime was believing in the Catholic faith. Both his head and that of Somerville were displayed on London Bridge.

There is one theory that Arden had fallen foul of his neighbour, Robert Dudley, Earl of Leicester, because Arden refused to wear Leicester's livery, accusing him of being an adulterer. Neither would he sell the earl land he wanted. Leicester, of course, was a very close friend of Queen Elizabeth. It must also be remembered that Leicester, a Puritan, lived in the stronghold county that housed the Catholic recusancy families of Throckmorton, Catesby and Tresham.

The de la Pole family

The de la Pole family was a real thorn in the side of the first two Tudor monarchs.

Edmund was the son of John de la Pole, the 2nd Duke of Suffolk and first cousin to Henry VII's queen, Elizabeth of York. When his father died, Edmund's elder brother, also called John, succeeded him as Earl of Lincoln. Richard III, on the death of his own son, had named Lincoln as his successor. Although initially the family was loyal to the new Tudor dynasty, John the younger joined the 1487 rebellion on Lambert Simnel's side and was killed at the Battle of Stoke.[5]

After John's death Edmund became not only his successor but also a leading Yorkist claimant to Henry VII's still shaky throne. It must be remembered that Edward, Earl of Warwick, also a nephew of Edward IV and Richard III, and a symbol of Yorkist hopes, was a prisoner in the Tower of London.

In 1492 Edmund agreed to renounce his claim to the dukedom of Suffolk and become Earl of Suffolk instead, as part of the agreement with Henry VII, ratified by an indenture.[6]

As part of that agreement, Henry gave Edmund, upon payment of £5,000, a portion of the land forfeited by the Earl of Lincoln in 1487. You have to hand it to Henry, he never stopped looking for, or taking advantage of, an opportunity to swell the royal coffers.

Polydore Vergil described Edmund as 'bold, impetuous and readily aroused to anger', attributes considered normal in noblemen and considered normal today in some quarters with regard to the wealthy and titled.[7] However, although his character was well suited to jousting, at which he was considered very able, it was not a good match with the reality of his circumstances under the new Tudor monarch.

In 1494 a certain Perkin Warbeck was parading around Europe masquerading as Richard of York, the younger son of Edward IV, and calling himself Duke of York, Henry promptly installed his own younger son, Henry, as Duke of York. Warbeck went to Scotland, being feted by James IV despite Henry VII's efforts to distract him. Incensed by James' intransigence, Henry decided to go to war with his northern neighbour and levied taxes to raise the necessary finance.

Cornwall, although part of Britain, has always considered itself apart and independent and in 1497 it demonstrated this profound belief. The people of Cornwall had nothing against Scotland and didn't see why they should fund a war. To add insult to injury, the tin-mining industry was very important to Cornwall, so when Henry suspended previously granted privileges and issued new mining regulations, the Cornish decided enough was enough.[8]

Although they lacked effective leaders, the rebels marched to London and met with Henry's forces at the Battle of Blackheath on 17 June 1497. At this point, a Tudor victory was by no means certain. Henry's queen and children, including the young Prince Henry, fled first to Margaret Beaufort's house at Coldharbour, but when the rebels approached London, Queen Elizabeth fled to the Tower.[9]

Whilst this is an important part of Henry VII's history, it is also pertinent to his successor. At that time, Henry, Duke of York, was almost six years old and not just his dukedom but his life hung in the balance for five days. What must it have been like for such a young child to know that, should the rebels defeat his father, his own life would be forfeit? And what effect did that have upon his later view of anyone who posed a threat to his throne, and, in consequence, fed his absolute need to father sons?

The Cornish rebels were easily defeated although Henry VII did agree to restore the tin-mining rights. Edmund of Suffolk was still behaving himself at this point and led a company of soldiers against the rebels.[10]

However, the lessening of his rank, plus the damage to his purse – Henry had magnanimously agreed Edmund could pay off the £5,000 fine at £200 per annum – had rankled for years. In 1498, he was indicted for murder, and although the whole incident was smoothed over, this was the last straw for Edmund. In July 1499, he escaped to Guisnes and then the Netherlands, in the hope that his aunt, Margaret of Burgundy, would help him.[11]

Using various inducements, Edmund was persuaded to return, whereupon Henry fined him another £1,000, but he was restored to his former place in the royal family. He was present when the treaty ratifying the marriage of Katherine of Aragon and Prince Arthur was signed and was scheduled to take part in the joust that followed the actual marriage.

One of the conditions laid down by Katherine's father, Ferdinand of Aragon, was that there must be no threat to the marriage or to Arthur when he came to take to the throne. By which, Ferdinand meant any Yorkist claimants. Henry obliged and executed the only son of George, Duke of Clarence, nephew to Edward IV, cousin to Elizabeth of York, and a simple-minded lad. And executed alongside the young Edward was Perkin Warbeck. Edmund once more fled to Europe to seek asylum with the Emperor Maximilian.[12]

Henry retaliated by arresting William de la Pole, Suffolk's youngest brother. In 1502 he sent William to the Tower, where he died some forty years later. Maximilian was bribed by the payment of 10,000 crowns not to help English rebels.

By this time Henry's eldest son, Arthur, was dead, his second son, Henry, was subject to illnesses, and his third son, also called Edmund, born in 1499, had died in 1500. Henry's options were limited and he could afford the 10,000 crowns bribe.

Suffolk was allowed to remain with Maximilian although he later left and was eventually imprisoned by Archduke Philip of Burgundy, aka Philip the Handsome, married to Katherine of Aragon's sister, Juana, Queen of Castile.

While sailing to Castile to secure Juana's inheritance, Philip was blown off course and became the unexpected and sudden guest of Henry VII. The English king must have been rubbing his hands with glee at this point. He took advantage of Philip's desperate need to continue his journey to exert pressure. Philip agreed to hand Edmund over to Henry with the proviso that none of the de la Poles should be harmed.

At this point, Henry had three de la Pole brothers ensconced in the Tower of London. And there they stayed. Montaigne's essays state that Henry's will instructed his son to execute Edmund.[13] He was executed by Henry VIII but not until 1513, four years after Henry VII's death. The Tudor view seems to have been that the only good de la Pole was a dead de la Pole.

Meanwhile, Richard de la Pole, Edmund's younger brother, who found sanctuary with King Ladislaus II in Hungary, became quite as much a perceived threat to Henry VIII as Edmund had been to Henry's father. A furious Henry VIII demanded the traitor's return. Ladislaus ignored him. While there was a de la Pole left running loose, there was always the fear that the Wars of the Roses could return.

Richard was known as the 'White Rose', and in 1513 was declared King of England by the French king, Louis XII. This may have been the catalyst for two events. The first, Henry VIII's decision to execute Edmund and the second to marry Henry's youngest sister, Mary, to Louis, who was some thirty years her senior.[14]

Richard, a hardened soldier, travelled to Italy in 1517, allegedly to try and fund an invasion of England from Denmark. By 1522 he was back in France and plotting with Francis I. However, by 1525 Francis was at war with Emperor Charles V, Katherine of Aragon's nephew. Richard de la Pole fought for Francis at the Battle of Pavia and was killed. The emperor sent a message to Henry to tell him the White Rose had been killed in battle and that he had himself seen Richard's body.

Henry's response was 'All the enemies of England are gone'.[15]

Tavern Talk:
It was considered treason for anyone to say anything derogatory about the monarch and Henry VIII never wanted to be thought of as anything other than the handsome, charismatic 'perfect gentil knight' of his youth. However, he is thought to have owned the first stairlift. According to David Starkey, when researching Henry's list of possessions, there is mention of a 'stairthrone' in Whitehall Palace that hoisted the king up the stairs. Starkey believes it worked via a block and tackle system. A well-kept Tudor secret.

Uprisings

The 'Amicable Grant', was an uprising in 1525 that sort of was and wasn't a proper revolt.

Governments since the time of Edward I had another string to their fiscal bow, which was a loan from the king's subjects to the king on the understanding that it would be repaid. These loans were calculated and charged on the current value of goods and chattels. This valuation became the amount of tax to be paid.[1]

When Edward I introduced it, this system had been regarded as state-of-the-art legislation. However, by the late fifteenth century it was no longer fit for purpose. It had always relied on parliamentary levies which subjects were forced to pay but which equally the government had to pay back.

Henry VII tried to modify the system and some of the changes made were factors in various uprisings in 1489 and 1497. If we fast forward to the second decade of Henry VIII's rule, the situation was that loans for the king's war, made in 1522 and 1523, had still not been repaid by 1525. While this did not help the king's reputation, nobody blamed Henry. They blamed Cardinal Wolsey. And the story of the Amicable Grant fiasco would not be complete unless it takes into account the wily cardinal. The 1525 uprising became the centre of a perfect storm for him.

There had been a time when the young Henry wanted nothing more than to spend all day, every day, hunting, jousting, performing in masques etc., and leaving the business of running England to Wolsey. The cardinal had taught the young Henry everything he knew about administration and statecraft. Henry, still only in his early twenties, was an apt pupil but the pivotal thing Wolsey taught Henry was that too many governmental cooks spoiled the broth: that the management of the realm was much safer being under the control of 'one man'.[2] Of course, by 'one man', Wolsey meant himself.

By 1522/23 everything was still going splendidly for Wolsey. Until a certain Lady Anne Boleyn fell for Lord Henry Percy, heir to the Earl of Northumberland, and he fell for her. The two had a secret engagement. According to some accounts, they went through a form of marriage, but this has never been confirmed. Whatever the true situation, Henry VIII's roving eye had also fixed on the Lady Anne. He had already bedded her sister, Mary, and confidently expected to bed Anne, too.

The king ordered Wolsey to end Anne's relationship with Percy and the latter was quickly married off to Mary Talbot. Wolsey thought Anne a chit of no account, one of his king's here-today-gone-tomorrow affairs. What a shock both Henry and Wolsey were in for. The cardinal made a deadly, intractable, enemy in Anne the day he split up the young lovers. Mistake Number One.

Fast forward to 1525. Henry is by now seriously – SERIOUSLY – infatuated with Anne. He wanted to impress her by taking advantage of the international situation. Francis I had been taken prisoner by Charles V, the Holy Roman Emperor, after the Battle of Pavia. Henry was never going to have such a golden opportunity to once more add the crown of France to that of England, something that had died with Henry VI a century before. He wanted to invade France. But – big but – Henry VIII lacked the funds to go to war.

He ordered Wolsey to levy a tax to pay for his war. Wolsey, still confident Anne Boleyn was of little consequence, did as he was told. The 'Amicable Grant' was a forced loan and demanded one third of the value of goods and chattels belonging to the clergy and one sixth belonging to laymen. Wolsey's big mistake was that he levied the tax without parliamentary approval. Mistake Number Two.

This unexpected levy outraged the people. There was large-scale civil unrest in Essex and Suffolk. Wolsey had simply imposed an order for the Amicable Grant to be paid, it was not approved by Parliament, and there was no assurance that the monies loaned would be repaid.[3] Furthermore, the amount being demanded was incredibly high, expected to yield around £333,000 (£386,465,259.98 in 2021). And all for the vainglory of Henry VIII, with the added prospect of impressing Anne Boleyn and persuading her to slip off her linen smock.

To add insult to injury, the levies from 1522/23 were still being collected. The country was penniless and here was Cardinal Wolsey, already unpopular, demanding money people didn't have. Widespread protests followed.

Many of the clergy told Archbishop Warham they were not inclined to pay. The monastery in Ely said they would be pleased to sell their goods and animals but there was nobody in the county who had any money to buy them.[4] Across the country, reactions ranging from reluctance to outright refusal led to a taxpayer strike which started in Suffolk and spread.

The government made concessions, especially when it was made clear that the protesters had no issue with the king.

The request for money was a benevolence and not a 'proper' tax. The people wanted to decide, as had been the custom with past grants, how much to pay, not have it decided for them. The government halved the amount being requested.

This didn't go down well either because the way the whole situation had been conducted contravened the 1484 Act. In the end, Henry had a very public meeting with the protest leaders who begged for forgiveness and, in his role as beneficial father of the country, he pardoned them.[5] In reality, he was forced to back down, listen to his subjects and give up the whole idea of going to war. And Anne Boleyn was in no mood yet to remove her smock.

Three things that began Wolsey's inevitable downfall were firstly that Anne Boleyn was not a stupid woman and now had Henry's ear. There is little doubt that she persuaded the king to put the blame for the whole Amicable Grant debacle on Wolsey and further increase his unpopularity. Secondly, Wolsey had grown too confident, not just where Anne was concerned, but in his power to enact something as contentious as tax-gathering without parliamentary approval.

But possibly the most telling consequence was that Wolsey's apt pupil believed the governance of the realm was indeed better in one man's hands and those hands should belong to the king. From that moment on, Wolsey's days were numbered. And we can see so clearly just how Henry's view of governance changed by comparing 1525, when he listened to his subjects and retreated, to his behaviour eleven years later during the 1536/7 Pilgrimage of Grace uprising, which also had a tax-gathering element to it.

By that time, not only had Henry stopped listening to anyone, he was also on his third wife, still with no son, and frightened of the power that the people could wield. He slaughtered as many as he could of those involved in the Pilgrimage of Grace, despite promises that they would be pardoned.

Vagrancy

In the following paragraphs, mention will be made of beggars and vagrants. To clarify the difference, the definition of a beggar is 'a person who begs', while that of a vagrant is 'a person without home or job'. Many people in the Tudor era were both.

Not everyone in the reign of Henry VII was delighted by the end of the Wars of the Roses. Some seventeen or so battles had been fought over thirty years. Even after the Battle of Tewkesbury in 1471 left the exiled Henry Tudor as the only possible threat to the Yorkist throne, the nobles still retained their armed militia. Henry VII saw them as a threat and forced the aristocracy to dismiss their armed retainers.

As the sixteenth century progressed vagrants with a military background became more numerous for the obvious reason that demobilised soldiers and sailors flooded the labour market when peace broke out. According to Edward Hext, a JP from Somerset, they numbered up to 300 or 400 to a shire and were constantly robbing the locals.[1]

Provost-marshals were appointed to apprehend and punish them. Upon discharge, ex-soldiers and sailors were given a sum of money for their homeward journey and a licence to travel unmolested, provided they followed a specific route and arrived within a defined time.

Naturally, people being what they are, many vagabonds without a military background sensed the opportunity for gain and pretended to be soldiers. This caused such confusion that the authorities were ordered to interrogate everyone. Genuine cases were provided with assistance. Frauds were punished.

The rising population was another cause of poverty. Sadly, the rising numbers were not matched by a corresponding rise in employment opportunities. The situation varied from area to area. London, unsurprisingly, was very much affected by this. In contrast, Norwich and York, two of the largest provincial cities, were not.[2]

With the rising population came an increasing demand from the towns for agricultural produce. This encouraged landowners to undertake more intensive and more efficient farming methods, and, in some cases, this increased efficiency led to surplus labour being summarily dismissed.

The cloth-producing areas, for example, in East Anglia, Yorkshire and the West Country, suffered a less acute problem because of steadily increasing demand from abroad. However, the cloth industry was affected by external events. It only needed a sudden bout of plague, an outbreak of war in Europe or a series of bad harvests to reduce purchasing power. This could cause a sudden fall-off in demand, setting up a chain reaction which resulted in wholesale unemployment for those least able to deal with it.[3]

Booms and slumps were a feature of the first quarter of the sixteenth century, and even if a man could temporarily weather an economic storm there was no guarantee that his original job would still be waiting for him. The urban wage earner was particularly vulnerable in this respect and far more likely to have to resort to begging than his rural equivalent.

Enclosures were also a major factor in the cause of poverty. Far greater profits could be made from enclosing a patch of land than any other source of income. Landowners believed if they enclosed their land and turned it over to sheep farming, they could expect to make a profit one and a half times more than they had been making previously. This was in an age when English wool was still in high demand from Europe.

Because of this, many landlords pulled down houses on their land, sometimes around their tenants' ears. John Hales declared these actions to be a great social evil. On some occasions, landlords depopulated whole villages so they could turn over their land to farm sheep. Deprived of their livelihood these people had no other option but to join the ranks of itinerant vagabonds and beggars.[4]

This was not the case with every landlord, of course. However, when all factors were taken into account it is undeniable that the situation presented the authorities with a real problem. In Leicestershire alone one village in three was affected, far more than the general three per cent statistic in the rest of the Midlands. The people thus affected, facing imminent or ultimate eviction, were particularly vulnerable. In the Midlands, conversion of arable to pasture was still a paying proposition but it depended to a large extent on the type of holding concerned.[5]

If Joe Bloggs held sound title to his land, which authorised him to pass it on to his heirs, and if his rent was fixed and his landlord was debarred from imposing an inflated entry fine (a modern equivalent would be 'key money') on his successor, Joe was normally safe. But few people were as fortunate as him. Some held leases of a specified length and once that period of tenure expired, they faced either eviction or the imposition of an extortionate entry fine into a new contract.

Price rises continued almost unabated through the whole of the sixteenth century. By the 1550s, prices in England had doubled from the early decades and there was a five-fold increase in grain prices. One major factor in this may well have been the debasement of the 1540s, which resulted in the silver content of the coinage being reduced by more than two thirds between 1543 and 1551. One of Henry VIII's nicknames was 'Old Copper-Nose' and this reflected people's opinions of him debasing the coinage.

England was in a situation where the population was rising. Various events like the sweating sickness – something that came in and went out with the Tudors – plague, flu epidemics, and political changes had resulted in less employment, and then the coinage was debased. Debasement of the coinage stimulated further sheep-rearing and thus more enclosures.[6] By the second half of Elizabeth's reign, her government's insistence on compulsory contributions to poor relief ensured that the poorest among the people were given some assistance.

Plague was a perennial scourge, whether of the bubonic or the pneumonic variety. The Black Death first came to England in 1348 and made its welcome exit in 1666. Between those times England was seldom free from it in one area or another. Sometimes it affected much of the kingdom, but more frequently it was selective. London might be rife with it but Bristol would be completely free; York might be unscathed while Norwich was decimated. Between 1579 and 1580 the population of Norwich was reduced by a third and the city experienced a serious outbreak every five years until 1603. The first outbreak killed 6,000 of its citizens. In the onslaughts of 1588 and 1593, and also in the last year of Elizabeth's reign, a further 3500 perished in each onslaught.[7]

The poor, as ever, were the biggest sufferers. They were crowded together in packed tenements with very little opportunity to flee from the contagion, and were therefore far more vulnerable than the wealthy. However once begun, plague spread like wildfire. The death of the head of the household meant that the family had lost its major wage earner. His wife, and those of his children who were old enough, would try to continue working until they too were afflicted, but their meagre earnings would be nothing like the income they had lost through the death of the husband and father.

Wealthier people fled in increasing numbers from stricken areas, which meant the richer employers left, resulting in job losses. In late Elizabethan times this exodus by employers also meant there were fewer people contributing to the poor rate, so again the poor suffered.

Looking at this in a very cold, clinical way, the plague aided money-starved local authorities. If the ranks of the poor had been decimated, there were fewer vagrants to deal with, and fewer destitute people to draw on already depleted funds. This advantage, small as it was, was offset by the numbers that became temporarily or permanently unemployed as a result of the outbreak, but if both factors were weighed in the balance, the city fathers seldom emerged the losers financially.[8]

On average there was harvest failure every four years. Sometimes the harvests were just deficient or disastrous for two or three consecutive years. This happened in the very early 1550s. It meant the majority of the poorer people in those areas were short of food and drink for that period of time. Naturally, a failed harvest led to a rise in the price of food. In this period, the labouring classes made up between half and two thirds of the population and they were particularly hard hit. Few had guaranteed regular employment. They were at the mercy of the climate, the seasons, falling demand and anything which meant that their meagre earnings would have to be stretched still further.

As the century progressed, perhaps a third of the population in cities and a fifth in rural districts were on or just below the poverty line. A similar number were barely above it. Food riots were common and the authorities, at both local and national level, had to keep a constant watch on the corn market, permitting the export of grain in one place while forbidding it in another and trying to maintain supplies. Failure to do so could well have led to insurrection. The disastrous famines of the 1590s led directly to the Elizabethan Poor Laws of 1598 and 1601.

When we examine the effects of the dissolution of the monasteries, however, the outcome for the normal man and woman in the street – the commons – was equally disastrous. Thomas Cromwell negotiated with all the abbots and priors of the monasteries that they would be given pensions. However, even as the king's workmen were physically destroying the very stones of the monasteries, the ordinary nuns and monks were thrown out and had no other recourse but to become vagrants and beggars.[9]

The other main disaster as far as the commons was concerned was that monasteries and nunneries had provided safe overnight housing when they were on a journey. It meant that, although people could still stop at an inn, some could not afford the inflationary prices and the standard of the accommodation was often appalling. They immediately lost the ability to travel, sometimes for work. For example, many towns had an annual fair and many of the travelling hawkers traditionally stayed at the local abbey, somewhere they knew was safe. This gave them not just time to plan their onward journeys but also time to attend services.

If most of the monks were in a relatively satisfactory position pension-wise, sadly, the nuns were not. The extremely small pensions they were paid, often a year in arrears, did not give them any financial independence and they had few obvious ways of supplementing their income. They could marry, of course, and when clerical marriage was legalised in the reign of Edward VI some nuns took advantage of this.

These unions were very short lived because when Mary came to the throne the new government insisted on the marriages being dissolved. There are no figures to say how or if any of the couples were reunited when Elizabeth came to the throne in 1558. A few nuns might have wealthy relatives, but the fate of most of them is obscure. One can only imagine that some of these had to resort to begging. Or worse.

With the fall of the monasteries, monastic charity also stopped. The care of the poor had been a duty that had fallen on the religious houses. They had a general obligation to distribute all food left over after meals to the local paupers at the gates.

At St Benet's Holm in Norfolk there were bitter complaints in 1526 that the dogs in the house were eating scraps and leaving nothing for the poor. By contrast, it was reported in 1519 that paupers at Markby in Lincolnshire were not only well fed but actually invited into the canons' hall for their scraps instead of being fed at the gates.[10]

The provision of food was a daily duty and the numbers fed obviously varied according to the size of the monastic house. Syon in Middlesex apportioned no more than 0.3 per cent of its monastic income. At the other end of the scale, Fountains Abbey in Yorkshire used 1.7 per cent of its income for the poor. Norwich Cathedral Priory used 8.4 per cent of its funds for the poor and Great Malvern in Worcestershire as much as 11 per cent. Most generous of all was Whalley in Lincolnshire where out of a total income of £551, £122, or just over 22 per cent, was spent on poor relief.[11]

The *Valor Ecclesiasticus*, which recorded such charities when assessing the monasteries for the new Royal tax in 1535, was only concerned with the amount of obligatory charity. It made no allowance for the generosity of the monks and nuns in other ways.

Robert Aske, the leader of the Pilgrimage of Grace in 1536, was convinced that the north at least maintained much of the relief of the common people by the succour of the abbeys. His testimony was supported by others. The abbeys and monasteries felt the financial squeeze as much as anybody else and they could be as financially rapacious as any landlord.

The last Abbot of Byland Abbey, John Ledes, demanded an admission fee equivalent to two years rent instead of the customary three months for the renewal of one tenant's lease, for example. Another (unnamed) abbot wanted to give a holding to one of his kinsman. The then tenant of the holding, Thomas Brown, was deaf, lame and blind. His wife grew almost demented with anxiety over the threats of the abbot. The couple were eventually evicted and there seems to be no record of their subsequent fate. It is more than likely they joined the ranks of vagrants and beggars.[12]

As far as ordinary people were concerned, most believed that vagrants were indolent or had been born with a character defect that led them to be idle drunkards. Many people felt threatened by them, believing they carried disease, most worryingly, plague. They were also perceived as preferring to live a life of crime. And, since some were ex-servicemen, people believed they were likely to incite rebellions.

One example that highlights this fear is the book written by Sir John Cheke citing the rebels in Kett's Rebellion in Norfolk in 1549. Titled *The Hurt of Sedition*, Cheke rants against the rebels and claiming that they 'stir up uproars of people, hurly-burlies of vagabonds, routs of robbers ... [who would] swarm in every corner of the realm, and not only lie loitering under hedges, but also stand sturdily in cities, and beg boldly at every door, ... stand in the high way to ask their alms whom you be afraid to say nay unto honestly, lest they take it away from you violently.'[13]

Unsurprisingly, the rise in population during the sixteenth century and the changing circumstances of economic growth led to many people being made homeless and jobless. This resulted in a rise in the level of poverty, and with that came a rise in crime.

Using two examples, one urban and one rural, the cloth industry, which was based in urban areas, had been thriving, but it suffered a slump. Since the industry was centred in towns, the numbers of men who lost their jobs and often their homes led to a serious situation for the authorities. This was exacerbated by the debasement of coinage in the 1540s and 1550s. It led to inflation and the price of food and other goods rose. Some people were forced to leave their homes in search of food and jobs.

The Elizabethan poor laws put the onus on the urban authorities to ensure that the poor were fed. However, the money for that came from rates paid by local employers and the more the numbers of poor rose, the more employers had to pay to feed them. Likewise, when there was an epidemic of either plague or influenza, the poor were the first victims, and so as numbers fell employers paid less.

In rural areas tenant farmers were reliant on their harvests to survive. During the six years of Edward VI's reign, 1547 and 1548 had good harvests. However, the years 1549-51 had disastrous harvests and 1552 was only an average harvest. This means that half the harvests in Edward's reign, especially when we remember that cereal crops made bread and ale – the staples – left people short of basic food and drink.[14] This led to farmers either flocking to the towns to find work, thus depopulating rural areas, or trying to recoup their losses by steep rises in rent, called rack-renting.

Thomas Harmon classified vagabonds and rogues according to the activities they specialised in. The most common types were:

- Angler: used a hook on the end of a long wooden stick to steal clothes/valuables;
- Clapper dudgeon: used arsenic on their skin to make it bleed, hoping to attract sympathy while begging;
- Doxy: stole chickens by feeding them bread tied to a hook; carried stolen goods in a large sack on their back;
- Counterfeit crank: dressed in tatty clothes and pretended to have fits, sucking soap to fake foaming at the mouth;
- Abraham man: pretended to be mad.

He also classified vagabonds as 'wandering beggars who turned to crime and rogues, who were inherently dishonest and turned to crime'.[15]

The situation became a vicious circle, especially when the influx of people from rural areas to the towns made feeding everyone extremely difficult. It must be borne in mind that town officials seldom came out of any enterprise poorer than when they went in. Not unlike today, poverty was mostly considered to be self-inflicted, but the poor laws only partly helped those who were unable to work due to age, disability, or infirmity. These were called impotent poor. Able-bodied poor were those who were physically able to work; they were often forced to work to prevent them from becoming vagabonds and beggars or vagrants.

To put this into a twenty-first century context, their situation was the modern equivalent of 'if you have no home, you have no address. No address means no bank account. No bank account means no job and, circling back to where we started, no job means no home.'

While today we have many charitable organisations who do their utmost to ensure people do not starve, in Tudor England the laws were less sympathetic and there were far fewer philanthropists.

In 1495 vagrants were put in the stocks for three days and then sent back to the parish of their birth.

In 1531 they were punished in the stocks and sent back to the parish of their birth, but repeat offenders were punished more harshly. The act did distinguish between those who were able-bodied and those who were not. It gave the impotent poor licences to beg but no other provision. It also ignored the fact that a man might want to work but be unable to find it.[16]

In 1535 it was recognised that there was insufficient work for every man. Possibly devised by William Marshall, one of Thomas Cromwell's advisors, it was proposed that a programme of public works on roads, forts, harbours, and rivers be set up, with reasonable wages, to help the unemployment situation. It was to be funded by taxes on income and wealth. Henry VIII was known to support the bill, but it was castigated in Parliament and the final outcome fell far short of what had been intended.

In 1547 the Duke of Somerset attempted to use legislation to punish the unemployed. Vagrants could have 'V' branded on their foreheads and be put into slavery for two years. If they escaped, the slavery sentence was for life. Repeat offenders were hanged. This law was repealed in 1550 mostly because it was unenforceable and JPs were reluctant to carry out what were perceived to be excessive punishments. Instead, another act in 1552 made town and parish authorities responsible for appointing two men to 'gently ask' for contributions. Those who refused were then exhorted by their local cleric, and if that failed, they would be threatened by a visit from the bishop in order to 'induce and persuade them'. In fact, from 1563 onwards parishioners could not only be brought before the bishop, but, if they continued to refuse to pay contributions, they were imprisoned until they did.[17]

In 1572 the Vagabonds Act introduced severe punishments against vagrants. These included being put into the stocks or pillories, being whipped, being bored through the ear, and, if habitual offenders, being executed.[18] There is evidence in the Middlesex records that between 1572 and 1575 forty-four vagabonds were branded, eight put into servitude and five hanged.[19]

The 1601 poor law formalised all previous acts. A compulsory contribution was introduced and those who refused or tried to evade it were jailed. Begging was made illegal. Almshouses came into being to look after the impotent poor. By the time of Elizabeth's death, there was the foundation of the welfare state, but it did not end poverty. In fact, most relief for the poor continued to come from private charities and that nurtured the growth of philanthropists.[20]

Witchcraft

'But my affection was not caus'd by Art; the witch that wrought on mee was in my brest.'

Poem by Sir Francis Hubert, who died in 1629.

Essex has, throughout history, appeared to be a hotbed for witches and the paranormal, both in fiction and non-fiction – the latter from the earliest pamphlets.[1]

In Lambeth Palace there is the only extant copy of a pamphlet on the examination of certain witches in Essex on 26 July 1566.[2]

Usually, women or elderly widows were vulnerable to being called witches, but this does not mean that witches and witchcraft existed in the form in which people believed it did. Right up until the Second World War, people believed in the village witch or wise woman who could put a hex on anyone who upset her. It all goes back to superstition and alleged witches are still with us.

Whatever the reality, people really did believe in witches – and not just ordinary people. Henry VIII decided that Anne Boleyn must have captivated him by witchcraft, since he could not possibly have ever been led by the contents of his codpiece, could he? James I/VI totally believed in witches. All it takes is for a belief to spread and take on a reality that cannot be dismissed.

That there was an organised cult of pagan belief with rituals for making things happen to people, animals and crops cannot be gainsaid. And from that stems the way in which organised religion dealt with this enormous threat to its supremacy. Unsurprisingly, the church declared such pagan rites to be Devil worship and the people who allegedly performed these rites – with covens of thirteen, naturally – were witches who had made a compact with the Devil.

Their aim was diametrically opposed to that of the church, which majored on the soul's journey through Purgatory and into heaven by means of being God-fearing, obedient and good whilst on earth. Witches, the church declared, only cared about having pleasure and power and since they sold their souls to the Devil in order to obtain these earthly treasures, cared nothing for their souls.

The first English statute regarding witchcraft was in 1542 under Henry VIII. By then he had not just been bewitched by Anne Boleyn, but also by her Howard cousin, Katherine, who possibly went further and cuckolded him with Thomas Culpepper.

In 1547 Edward VI, Henry's boy-child heir, repealed many of his father's statutes, including the 1542 one. It was not until 1563, under Elizabeth, that the legal situation regarding witches returned to its 1542 status. Despite a few conjurers being punished, it was not until 1560 that two people were accused of witchcraft at the Essex Assizes.

The 1563 Act against Conjuracions Inchantments and Witchcraftes was replaced in 1604 by a much more severe act, probably as a nod to the beliefs of James, the new king. The 1563 act laid down a penalty of death for anybody found guilty of invoking evil spirits or by using sorcery to kill someone. Any accomplices were also to suffer the death penalty. For lesser offences, such as causing injury to people or property, the offender was imprisoned for a year, with four sessions of six hours each in the pillory for a first offence. Any subsequent offence was a death sentence.

Life imprisonment and forfeiture of goods was the punishment for a second offence where the 'witch' had said where treasure or lost property could be found, or for intending 'to provoke any person to unlawful love'.[3]

Both the 1563 and 1604 statues stated that those found guilty were barred from any rights of clergy and sanctuary.

A legend has come down through history that all witches were burned. Not so. Death was by hanging unless the crime was considered petty treason in which case, the penalty *was* burning. One Essex JP threatened that witches who did not confess 'shall bee burnt and hanged'.[4] One assumes not in that order!

Witchcraft was considered, legally speaking, as a 'crime apart', similar to poisoning, since both were committed in secret. As such, it did not need testimony or witnesses to the act, just suspicion and common fame, in other words hearsay, about the suspect's reputation.

Moreover, witches did not have to be present at the scene of the crime. They could be miles away, so, because evidence was almost impossible to come by, special provision had to be made in law to deal with their alleged offence.

The character of the accused was a vital part of the evidence. An examining magistrate needed to know whether the suspect's family was wicked, or if she was courteous and respectful, or someone who initiated arguments and strife. The magistrate would ask if the suspect was hard-working and not a vagrant, whose company she frequented, and the opinion of locals as to her character.[5]

In other words, a suspect's entire social class and interaction was on trial. If the suspect was married and/or had children, their spouse and offspring could be interrogated, something contrary to common law.

There were several distinct points of evidence to be considered.[6] These included:

- Enough suspicion for the suspect to be brought before a magistrate;
- That there was a 'strong presumption' of guilt, or several presumptions, which, when put together, made enough of a case for conviction;
- The reputation of the accused; somebody who claimed to have been injured by them or a 'known malice' towards a witness, which was followed by a disaster;
- A suspected witch, who had remained floating when thrown into water – a case of heads we win, tails you lose;
- An implicit confession, such as 'you shouldn't have upset me';
- Over-diligent interest in a sick neighbour;
- A deathbed accusation by a supposed victim;
- An unnatural mark on the body of the alleged witch;
- Witnesses to a witch making a pact with the Devil;
- Being seen to entertain familiars – God help the lonely widow who spoke to her cat.

Richard Bernard, a Puritan clergyman wrote *A Guide to Grand Jurymen*, published in 1630, so outside the Tudor era, but it stated that if a supposed witch gave an apple to a child and that child later became ill, so long as there was known malice between them, there was enough proof for execution. In the Essex Assize records, the main evidence became that of known malice.

One such accusation became a case of neighbours jumping on the 'I refused to lend her money/give her some herbs' bandwagon, which ended up with the accused being hanged. Standing on the execution ladder the woman stated that she had never harmed anyone.[7]

Since a confession was rock-solid evidence of guilt, justices and magistrates went to considerable lengths to pressure the accused. Some were pressured so much they suffered mental breakdowns. Not only did confessions satisfy society's need for the absolute truth, but it also doubtless assuaged any feeling of guilt and shame on the part of the judiciary and witnesses who had perjured themselves out of malice towards the accused.

CASE STUDY

Agnes Waterhouse[8]

Henry VIII kickstarted the hysteria regarding witches and witchcraft, which a century later grew to horrendous proportions under the aegis of Witchfinder Matthew Hopkins during the seventeenth-century English Civil War. Exaggerated tales of witchcraft augmented the story-telling tradition.

However, the first witch to be put on trial and executed was Agnes Waterhouse, sometimes called Mother Waterhouse, who, with her daughter, Jone (Joan), and a friend, Elizabeth Francis, was charged with witchcraft. The three women were also accused of consorting with their familiar, a cat called Satan, who was able to metamorphose from a cat to a toad or a dog.

To twenty-first century readers, the story is beyond preposterous. Shakespeare did not have to travel far for his ideas.

In 1566 these three – that sounds familiar – were put on trial. Agnes was singled out as causing William Fynne to fall ill and later die. To make sure of a guilty verdict, she was also charged with killing livestock and causing the death of her husband. Agnes was found guilty but her daughter, charged with the same offences, was not, which has led some commentators to believe that she negotiated the sixteenth-century equivalent of a plea bargain. It was Joan's testimony which was central in obtaining a guilty verdict. Against her own mother. Nice girl.

The information on the trial, held in Chelmsford, is detailed in the pamphlet referred to earlier that is now housed in Lambeth Palace. It was written by John Phillips, and while not complete, does give an outline of what happened.

There were two hearings, the first before Thomas Cole, an archdeacon of Essex, and Sir John Fortescue, a future Chancellor of the Exchequer to Elizabeth I. The second hearing was attended by Elizabeth's attorney, Sir Gilbert Gerard, and a justice of the queen's bench, John Southcote. The seniority of the examiners denotes the perceived gravity of the crime.

Elizabeth Francis, the friend, was questioned first. She admitted to possessing the cat, telling the court it had been a gift from her grandmother, Mother Eve of Hatfield Peverell, who taught the twelve-year-old Elizabeth witchcraft. She confessed that she had kept the cat for fifteen or sixteen years before she gave it to Agnes. She further confessed that the cat could speak using a strange, hollow voice and would do anything in exchange for a drop of blood.

But Elizabeth did not stop there. She admitted to stealing sheep and killing a wealthy man called Andrew Byles who refused to marry her after making her pregnant. However, Satan, the cat, came to her rescue and told her what concoction she should make and drink to cause a miscarriage. When she made a later, unhappy marriage, she said she had willed the cat to kill her baby daughter and make her husband lame. This latter admission defies logic; surely, if she could kill people, then eradicating her husband should have been a piece of cake.

And cake is what enters the equation next, because Elizabeth gave the cat to Agnes in exchange for a cake. It was Elizabeth who accused Agnes Waterhouse, but even after so many heinous confessions, she was not executed until after a second conviction some thirteen years later. According to a later pamphlet from her 1579 trial, Elizabeth and Agnes were not friends but sisters.

Under questioning, Agnes told of how she tried to get Satan to kill a pig, just to see if it could. However, she wanted to use the cat's bed for something else, so turned the cat into a toad. Some sources, according to the pamphlet, stated that the cat turned itself into a toad. Agnes denied that she had ever managed to kill anyone.

The chief testimony against Agnes came from a neighbouring child, also called Agnes. Little Agnes declared that the witch had used the cat – now in toad form – to haunt her with a great horned dog. With the help of what must have been a wonderful imagination, the child described the dog as having a face like an ape, with a whistle around its neck and horns on its head. The demon – for it must have been one – asked her for some butter, which she refused, so the dog/demon got the key to the milkhouse, unlocked it and stole the butter. The demon next threatened to stab her to death. Courageous Little Agnes then asked who its owner was and the demon wagged its head towards the house belonging to Agnes Waterhouse.

Needless to say, Agnes, the witch, was found guilty. She was executed on 29 July 1566. What may have appeared to confirm her guilt further was that when questioned about her church attendance, she said she prayed often but always in Latin because the cat forbade her to pray in English. Since Latin services smacked of Catholicism, everyone felt vindicated anyway. This author has a sneaking hope that Little Agnes went on to have a horrible life.

Elizabeth Stiles[9]

One of the earliest British witchcraft pamphlets was published in 1579, *A Rehearsall both Straung and True, of Hainous and Horrible Actes Committed by Elizabeth Stile, alias Rockingham, Mother Dutten, Mother Deuell, Mother Margaret, Fower Notorious Witches.*

This records the case of a sixty-five-year-old widow from Windsor who had been charged previously for being a witch. It didn't help that she was a bad-tempered old crone who would fulminate against anyone who refused to give her alms. Of course, what guaranteed the accusation of witchcraft was that she kept a pet rat.

A local innkeeper refused her appeal for food and soon after, he fell ill – nothing to do with possibly sampling his wares a little too enthusiastically. He was convinced Stiles had cursed him and so set about trying to break the spell she had obviously put on him. He used one of the criteria for testing the existence of a witch, called pricking.

Upon him scratching her, she bled. Not surprising since she was obviously not well-fed, probably unhealthy, and, being old, her skin would be thin. However, she bled and the innkeeper recovered, which plays towards recovery from a monster hangover for this author.

Mother Stiles was arrested. She described how, with three other witches, she created a doll in the image of her intended victim and stabbed it with pins. These four women also associated with a man called Father Rosimunde, who was, allegedly, able to shape-shift into any animal he desired.

It will cause the reader no surprise to learn that the four women were found guilty and hanged on 29 February 1579. What is interesting, however, is that, in common with Agnes Waterhouse, there are overtones of Catholicism in their depositions to the courts. For Agnes, it was praying in Latin and for Elizabeth and her associates the Father Rosimunde connection.

These two cases reinforce the standard definition of a witch. A woman, spinster or widow. Old. With a pet. And if, like Mother Stiles, she is not the kindest person on the planet, she must be a witch.

Which begs a question. Why did the women confess to something of which they were palpably innocent? It was all very well making the locals a bit unsure about you to the extent they would bring round little presents like honey and bread, but to stand in a court of law and confess you had a cat that could turn into a toad and talk to you makes absolutely no sense at all.

Except that when you consider the onus on the judiciary was to obtain a confession at all costs, regardless of guilt or innocence, things look different.

Those accused of witchcraft:

- Were tortured by sleep deprivation, often being made to stand for two days before being interrogated, by which time most of them were hallucinating and incoherent;
- Suffered water torture;

- Were often stripped naked to be examined for the teat Satan fed from;
- Were brutalised with pilliwinks, better known as thumbscrews which would crush fingers and toes and render the sufferer crippled;
- Had ropes fastened around their heads and pulled tight to inflict injuries to the facial bones;
- Underwent 'pricking', thought to be the real tell-tale evidence, when the skin would be pricked or scratched to see if they bled and, if they did, if the person who had been bewitched by them recovered;
- Pressed under heavy weights;
- Were tortured by the Heretic's Fork, which was a two-pronged length of metal placed between the breastbone and under the chin and then the victim was hung from the ceiling.

Is it any wonder that we read so many stories of confessions? They might have assuaged consciences in some quarters but all they really did was contribute to public hysteria and focus hatred on one particular section of the community.

Tavern Talk:
Mother Stiles, executed for witchcraft, was accused of consorting with Father Rosimunde (see above). Rosimunde claimed to be able to change into any animal he desired. The proper name for this ability is 'Therianthropy'. Try saying that after a few gins.

Xenophobia

The definition of xenophobia is 'dislike of or prejudice against people from other countries'.

Until very recently, prejudice, whether of creed, gender or race was not illegal, but it cannot be denied that it has been the cause of people breaking the law as the following case study highlights.

Evil May Day 1517[1]

The English are a funny breed. Probably because we are an island race, we have a history of xenophobia. In 1517, reasonably early in Henry VIII's reign when he was more or less still happy with his wife, Katherine of Aragon, there occurred a riot in London that majored on people's prejudices and fed on tension and rhetoric.

By the beginning of the sixteenth century London was already a cosmopolitan city with a goodly number of migrant workers, mainly from France and Holland. These men were primarily artisans, working as weavers or in the cloth industry. They came to England by royal invitation with letters of protection issued by the monarch. By doing this, the English cloth industry gained a boost from the influx of skilled foreign workers.

There was also a high proportion of shoemakers or cobblers. A shoemaker or cordwainer was permitted to work with new leather to create shoes, whereas a cobbler was forbidden to work with new leather and had to make repairs using old leather.

Of course, the royal protection was not the only factor in the arrival of these workers and not all were artisans. Some were driven to move by warfare or suppression. Others were wealthy merchants and bankers who not only loaned the king money but imported goods like silk and spices and exported English wool. They often congregated in districts or lived in the houses of the rich.

Some lords were granted liberties, which meant that they were left to run their own affairs with very little interference from the authorities, or sometimes even the king. These arrangements were invariably vague and led to many legal disputes. Some 'aliens' became prominent and very unpopular due to their arrogance and perceived eminence. One of these was John Meautys. His house was on Leadenhall Street and he was known to shelter his countrymen, including pickpockets, from the law.

Resentment grew, and with reason, since these foreign merchants were thought to be using their royal liberties and connection with the king to the detriment of English traders and merchants.

In April 1516 a paper complaining about aliens taking advantage of the king and growing rich by dominating the wool trade, was nailed to the door of St Paul's Cathedral. In the early months of 1517 the Earl of Surrey was approached by the Mercers' Company and asked for help in subduing aliens who broke city laws. Then came May Day.

May Day Eve was a holiday in which boisterous young men and women proceeded to make merry with noisy celebrations. 1517 was a little different. The chronicler, Edward Hall, was a Tudor lawyer and Member of Parliament. In his account of *Evil May Day*, he condemned the rioters for their violence and insubordination. However, he does display a degree of sympathy in his account.[2]

What Hall tells us is that two weeks before the riot, a Dr Bell (or Beal according to some sources) made an inflammatory speech at St Paul's Cross. The speech had been either written or instigated by a broker called John Lincoln, who had apparently convinced Bell that the city's economic problems stemmed from an influx of foreigners.

Bell called on Englishmen to defend themselves and their way of life against these aliens; that they were taking bread from the mouths of poor fatherless children. He accused them of stealing the livings of English workers and merchants. He exhorted his listeners to attack the immigrants who lived in the city. In the two weeks preceding the riots there were occasional attacks on foreigners and rumours abounded that on May Day all the aliens would be killed.

On 30 April the mayor, John Rest, a member of the Grocers Company, announced a 9pm curfew to try and alleviate the situation. One alderman, John Mundy, saw a group of young men in Cheapside and told them to disperse. The ferocity of their response forced him to flee.

A few hours later a mob of approximately 1,000 apprentices congregated in Cheapside. It is interesting that their first action was to march to Newgate Prison and free prisoners who had been locked up for attacking foreigners. The mob then travelled to St Martin le Grand attacking and robbing the shops of foreigners as they went. Their destination was an area north of

St Paul's where foreigners made up a considerable percentage of the local population. At this point they were intercepted by Sir Thomas More, who was then the under-sheriff of London.

More tried to persuade the rioters to disperse and go home. However, as soon as he had calmed the situation, people who lived in the area began to bombard the crowd with anything they had to hand, including stones and bricks. The rioters smashed and damaged everything they could reach and many houses were vandalised.

According to Edward Hall, the mob then ran to Cornhill by Leadenhall to the house of the aforementioned John Meautys who was much hated. The house was ransacked and the protesters then set about trying to find the man himself. Had they found him, there is no doubt they would have 'stricken off his head' Hall tells us.

Instead, they then ran to a group of buildings near Aldgate, home to a large number of foreign shoemakers and cobblers who were attacked. Boots and shoes were thrown into the street.

Two noblemen arrived in London with soldiers to restore order. One of these was the Duke of Norfolk who brought his private army of about 1,300 retainers. The other was probably Norfolk's son, the Earl of Surrey. By mid-afternoon, the riot had died down. Some 300 people were arrested and many were sentenced to death for treasonously attacking foreigners considered to be under the protection of Henry VIII.

There are various accounts of the immediate aftermath. One stated that Henry was awoken in the middle of the night at Richmond, another that the Lieutenant of the Tower of London ordered his men to fire at the city, something that made the city elders very angry.

In the end, only about fifteen people, including John Lincoln, were hanged, drawn and quartered. Executions took place at St Martin's Gate, Ludgate, Aldgate, Bishopsgate, Doggate, St Manguns, Leadenhall in the Poultry and at the standard in Cheapside. John Lincoln was executed with another felon at Newgate.

Naturally, Henry, a man who adored grandstanding, made the most of the situation for his own vainglory. On 22 May he ordered the prisoners to be brought into his presence at Westminster Hall. Nobles present begged him to pardon the prisoners, all of whom were wearing halters. Only when Cardinal Wolsey and then Henry's wife, Katherine of Aragon, sank to their knees before the king, beseeching him to spare the prisoners' lives for the sake of their families, did he magnanimously agree, at which point there was 'much rejoicing and weeping'.

Zealots

The definition of a zealot is 'a person who is fanatical and uncompromising in pursuit of their religious, political, or other ideals'.

There are several sections in this book that describe what happened to religious zealots. However, political zealots were thinner on the ground. The post-Reformation decades were particularly fraught, and not just for ordinary people. There is plenty of evidence to suggest that Anne Boleyn was very much aware that her leanings towards the 'new' religion were well known and that not only could Henry VIII have her burned but some of his advisors were advocating it.

Stephen Gardiner, Bishop of Winchester and a Catholic zealot, tried his hardest to entrap Henry's last wife, Katherine Parr, who was known to have Protestant leanings. Katherine outwitted him by throwing herself to her knees in front of her husband and assuring him she had merely been trying to divert his attention away from the pain of his ulcerous leg. Had she not, it is likely Henry would have sent her to the fire because by that time he was not just a tyrant but a paranoid one seeing threats everywhere, much like his father.

One zealot who is often regarded as a good fair man, propagated by the character in Robert Bolt's *A Man For All Seasons* was Thomas More. However, Bolt's character bears no resemblance to Hilary Mantel's More in *Wolf Hall*.

There is no doubt that More was a complicated and often troubled man. But he was also a man who, some might say, was willing to compromise his own integrity to stay in power. He was Henry VIII's Chancellor at the time when the king was trying to divorce Katherine of Aragon and marry Anne Boleyn. More completely disagreed with the divorce but stayed working for Henry.

He was, however, an ardent Catholic. It was only when he had to choose, not his religion, but who was the supreme power in that religion, that he decided his king did not come first. Henry was absolutely determined that everyone in England should acknowledge him as the Supreme Head of the church. For More that was one step too far. It was, after all, the difference between being a Roman Catholic and an Anglo Catholic. In other words, More believed that the Pope was a direct successor of St Peter, the leader of the apostles: the king was not.

More did not come to prominence until around 1518 when Cardinal Wolsey replaced Richard Pace, Henry VIII's principal secretary, with More, who, Wolsey believed, would be more trustworthy. Henry and Thomas More were in each other's company a lot of the time and More became as much of a friend as a servant could be to his king.[1]

More and Wolsey accompanied Henry to the Field of the Cloth of Gold in 1520. While the two kings and guests were feasting, More was tasked with talking to the envoys of Charles V, the new Holy Roman Emperor. Wolsey also sent him to talk to the merchants in the Hanseatic League and settle commercial disputes.

By August 1521 More was disillusioned not just with Wolsey but also Henry. He thought the unofficial bargain Henry had entered into with Charles – that they would invade France provided Wolsey was made Pope when the then incumbent died – was corrupt and that Wolsey was putting his own interests ahead of those of peace in Europe. The rigged trial of Edward Stafford, Duke of Buckingham, in 1521 furthered his disillusion. More was then sent into London to threaten citizens loyal to Buckingham, something that, for him, echoed the actions of Richard III in 1483.

Despite this, he stayed in the royal household. He helped write rebuttals to the works of Martin Luther and was active in the burning of heretical books. By 1528 More was active in finding and prosecuting heretical publishers. Robert Barnes, a Lutheran publisher, was forced to perform a public penance and then abjure the realm. More also imprisoned a London draper called Humphrey Monmouth, although the raid on Monmouth's house revealed no Lutheran books.

More wrote *Dialogue Concerning Heresies*, in which the Messenger character sets forth his Lutheran beliefs, enabling the author to rebut them. It was probably whilst writing this that More became convinced that the unity of the Catholic church was of overriding importance.

When Wolsey fell in 1529, More became Henry's Chancellor. It was a poisoned chalice, putting him betwixt his zeal to eradicate Lutheranism and Henry's divorce. When a Cambridge reformer was burned at the stake More ordered a judicial review and forced witnesses to answer his questions on oath. In that way he could conclude that Thomas Bilney had indeed been a dangerous heretic and therefore deserved to die – even though the victim recanted just as the fire was lit.[2]

Thus began a war between More and the heretics. He kept George Constantine, who had imported forbidden books, in the stocks at the gate of his house in Chelsea. After a week, the man freed himself and fled to Antwerp. More then trapped James Bainham, a lawyer who had been overheard calling Thomas Becket a traitor. Richard Bayfield, a book-dealer, was handed over to a church court who obligingly sentenced him to burn. Bayfield was bound in chains, the fire wasn't properly lit and the poor man died in excruciating pain very slowly.[3]

By zealously searching out all possible hotbeds of heretics, More, like Queen Mary twenty-five years later, believed he was doing God's work. His one-time friend, Erasmus, on hearing on how More was wielding his power as Chancellor, was appalled that the author of *Utopia* could behave in this fashion. More himself wrote that he had been 'grievous to thieves, murderers and heretics' and wanted everyone to know it. Furthermore, he wrote that as far as heretics were concerned he wanted 'to be as hateful to them as anyone can possibly be'. How very Christian!

In May 1532 the bishops yielded unconditionally to Henry's Act of Supremacy. More resigned as Chancellor. He refused an invitation to Anne Boleyn's coronation since he believed that she was committing adultery. He refused to recognise Cranmer's annulment of Henry's marriage to Katherine of Aragon.

By 1534 Henry VIII was in a perpetual state of apprehension and anxiety. Contrary to her promise to give him a son, Anne had only given him a girl. However, she was pregnant again so there was still hope of a son. Henry demanded that everyone must sign the Act of Succession, one tenet of which was that Henry's marriage to Anne was legal and valid. More refused to sign.

Despite heavy pressure, he repeatedly refused to sign. He was sent to the Tower of London. By November 1534, Parliament recognised Henry as Supreme Head of the Church of England. The Act contained a new oath. More refused to sign that, too. After that, he was a dead man walking. He was put on trial, found guilty of treason, and executed in July 1535.

Was More a zealot? Certainly within the strict meaning of the term, yes, he was. He was also a complicated man who could often see both sides of an argument, unless, of course, it was an argument about religion.

However, his legacy has come down to us depicting a man with heroic moral principles. Henry may have maintained that More betrayed him, but this author believes the king's savagery was driven more by his desperation to have a legitimate male heir than a point of principle.

Afterword

Love them or loathe them, the Tudor monarchs changed the face of England forever in so many ways. Henry VII brought peace and stability to a land riven for thirty years by the Wars of the Roses. He also developed sophisticated methods of stripping money from citizens and using financial and legal powers to strip power from his nobles. He left England's royal coffers full to bursting.

His son, Henry VIII, took around a dozen years to empty those coffers, but he also made England a centre for art and trade. However, arguably the most decisive event in England's history since the Norman invasion of 1066 occurred on Henry VIII's watch: the Reformation and resulting Dissolution of the Monasteries. In some quarters their effects were still being felt in the early twentieth century. Religious differences led to revolts and uprisings on each side of the religious divide, all put down with incredible ferocity. For all that, Henry was a Catholic, albeit an Anglo-Catholic. He burned Protestant heretics just as his elder daughter did, only not as many. England became something of an Orwellian land, and nowhere is that better demonstrated than by the fact that on the day Henry VIII died, England was still a Catholic country, but within a week, under his nine-year-old son, Edward VI, it was well on the way to becoming a Protestant nation. Not until Elizabeth I's often pragmatic approach was some kind of stability established.

How did all this affect law and order? Where does justice come from? In modern times, it comes from the people through elected representatives who appoint judges. In Tudor England justice came down directly from the monarch, who was, of course, appointed by God. Nowadays we think nothing of challenging the law, questioning its purpose, and trying to build better laws. In the sixteenth century, challenging the law was almost a suicidal act.

Tudor England gave the country many different types of courts, for different strata of society. Whereas the royal court would judge rich and powerful transgressors, local manor or leet courts would be more concerned with using the offender's local standing to pull him or her into line. Ecclesiastical courts dealt with the punishment of sin.

However, social status was, as it has always been, the guide to how offenders were dealt with. When town mayors took the oath 'to do every man right', they meant that as it pertained to that man's social standing and wealth, or lack of it.

By the time men like Lord Burghley and Walsingham were leading Elizabeth's Privy Council, theirs were the voices that led to the poor laws, trying to improve the lot of the common man and be just. When Elizabeth breathed her last, she left behind 118 years of gradual improvement in the structure of law and order.

That, of course, takes no account of the prime motivations of people. No law has ever driven out greed, the pursuit of power and riches at whatever cost, arrogance, narcissism, and all the other traits we humans possess.

What is clear is that the Tudor monarchs were central to the improvements made during the sixteenth century. And to see in stark clarity the truth of that is to compare it with what happened after Elizabeth.

In one respect, Elizabeth's execution of Mary, Queen of Scots, an anointed sovereign and mother of James I (and VI of Scotland), could be viewed as a precedent for what happened less than fifty years after her death. However, James himself was more culpable. His habit of constant self-indulgence, egotism, ignoring state business, giving power to sycophants and male favourites, and caring little for his realm, soon made England the perfect hotbed for the rise of what would become the Commonwealth of the mid-seventeenth century and the murder of a king.

Select Bibliography

Andrews, William, *Bygone Punishments*, ebook, Project Gutenberg, 2009

Barrett & Harrison, *Crime and Punishment in England: A Source book*, Routledge, 2005: ISBN 978-1857288728

Bayani, Debra, *Jasper Tudor: Godfather of the Tudor Dynasty*, MadeGlobal Publishing, 2015: ISBN 978-8494372100

Bellamy, John, *The Tudor Law of Treason*, 1979, Routledge Revivals: ISBN 9780415712842

Bellamy, J, *Strange Inhuman Deaths*, Sutton Publishing, 2005: ISBN 9780750938631

Bennett, H S, *The Pastons and their England*, Cambridge University Press: 1922: ISBN: 9780521398268

Besant, Walter, *London in the time of the Tudors*, 1904

Bicheno, Hugh, *The Wars of the Roses*, Head of Zeus, 2019: ISBN 9781789544725 P 527

Blackstone, William, *Commentaries on the law of England, Vol 4*, P 319-24

Borman, Tracy, *The Private Lives of the Tudors*, Hodder & Stoughton, 2016: ISBN 9781444782899

Bucholz, Robert, *Early Modern England 1485-1714: A Narrative History, 2nd Edition*: Chapter Five

Clegg, C S, *Press Censorship in Elizabethan England*, Cambridge University Press, 1997: ISBN 9780521545860

Crawford, Anne, *Letters of the Queens of England 1100-1547*, Sutton Publishing, 1994: ISBN 0750916060

Curtler, W, 2005 ebook *A Short History of English Agriculture* https://www.gutenberg.org/files/16594/16594-8.txt

Duffy, Eamon, *Saints, Sacrilege and Sedition: Religion and Conflict in the Tudor Reformations*, London, Bloomsbury, 2012

Durston, Greg, *Jacks, Knaves & Vagabonds*, 2020, Waterside Press

Elgin, Kathy, *Crime and Punishment (Shakesepeare's World)* (sic), Cherrytree Books, 2008: ISBN: 9781842345399

Emerson, Kathy Lynn, *A Who's Who of Tudor Women* (Kindle Edition)

Farrar, James Anson, *Crimes and Punishments*, Chatto & Windus, 1880

Foxe, John, *Book of Martyrs*

Froude, James A, *The Reign of Queen Mary*

Goodchild, S Tewkesbury, *Eclipse of the House of Lancaster 1471*, Pen & Sword, 2014, ISBN 9781844151905 P63/4

Guy, John, *Thomas More; A very brief history*, SPCK Publishing, 2017, Unabridged edition: ISBN 978-0281077380

Hall, A C, 'Tudor England 1485-1603', *Crime in Its Relations to Social Progress*, New York, Chichester, West Sussex, Columbia Uni Press, 1902

Hayward, Maria, Richa Apparel, *Clothing and the Law in Henry VIII's England*, Routledge, 2016

Hester, Marianne, *Lewd women and wicked witches : a study of the dynamics of male domination*, Routledge, 1992: ISBN 0415070716

Harmon, Thomas, *A Caveat or Warning for Common Cursetors*, 1566

Innes, Arthur, *England Under the Tudors*

Kesselring, K J, *Mercy and Authority in the Tudor State*, Cambridge Studies in Early Modern British History, 2003: ISBN 9780521819480

Kors, Alan Charles, Peters, Edward, *Witchcraft in Europe, 400-1700: a documentary history*, University of Pennsylvania Press, 2001: ISBN 0812217519

Licence, Amy, *Cecily Neville: Mother of Kings*

MacCulloch & Fletcher, *Tudor Rebellions*, Routledge, 2020: ISBN 9780367345525 P 22

MacFarlane, Alan, *Witchcraft in Tudor and Stuart England*, Routledge, 1971: ISBN 9780415196123

Mantel, Hilary, *Mantel Pieces*, Fourth Estate, 2020: ISBN 9780008429973

Matusiak, John, *The History of the Tudors in 100 Objects*, History Press, 2016: ISBN 9780750991254

Mchangama, Jacob, *Free Speech: A Global History from Socrates to Social Media*, Basic Books UK, 2022

Mortimer, Ian, *The Time Traveller's Guide to Elizabethan England*, Vintage 2021: ISBN 978-0-099-54207-0

Moore, John, *The Tudor Murder Files*, Pen & Sword, 2016: ISBN 9781473857032 pp71-79

Morris, Tom, *The Alchemists: Thomas Charnock*, Smashwords, 2012

O'Day, Rosemary, *The Tudor Age*, Routledge, 2010: ISBN 9780415445658 P 2

Penn, Thomas, *Winter King*, Penguin, 2012: ISBN 9780141040530 P 21

Pierrepoint, Albert, *Executioner Pierrepoint: And Autobiography*, Eric Dobby Publishing, 2005: ISBN 9781858820613

Select Bibliography

Pound, John, *Poverty and Vagrancy in Tudor England*, Longman, 1978: ISBN 0582314054

Pratchett, Terry, *The Truth*, Corgi, 2013: ISBN 9780552167635

Ross, Charles, *Edward IV*, Yale University Press, 1997: ISBN 0300073720 P 168

Reilly, S A, *Our Legal Heritage: the first thousand years 600-1600, 2nd edition*, 1999, Ch 7

Ridley, Jasper, *A Brief History of the Tudor Age*, Robinson, 2002: ISBN 9781841194714 P79

Ridley, Jasper, *Elizabeth I*, Constable, 1987: ISBN 009466370 P 210

Ryrie, Alec, *The Sorcerer's Tale,* Oxford University Press, 2008: ISBN 9780199229963

Salgado, Gamini, *The Elizabethan Underworld*, Folio Society, 2006

Sellar, W, *1066 and All That*, Methuen, 1998: ISBN 9780413772701

Sharpe J A, *Crime in Early Modern England 1550-1750*, Longman, New York

Sharpe, J A, *Witchcraft in Early Modern England: 2nd edition*, Routledge, 2020: ISBN 9780429300318

Starkey, David, *Henry, Virtuous Prince*, Harper Perennial, 2009

Starkey, David, *Elizabeth*, Vintage, 2001: ISBN 0099286572 P72/3

Thornton, T & Carlton, K, *The Gentleman's Mistress*, Manchester University Press, 2019: ISBN 9781526114068 Ch 3

Weir, Alison, *Lady in the Tower*, Jonathan Cape, 2009: ISBN: 9780224063197

Weir, Alison, *Elizabeth of York: The First Tudor Queen*, Jonathan Cape

Endnotes

Introduction

1. Sellar, W, 1066 and All That, Methuen, 1998
2. Hall, AC, Tudor England 1485-1603, Crime in Its Relations to Social Progress, New York Chichester, West Sussex, Columbia Uni Press, 1902, pp195-226
3. Hall, AC, Tudor England 1485-1603
4. Hair, P E H, Homicide, infanticide and child assault in late Tudor Middlesex, Local Popul Stud. 1972, 9: 43-6

Justice from the Romans to the Tudors

1. Monty Python What have the romans ever done for us (Nl subs) – YouTube (https://www.youtube.com/watch?v=2ozEZxOsanY)
2. Roman law | Influence, Importance, Principles, & Facts | Britannica (https://www.britannica.com/topic/Roman-law)
3. Appendix 2: Inscriptions of Roman London, British History Online (www.british-history.ac.uk/rchme/london/vol3/pp170-178)
4. Fordham Law Review Volume 29 Issue 3 Article 2 1961 The Roman Contribution to the Common Law Edward D. Re
5. Merrill, Kelse Bright, GECNAWAN THOU GEWEORTH- TO KNOW YOUR WORTH: EXAMINING VARIATIONS OF WERGILD IN ANGLO-SAXON ENGLAND: 600 C.E.-850 C.E. (2019). Open Access Master's Theses. Paper 1725. https://digitalcommons.uri.edu/theses/1725
6. UKEssays. (November 2018). The Law Code of King Alfred the Great. Retrieved from https://www.ukessays.com/essays/history/the-law-code-of-king-alfred.php?vref=1
7. Fordham
8. Ibid
9. Ibid
10. Vincent, Nicholas, A Brief History of Britain: Birth of a Nation Constable & Robinson: 2011, p186

11. Magna Carta, Definition, History, Summary, Dates, Rights, Significance, & Facts, Britannica, https://www.britannica.com/topic/Magna-Carta
12. Reilly, S A, Our Legal Heritage: the first thousand years 600-1600, 2nd edition, 1999, Ch 7
13. Ibid

The Role of Superstition in the Justice System

1. ABOUT EDMUND ‹ SECRET SUFFOLK http://secretsuffolk.com/about-edmund/
2. Devine, Pamela, Beliefs and Superstitions: Medieval Graffiti
3. Blackstone, William: Commentaries on the law of England. Vol 4, Ch 8
4. Ibid
5. Rosedale, Monastic Matrix (st-andrews.ac.uk) https://arts.st-andrews.ac.uk/monasticmatrix/monasticon/rosedale
6. Revealed: How Hitler's defeat really was down to the stars, Daily Mail Online https://www.dailymail.co.uk/news/article-528251/Revealed-How-Hitlers-defeat-really-stars.html
7. Blackstone, William, Commentaries on the law of England, Vol 4, Ch 27

The Power of the Press

1. Pratchett, Terry, The Truth, Corgi, 2013
2. Da Costa, Alexandra, A Hunger for News: Pamphlets and Broadsheets
3. The Will of Henry VII, https://henrytudorsociety.com/the-will-of-henry-vii/
4. Ibid
5. Ibid
6. Ibid
7. Clegg, C S, Press Censorship in Elizabethan England, CUP, 1997, p66
8. Raven, James, The Business of Books: Booksellers and the English Book Trade 1450-1850, Yale UP, 2007, p62
9. Jacob Mchangama: Free Speech: A Global History from Socrates to Social Media: Basic Books UK, 2022
10. Ibid
11. Nichols, Chronicle of Queen Jane, Camden Soc., 1850, p33
12. Loades, D. M., The Press Under the Early Tudors: A Study in Censorship and Sedition: Transactions of the Cambridge Bibliographical Society 4, no. 1, 1964, pp29-50
13. Borman, Tracy, The Private Lives of the Tudors, Hodder & Stoughton, 2016 P258-260

14. The Press Under the Early Tudors: A Study in Censorship and Sedition: Transactions of the Cambridge Bibliographical Society 4, no. 1, 1964, pp29-50
15. Ibid
16. Ridley, Jasper, Elizabeth I, Constable, 1987

Prisons in England

1. Winter, Christine, Prisons and Punishments in Late Medieval London: PhD Thesis, Royal Holloway, University of London, 2012
2. Ibid
3. Mortimer, Ian, The Time Traveller's Guide to Elizabethan England, 2021, Vintage
4. Mortimer, Ian, p304
5. Prisons (tudorplace.com.ar)
6. Mortimer, Ian, p307
7. Griffiths, Paul, Contesting London Bridewell, 1576–1580, Journal of British Studies 42, no. 3, 2003, pp283–315
8. Ibid
9. Mortimer, p307
10. Griffiths, Paul
11. Roberts, Leonard A, Bridewell, The World's First Attempt at Prisoner Rehabilitation Through Education', Journal of Correctional Education 35, no 3, 1984, pp83–85
12. Contesting London Bridewell, 1576–1580, Journal of British Studies 42, no. 3, 2003, pp283–315

Population

1. Blanchard, Ian, Population Change, Enclosure and the Early Tudor Economy, 1970 Econ. Hist. Rev. Vol 23, No 3, pp 427-445
2. Ibid
3. Tudor Population Figures & Facts - Key Information (englishhistory.net)
4. Truman, C N, Henry VII and the Economy, www.historylearningsite.co.uk
5. Ibid
6. Cornwall, Julian: English Population in the early 16th century, 1970, Econ. Hist. Rev. Vol 23, No 1, pp 32-44
7. Ibid
8. The Battle of Towton (historic-uk.com)

9. Penn, Thomas, Winter King, Penguin, 2012
10. Truman C N, Henry VII and Extraordinary Revenue www.historylearningsite.co.uk

Policing in Tudor England

1. Penn, Thomas, p275, 329
2. Courts & Justice in Tudor England (agecrofthall.org)
3. Blackstone, William, Ch 13
4. Courts & Justice in Tudor England (agecrofthall.org)
5. Keaton, YouTube https://www.youtube.com/watch?v=ZZnuuov9vis
6. C N Truman, Henry VII And JP's, historylearningsite.co.uk
7. Gregory, Candace, Sixteenth-Century Justices of the Peace: Tudor Despotism on the County Level, http://people.loyno.edu/~history/journal/1990-1/gregory.htm
8. Hamil, Frederick Coyne, Presentment of Englishry and the Murder Fine, Speculum 12, no. 3 (1937): 285–98. https://doi.org/10.2307/2848624.
9. Jacks, Knaves and Vagabonds: Crime, Law, and Order in Tudor England (Crime History Series): 2020: Ch 4
10. Ibid
11. Ibid
12. 1360, 34 Edward 3 c.1: Justices of the Peace, The Statutes Project
13. Artificers, statute of Encyclopedia.com

Punishments

1. Masschaele, James, The Public Space of the Marketplace in Medieval England, Speculum 77, no. 2 (2002): 383–421
2. Ibid
3. Ibid
4. Ibid
5. A Grim And Gruesome History Of Public Shaming In London: Part 1, Londonist, https://londonist.com/2015/12/publicshaming1?ref=related_links
6. Ibid
7. Ibid
8. Ibid
9. Hanged by the neck until dead. The process of judicial hanging (capitalpunishmentuk.org)
10. Starkey, David, Six Wives: The Queens of Henry VIII, Chatto & Windus, 2003, p561

11. Ibid, p566
12. Letter from Thomas Cranmer to King Henry VIII, 3 May 1536, on Anne Boleyn's Arrest (luminarium.org)
13. Chilling find shows how Henry VIII planned every detail of Boleyn beheading Monarchy, The Guardian
14. Weir, Alison: Lady in the Tower, Jonathan Cape, 2009, p252
15. Ibid, p255
16. http://garethrussellcidevant.blogspot.com/2010/05/may-18th-1536-threshold-of-eternity.html
17. Weir, Alison, p261
18. Ives, Eric, The Life and Death of Anne Boleyn, Blackwell, 2004, p358
19. Weir, Alison, p271
20. https://guillotine.dk/pages/30sek.html
21. https://www.livescience.com/39219-can-severed-head-live.html
22. https://www.news18.com/news/buzz/research-shows-brain-continues-to-function-for-few-moments-even-after-decapitation-4417097.html
23. Richard Roose, The History Jar
24. Stacy, William R, Richard Roose and the Use of Parliamentary Attainder in the Reign of Henry VIII, The Historical Journal 29, no. 1 (1986), 1–15, http://www.jstor.org/stable/2639253.
25. Moore, J, The Tudor Murder Files, Pen & Sword, 2016, p53
26. Stacy, William R, Richard Roose and the Use of Parliamentary Attainder in the Reign of Henry VIII, The Historical Journal 29, no.1 (1986), pp1–15, http://www.jstor.org/stable/2639253.
27. Sadowski Pietro, Mosaic: An Interdisciplinary Critical Journal, 53/3, Sep 2020, pp139-154
28. https://www.ranker.com/list/what-being-boiled-is-like/laura-allan
29. A Grim and Gruesome History Of Public Shaming In London, Part 2, Londonist
30. Ridley, Jasper, A Brief History of the Tudor Age, Robinson, 2002, p79
31. Daybell, James, Gender, Obedience, and Authority in Sixteenth-Century Women's Letters, The Sixteenth Century Journal 41, no. 1 (2010), pp49–67, http://www.jstor.org/stable/27867637.
32. Blackstone, William, Ch 6
33. The Witches of Lynn, Norfolk Record Office (norfolkrecordofficeblog.org)
34. Mortimer, pp305-6
35. Hanged by the neck until dead, The process of judicial hanging (capitalpunishmentuk.org)
36. Pierrepoint, Albert, Executioner Pierrepoint: An Autobiography, Eric Dobby Publishing, 2005

37. Was Henry VIII the Worst Monarch of All Time?
38. Kesselring, K J, PhD Thesis: To Pardon and To Punish: Mercy and Authority in Tudor England: Queen's University Ontario, 2000
39. The Execution Sites of London, Historic UK (historic-uk.com)
40. Tarlow S., Battell Lowman E. (2018) Hanging in Chains: Harnessing the Power of the Criminal Corpse, Palgrave Historical Studies in the Criminal Corpse and its Afterlife, Palgrave Macmillan, https://doi.org/10.1007/978-3-319-77908-9_6
41. De la Croix, Jersey, Ses Antiquités, Ses Institutions, Son Histoire, vol. iii. pp342, 343
42. Bygone Punishments, Project Gutenberg, 2009
43. Ibid
44. Wright, Jonathan, The World's Worst Worm: Conscience and Conformity during the English Reformation, The Sixteenth Century Journal 30, no. 1 (1999), pp113–33, https://doi.org/10.2307/2544902.
45. Mortimer, p236
46. Henry VIII and the Carthusian Monks, The Tudor Society
47. Blackstone, William, Commentaries on the law of England, vol 4, pp319-24
48. LaRocca, John J, Time, Death, and the Next Generation: The Early Elizabethan Recusancy Policy, 1558-1574, Albion: A Quarterly Journal Concerned with British Studies 14, no. 2 (1982), pp103–17 https://doi.org/10.2307/4049186.
49. Peine forte et dure, Wikipedia
50. Ibid
51. Andrews, William, p243
52. Londonist Part 2
53. Mortimer, Ian, p309
54. Barrett & Harrison, Crime and Punishment in England: A Source book, Routledge, 1st edition, 3 Aug 2005, Ch 2
55. Durston, Greg, Ch 13
56. Ibid
57. Goodchild, S, Tewkesbury: Eclispse of the House of Lancaster 1471, Pen & Sword, 2014
58. Durston, Greg, Ch 13
59. Sharpe, J, A Fiery & Furious People, Random House, 2016, p238
60. Mortimer, Ian, pp308-10
61. Mortimer, Ian, p311
62. Barrett & Harrison Ch 2
63. Ibid

64. Mortimer, Ian, pp307-9
65. Elgin, Kathy, Crime and Punishment (Shakespeare's World), Cherrytree Books, 2008
66. Mortimer, Ian, pp307-9

PART TWO: CRIMES AND CASES

Alchemy

1. Morris, Tom: The Alchemists: Thomas Charnock: Smashwords 2012
2. Ryrie, Alec: The Sorcerer's Tale: Oxford University Press: 2008: ISBN: 9780199229963

Animal Theft

1. Jacks, Knaves and Vagabonds:Crime, Law, and Order in Tudor England (Crime History Series): 2020: Ch 19
2. Durston, Greg, Ch 19
3. Ibid
4. Crime In Tudor and Stuart Epsom and Ewell, Epsom & Ewell History Explorer (eehe.org.uk)
5. Curtler, W, A Short History of English Agriculture, 2005,
6. Wortley Axe, J, The Horse - Its Treatment In Health And Disease, Hewlett Press, 2008
7. The Fell Pony Museum, Horses and Cattle in Tudor Times (archive.org) Safety in the Wilderness
8. Durston

Begging

1. Clark, Elaine, Institutional and Legal Responses to Begging in Medieval England, Social Science History 26, no. 3 (2002) pp447–73, http://www.jstor.org/stable/40267786.
2. Clark, Elaine
3. Ibid
4. Burrows, Edith, Poor relief in Tudor England (1966), Honors Theses, https://scholarship.richmond.edu/honors-theses/1075
5. Rushton, N, Monastic charitable provision in Tudor England: quantifying and qualifying poor relief in the early sixteenth century
6. Burrows, Edith
7. Rushton, N

8. Ibid
9. Burrows, Edith
10. Pound, John, Poverty and Vagrancy in Tudor England, Longman, 1978, p4
11. Ibid
12. Ibid, p39
13. Ibid, p103
14. Daly, Christopher Thomas, Basilisks of the Commonwealth: Vagrants and Vagrancy in England, 1485-1553, (1986), Dissertations, Theses, and Masters Projects, Paper 1539625366, https://dx.doi.org/doi:10.21220/s2-y42p-8r81
15. Inflation calculator 1949-2021, Bank of England
16. Daly, Christopher

Blackmail

1. Crawford, Anne: Letters of the Queens of England 1100-1547: Sutton Publishing: 1994: ISBN 0750916060 P 206
2. Borman, Tracy, p189
3. Tudor Hackney Welcome Page (nationalarchives.gov.uk)
4. Ibid
5. Borman, Tracy, p2
6. Elizabeth I's favourite extorted by Daniells of Hackney, 1599, horridhackney.com
7. Ibid

Blasphemy

1. Atheism in Tudor England (spartacus-educational.com) https://spartacus-educational.com/Atheism.htm
2. Lowe, Ben, War and the Commonwealth in Mid-Tudor England, The Sixteenth Century Journal 21, no. 2 (1990) pp171–92, https://doi.org/10.2307/2541048.
3. Mantel, Hilary, Mantel Pieces, HarperCollins, 2020
4. Atheism in Tudor England, spartacus-educational.com
5. Accusations against Christopher Marlowe by Richard Baines and others, The British Library,bl.uk
6. The Marlowe-Shakespeare Connection, Marlowe and the Privy Council, http://marlowe-shakespeare.blogspot.com/2011/05/marlowe-and-privy-council.html
7. The Mysterious Death of Christopher Marlowe, https://www.mentalfloss.com/article/80556/mysterious-death-christopher-marlowe
8. Ibid

Coney-Catching

1. Barrett & Harrison, Crime and Punishment in England: A Source book, Routledge, 1st edition, (3 Aug 2005, Ch 2
2. Ibid

Defamation

1. A short history of slutshaming, after a woman told my employers I was a SLAG (inews.co.uk)
2. Horys, strumppettes and fyssenagges: Defamation in the Courts of Later Medieval England – Legal History Miscellany https://legalhistorymiscellany.com/2021/08/23/horys-strumppettes-and-fyssenagges-defamation-in-the-courts-of-later-medieval-england/
3. Ibid
4. Ibid
5. Lewis, Jenny, https://lichfieldbawdycourts.wordpress.com/2020/01/21/sabbath-breaking-in-swynnerton/

Embezzlement

1. Smuggling, Fraud and Embezzlement: Corruption in the 16th Century Customs House, by James Wilkes, PublisHistory Blog, wordpress.com
2. Nef, John U, Richard Carmarden's 'A Caveat for the Quene' (1570), Journal of Political Economy 41, no. 1 (1933), pp33–41, http://www.jstor.org/stable/1822872.
3. Smuggling, Fraud and Embezzlement: Corruption in the 16th Century Customs House
4. Nef, John U
5. Smuggling, Fraud and Embezzlement: Corruption in the 16th Century Customs House

Fraud

1. Ryrie, Alec: The Sorcerer's Tale: Oxford University Press: 2008: ISBN: 9780199229963

Gangs

1. Bennett, H S, The Pastons and their England: Cambridge University Press, 1922, p116, 184

2. McMullan, John L, Criminal Organization in Sixteenth and Seventeenth Century London, Social Problems 29, no. 3 (1982), pp311–23. https://doi.org/10.2307/800162.
3. Salgado, Gamini: The Elizabethan Underworld, Folio Society, 2006, Ch 1
4. McMullen, John L
5. Ibid
6. Ibid
7. Ibid
8. Ibid

Heresy

1. Tudor Heretics (spartacus-educational.com)
2. Ibid
3. Kennedy, Michael, Portrait of Elgar, 2nd edn, p15
4. The Act of Settlement, The Royal Family https://www.royal.uk/act-settlement-0#:~:text=The%20Act%20applies%20to%20those,sixteen%20Realms%20in%20March%202015).
5. Defender of the Faith - Medieval manuscripts blog https://blogs.bl.uk/digitisedmanuscripts/2020/
6. https://tudortimes.co.uk/religion/cromwell-and-the-english-bible/the-great-bible
7. Katharine/Catherine/Katherine Parr - Facts & Information, englishhistory.net
8. To What Extent Was England Dominated By Spanish Interests During The Reign Of Mary? History Resource, https://www.tutorhunt.com/resource/5033/
9. The Illnesses and Death of Queen Mary I – The Freelance History Writer, https://thefreelancehistorywriter.com
10. Tudor Heretics, spartacus-educational.com
11. Rounding, Virginia, The Burning Time: Henry VIII, Bloody Mary, and the Protestant Martyrs of London, 2017, p287.
12. Tudor Heretics
13. George van Parris, https://spartacus-educational.com/George_van_Parris.htm
14. Mrs Joyce Lewes, Fox's Book of Martyrs, https://www.biblestudytools.com/history/foxs-book-of-martyrs/mrs-joyce-lewes.html

Insurrection

1. Ross, Charles, Edward IV, Yale University Press, 1997
2. Penn, Thomas
3. Williams, C H, The Rebellion of Humphrey Stafford in 1486, The English Historical Review, Apr 1928, Vol. 43, No. 170, pp181-189
4. O'Day, Rosemary, The Tudor Age, Routledge, 2010, p2
5. Williams, C H
6. Ibid
7. Bicheno, Hugh
8. Williams, C H

Infanticide

1. A-INFANT.PDF, http://www.alanmacfarlane.com/savage/A-INFANT.PDF
2. Billingham, J E, Piteous Performances: Representations and Context of Infanticide in Tudor and Stuart Literature of Stage and Street, PhD Thesis, University College, London, 2015
3. MacMillan, K, True Stories of Crime in Tudor and Stuart England, Routledge, 1st edition, 2 April 2015, Ch 27
4. Sharpe, J.A., Domestic Homicide in Early Modern England, Historical Journal 24 (1981), pp29-48
5. Hair, P E H, Homicide, infanticide and child assault in late Tudor Middlesex, Local Popul Stud, 1972, pp43-46
6. Sharpe, J
7. Hair, P E H
8. Sharpe, J
9. Sharpe, J

Infidelity

1. Partial defences to murder: loss of control and diminished responsibility; and infanticide: Implementation of Sections 52, and 54 to 57 of the Coroners and Justice Act 2009
2. The Short History of the Infidelity Defence in England, Legal History Miscellany
3. Legitimate rape – a medieval medical concept, History of science, The Guardian https://legalhistorymiscellany.com/2016/08/08/infidelity-defence/
4. Marriage in Tudor Times, by Sarah Bryson, The Tudor Society
5. The Short History of the Infidelity Defence in England, Legal History Miscellany

6. Thornton, T & Carlton, K, The Gentleman's Mistress, 2019, Manchester University Press
7. Bennett, H S, The Pastons and their England, Cambridge University Press, 1922
8. Thornton, T & Carlton, K
9. Ibid

Juvenile Crime

1. Bellamy, J, Strange Inhuman Deaths, p12
2. Durston, Greg
3. Teenagers in Tudor times, The History Press, extracted from Tudor Tales by Dave Tonge
4. Pound J, p99

Kidnapping and Abduction

1. TKR 12-9 (gla.ac.uk) Osborne, Emma; Review of Dunn, Caroline. Stolen Women in Medieval England
2. Starkey, David, Elizabeth, Vintage, 2001, pp72-73
3. 5 October 1549 - Protector Somerset issues a proclamation, The Tudor Society, https://www.tudorsociety.com

Larceny

1. Swinden, Cara, Crime and the common law in England, 1580-1640, 1992, Honors Theses, Paper 769.
2. https://www.bl.uk/collection-items/satire-on-watchmen-and-playhouses-in-dekkers-the-gulls-horn-book
3. Swinden, Cara
4. Kesselring, K J, Mercy and Authority in the Tudor State, Cambridge Studies in Early Modern British History, 2003
5. Swinden, Cara

Murder

1. Seeing Is Believing: The CSI Effect Among Jurors in Malicious Wounding Cases, CORE Reader
2. Galen, father of systematic medicine. An essay on the evolution of modern medicine and cardiology, PubMed, nih.gov
3. ANDREAS VESALIUS (1514-1564), stanford.edu

4. Durston, Greg
5. Kesselring, K J
6. Calderwood, W, The Elizabethan Protestant Press; publishing of Protestant literature in England, excepting Bibles and Liturgies 1558-1603, Doctoral thesis, University of London, 1977
7. Kesselring, K J
8. Blackstone, William
9. http://www.bbc.co.uk/news/mobile/magazine-13762313
10. Green, Thomas A, The Jury and the English Law of Homicide, 1200-1600, Mich. L. Rev. 74, 1976, pp413-499.
11. Moore, J, The Tudor Murder Files, Pen & Sword, 2016
12. Green, Thomas A
13. Langbein, John H, Historical Foundations of the Law of Evidence: A View from the Ryder Sources
14. https://www.macmillanlearning.co.uk/resources/pdfs/rsc-shakespeare/arden-of-faversham.pdf
15. Cust, Lionel, Arden of Feversham, Kent Archeological Society, 2017, https://www.kentarchaeology.org.uk
16. http://www.executedtoday.com/tag/alice-arden/
17. Cust, Lionel
18. Divorce & Remarriage in the Church Ch.11: Promises, Promises, http://www.instonebrewer.com/DivorceRemarriage/DRC/Summ-11.htm
19. Cust, Lionel
20. Weir, Alison, Elizabeth of York: The First Tudor Queen, Jonathan Cape, 2013
21. Bicheno, Hugh, pp603-606
22. Weir, Alison, p91
23. Ibid, p95
24. Penn, Thomas, pp34-9
25. https://www.britannica.com/event/Treaty-of-Medina-del-Campo
26. Penn, Thomas, pp42-3
27. The Downfall of Margaret Pole, Countess of Salisbury, by Alexander Taylor - The Tudor Society https://www.tudorsociety.com/the-downfall-of-margaret-pole-countess-of-salisbury-by-alexander-taylor/

Nuisance

1. Janet Loengard, The Assize of Nuisance: Origins of An Action at Common Law, The Cambridge Law Journal 37, no. 1 (1978), pp144–66, http://www.jstor.org/stable/4506065.

2. Elizabethan 'madmen' Part II: Nightmare neighbours and Tudor ASBOs, https://manyheadedmonster.com/2014/04/19/elizabethan-madmen-part-ii-nightmare-neighbours-and-tudor-asbos/

Organised Crime

1. Ryrie, Alec
2. Ibid
3. Sharpe J A
4. A Manifest Detection of Diceplay (jducoeur.org) http://jducoeur.org/game-hist/diceplay.html
5. Ryrie, Alec
6. Ibid
7. Ibid, p71
8. A Manifest Detection of Diceplay

Poaching

1. Unlawful Activity associated with Parks, https://www.kentarchaeology.org.uk/17/01/2013/06/245.pdf
2. Manning, Roger B, Patterns of Violence in Early Tudor Enclosure Riots, Albion: A Quarterly Journal Concerned with British Studies 6, no. 2 (1974), pp120–33. https://doi.org/10.2307/4048139.
3. Swinden, Cara

Poison

1. ExecutedToday.com, 1542: Margaret Davy, poisoner, https://legalresearch.blogs.bris.ac.uk/2021/05/to-marry-and-to-burn-punishing-domestic-treachery-in-medieval-england/
2. Once upon a time in history: Killing your husband in Tudor England, http://cupboardworld.blogspot.com/2012/08/killing-your-husband-in-tudor-england.html
3. Bellamy, J, Strange Inhuman Deaths, pp56-7
4. Gorrell, Robert Mark, John Payne Collier and the Murder of Iohn Brewen, Modern Language Notes 57, no. 6 (1942), pp441–44, https://doi.org/10.2307/2910347.
5. Marriage, Murder and the Streets of London: The Most Wicked Secret Murthering of John Brewen, Literary London Reading Group, https://literarylondonrg.wordpress.com/2016/04/03/marriage-murder-and-the-streets-of-london-the-most-wicked-secret-murthering-of-john-brewen/

Prostitution

1. Emerson, Kathy Lynn, A Who's Who of Tudor Women
2. Ungerer, Gustav, Prostitution in Late Elizabethan London: The Case of Mary Newborough, Medieval & Renaissance Drama in England 15 (2003), pp138–223, http://www.jstor.org/stable/24322659.
3. Ibid

Quarrels

1. Epsom & Ewell History Explorer
2. Pearson, Samuel ,Thou spekyst tresson, Popular Politics and Seditious Speech in the Henrician Reformation: Newcastle University Postgraduate Forum E-Journal, Edition 12, 2015
3. Ibid
4. Ibid

Recusancy

1. Blackstone, William
2. LaRocca, John
3. Ibid
4. Ibid
5. The Rising of the North of 1569 and the enduring geographical fault lines in English life, British Politics and Policy at LSE, https://blogs.lse.ac.uk/politicsandpolicy/the-rising-of-the-north-of-1569/
6. Lane, Michael David, Of Whims and Fancies: A Study of English Recusants under Elizabeth, 1570-1595, (2015). LSU Master's Theses, 4240, https://digitalcommons.lsu.edu/gradschool_theses/4240
7. BBC North, Yorkshire/Faith/The Pearl of York https://www.bbc.co.uk/northyorkshire
8. Margaret Clitherow: History of York, http://www.historyofyork.org.uk/themes/tudor-stuart/margaret-clitherow
9. Ibid

Riots

1. Fairlie, Simon, A Short History of Enclosure in Britain, The Land Magazine, https://www.thelandmagazine.org.uk/articles/short-history-enclosure-britain
2. Manning, R B, Patterns of Violence in Early Tudor Enclosure Riots, Albion, A Quarterly Journal Concerned with British Studies, 1972, 6(2), pp120–133

3. Ibid
4. Ibid
5. Ibid

Scolding

1. Sharpe, J, A Fiery & Furious People, Random House, 2016, p233
2. Ibid, p237
3. Ibid, pp234-5

Sedition

1. Manning Roger B,The Origins of the Doctrine of Sedition, Albion: A Quarterly Journal Concerned with British Studies Vol. 12, No. 2 (Summer, 1980), pp99-121
2. Ibid
3. Duffy, Eamon, Saints, Sacrilege and Sedition: Religion and Conflict in the Tudor Reformations, London, Bloomsbury, 2012 ,p33
4. https://www.nationalarchives.gov.uk/pathways/citizenship/citizen_subject/docs/act_rumours.htm

Sexual Offences

1. Hair, P E H
2. Spielmann, Richard M, The Beginning of Clerical Marriage In the English Reformation: The Reigns of Edward and Mary, Anglican and Episcopal History 56, no. 3 (1987), pp251–63, http://www.jstor.org/stable/42610201.
3. Durston, Greg
4. Legitimate rape – a medieval medical concept, https://www.theguardian.com/science/the-h-word/2012/aug/20/legitimate-rape-medieval-medical-concept
5. Durston, Greg
6. Ibid
7. Case6_DHC-QSB-Easter1598.pdf (exeter.ac.uk) https://humanities-research.exeter.ac.uk/womenswork/courtdepositions/downloads/Case6_DHC-QSB-Easter1598.pdf
8. Durston, Greg
9. McCarthy, K J, The Prosecution of Homosexuality in England and Ireland 1553-1991, https://www.academia.edu/

10. Lesbianism and the criminal law of England and Wales, OpenLearn, Open University https://www.open.edu/openlearn/society-politics-law/law/lesbianism-and-the-criminal-law-england-and-wales
11. Durston, Greg
12. Ibid
13. Ibid
14. Ibid
15. Ibid
16. Walter Hungerford and the Buggery Act: LGBTQ+ History and Punishment at The Tower of London, https://blog.hrp.org.uk/curators/walter-hungerford-and-the-buggery-act-lgbtq-history-and-punishment-at-the-tower-of-london/
17. Samaha, Joel B, Hanging for Felony: The Rule of Law in Elizabethan Colchester, The Historical Journal 21, no. 4 (1978), pp763–82. http://www.jstor.org/stable/2638968.

Spying

1. Isabella Hoppringle: Biography, on Undiscovered Scotland https://www.undiscoveredscotland.co.uk/usbiography/h/isabellahoppringle.html
2. Parry, William (d.1585), of London, History of Parliament Online http://www.historyofparliamentonline.org/volume/1558-1603/member/
3. Adams, Robyn, The Service I Am Here For: William Herle in the Marshalsea Prison, 1571, Huntingdon Library Quarterly 72, 2009, No 2, pp217-38
4. Gill, M P, William Herle and the English Secret Service, Thesis: Victoria University of Wellington, 2010
5. Gill, M P
6. Adams, Robyn

Sumptuary Laws

1. Sumptuary Laws, https://theodora.com/encyclopedia/s2/sumptuary_laws.html
2. Ingram, John Kells, Sumptuary Laws, In Chisholm, Hugh (ed.). Encyclopædia Britannica. Vol. 26 (11th ed.), Cambridge University Press, 1911, pp83–85.
3. Kirtio, Leah, The inordinate excess in apparel, Sumptuary Legislation in Tudor England https://www.readcube.com/articles/10.29173%2Fcons16283

4. Kirtio, Leah
5. https://www.nga.gov/collection/art-object-page.72.html
6. Hayward, Maria, Richa Apparel; Clothing and the Law in Henry VIII's England, Routledge,2016
7. Baldwin, Frances, Sumptuary legislation and personal regulation in England, John Hopkins University, 1926
8. Lyon, Karen, Sumptuary laws: Rules for dressing in Shakespeare's England, folger.edu
9. Hayward, Maria
10. https://thehistoricalnovel.com/2018/04/10/quotes-in-context-elizabeth-i/
11. Lyon, Karen
12. Ibid
13. Cooper, Charles Henry, Annals of Cambridge, Cambridge University Press, 2010, p346
14. Lyon, Karen

Theft

1. Thieves' cant, Wikipedia
2. Harmon, Thomas, A Caveat or Warning for Common Cursetors, 1566, https://archive.org/details/acaveatorwarnin00harmgoog

Treason

1. Bellamy, John, The Tudor Law of Treason, 1979, Routledge Revivals Ch 1
2. Ibid
3. Ibid
4. Edward Arden and the earl of Leicester, bham.ac.uk
5. Penn, Thomas, pp23-4
6. Starkey, David Henry, Virtuous Prince, Harper Perennial, 2009, p150
7. Ibid
8. Penn, Thomas, pp30-1
9. Starkey, David, p114
10. Edmund de la Pole, Earl of Suffolk (1472?-1513), http://www.luminarium.org/encyclopedia/edmunddelapole.htm
11. Starkey, David, p150-1
12. Ibid, p154
13. That Intention Is Judge of Our Actions - The Essays of Michel de Montaigne, https://hyperessays.net/essays/intent-is-the-arbiter-of-our-actions/

14. England under the Tudors: Richard de la Pole (d.1525), http://www.luminarium.org/encyclopedia/richarddelapole.htm
15. Shore, Miles F, Henry VIII and the Crisis of Generativity, The Journal of Interdisciplinary History 2, no. 4 (1972), pp359–90

Uprisings

1. Bush, Michael, Tax Reform and Rebellion in Early Tudor England, History 76, no. 248 (1991), pp379–400, http://www.jstor.org/stable/24421380.
2. Starkey, David, p367
3. Bush, Michael
4. Diarmaid MacCulloch, Anthony Fletcher: Tudor Rebellions, Routledge, 2020
5. Bush, Michael

Vagrancy

1. Pound, John, p30
2. Ibid, p6
3. Ibid
4. Samson, S A, Enclosures, Rebellion, and the Commonwealth Men, 1536-1549
5. Pound, John, p8
6. Osborn, Lewis, The Great Debasement, http://www.e-articles.info/e/a/title/The-Great-Debasement/
7. Larkey, S V, Public Health in Tudor England, American Journal of Public Health, November 1934, Vol 24, No 11
8. Pound, John, pp13-15
9. Ibid, p16
10. Ibid, p22
11. Ibid,
12. Ibid, p23
13. Daly, Christopher Thomas
14. Lawson, Peter, Property Crime and Hard Times in England, 1559-1624, Law and History Review 4, no. 1 (1986), pp95–127, https://doi.org/10.2307/743716.
15. Harmon, Thomas
16. Pound, John, pp39-40
17. Davies, C. S. L., Slavery and Protector Somerset; The Vagrancy Act of 1547, The Economic History Review 19, no. 3 (1966), pp533–49, https://doi.org/10.2307/2593162.

18. No rest for the wicked: Anti-vagrancy laws in Tudor England, 1495-1604, https://roguish.wordpress.com/2017/12/04/no-rest-for-the-wicked-anti-vagrancy-laws-in-tudor-england-1495-1604/
19. How Effective were the Tudors with Poverty, http://www.andallthat.co.uk/uploads/2/3/8/9/2389220/how_effective_were_the_tudors_with_poverty.pdf
20. Burrows, Edith, Poor relief in Tudor England, (1966), Honors Theses, 1075. https://scholarship.richmond.edu/honors-theses/1075

Witchcraft

1. Witchcraft pamphlet: A Rehearsal both Strange and True, 1579, British Library, London, Shelf mark: C.27.a.11.
2. The examination and confession of certaine Wytches at Chensforde, https://engole.info/examination-chensforde/
3. MacFarlane, Alan, Witchcraft in Tudor and Stuart England, Routledge, 1971
4. Ibid
5. Sharpe, J, Witchcraft in Early Modern England, 2nd edition, Routledge, 2020, Ch 3
6. MacFarlane, Alan
7. Ibid
8. The Trial of Agnes Waterhouse – Witchcraft in Essex, 1566, http://www.essexrecordofficeblog.co.uk/the-trial-of-agnes-waterhouse-witchcraft-in-essex-1566/
9. 10 Little Known Witch Trials From History, https://historycollection.com/10-little-known-witch-trials-from-history/4/

Xenophobia

1. Evil May Day: anti-alien riots in 1517, https://www.ourmigrationstory.org.uk/oms/londons-evil-may-day-riots
2. Evil May Day Riots, https://spartacus-educational.com/Evil_May_Day_Riots.htm

Zealots

1. Guy, John: Thomas More; A very brief history, SPCK Publishing, 2017: Unabridged edition, Ch 3
2. Ibid, Ch 4
3. Ibid

Index

Acomb 160
Act: Conjuracions Inchantments, 1563 205
Act of Settlement 96
Act of Succession 216
Act of Supremacy 216
Admiralty Law 52
Aethelbert 4
Aileston, Robert 166
Alexandre, Sébastien 49
Alfred 5
Allyot, Sibyl 109
Alva, Duke of 152
Amicable Grant 193-95
Anabaptists 98-99
Anjou, Duke of 20, 77, 178
Appleby, Sir George 99
Archery Law 124-5
Arden, Alice (nee Mirfyn) 126-31
Arden, Edward 188
Arden, Thomas 126-31
Arnold, John 150
Arthur, Prince of Wales 15, 190
Ashley, Sir William 67
Aske, Robert 49, 200
Askew, Anne 16, 96
Assize, Novel desseisin 6, 136
Assizes, Essex 107
Assizes, Exeter 167
Assizes, Home Circuit 107
Augustus, Emperor 4

Bacon, Francis 72
Bailly, Charles 177
Baines, Ralph, Bishop of Lichfield 100
Baines, Richard 77
Bainham, James 216
Baken, Agnes 82
Bakewell, Derbyshire 157
Bales, Peter 73
Ballads 14-20
Banburgh (Bawburgh), Thomas 82
Barber Surgeons 145
Barnby, Charles 112
Barnes, Robert 215
Bartholomew Fair 93-94
Basse, Ellis 167
Bayfield, Richard 216
Beadles 29
Beamond, John 165
Beaufort, Margaret 111
Beaurieux, Dr 41
Becket, Thomas 7
Bedoe, William 61
Beggars 66-69, 196-203
Beheading 36-41
Bell/Beal, Dr 212
Bellmen 32
Benefit of Clergy 22, 43, 124
Bernard, Richard 206
Bickley, Earth 166-7
Bickley, Richard 166
Bilney, Thomas 215

Index

Black Will 127-31
Blackheath, Battle of 1497 190
Blaybourne 132
Bocher, Joan 95, 98-99
Boiling to Death 41-44
Boleyn, Anne 15, 36-39, 107, 150, 193-95, 204, 214
Bolt, Robert 214
Bosworth, battle of viii, 132
Boughton, Joan 76
Bourchier, Anne 112
Bowker, Agnes 169
Boye, Brian 149
Brackley, Rachel 114
Bracton, Henry de 6
Bradshaw, George 127
Branding 44
Brewen, John 142-5
Brewing 92
Bridewell 22, 146
Broadsheets 14-20
Brown, Elizabeth 109
Brown, James 114
Brown, Thomas 201
Browning, Joane 167
Buckley, John 61
Bulmer, Joan 71
Burning to Death 45-46
Bushnell, George 166
Butler, Lady Eleanor 132
Butler, Thomas, Earl of Ormonde 72
Byland Abbey 201
Byles, Andrew 207
Byrd, Williams 84
Bywater, Nicholas 147

Calle, Richard 112
Canon law 8
Cant Speak (Theft argot) 185

Canute 5
Carmarden, Richard 84
Castiglione, Baptist 19
Caveat for Common Cursitors 185
Cawches, Katherine 97
Cecil, Sir Robert 78
Cecil, William, Lord Burghley 19, 84-85, 98, 136-37, 139, 172
Chancery, Court of 8
Chapuys, Eustace 38, 107, 118
Charles V, Holy Roman Emperor 37, 215
Charnock, Thomas 61
Charterhouse monks 49
Chaundler (Chandler), Margaret 109
Cheke, Sir John 18, 201
Chelmsford 207
Cherry, Henry 166
Chester 152
Cheyne, Sir Thomas 128
Clarence, George, Duke of 132
Clerke, Joan 165
Cleves, Anne of 70, 170
Clink Prison 23
Clitherow/Clitherow, Margaret 153-5
Cloth Industry 197, 211
Clothing legislation 180-84
Cobbler 211
Coke, Sir Edward 74, 94
Coldstream 172
Cole, Thomas 207
Como, Cardinal 174
Constable, Sir Robert 49
Constables, High 31
Constables, Parish 29, 32
Constantine, Emperor 4
Constantine, George 216
Constitutions of Clarendon 7

Conway, Sir Hugh 103
Conway, Sir John 173
Cootes, Helen 146-8
Corday, Charlotte 40
Cordwainer 211
Coroner 31
Cotell, Agnes 141
Counterfeit Crank 186
Court of Alderman 186
Court of Pie-Powder 94
Court, Bishop of London's Commissary 168
Court, King's 27
Courts, Bawdy Courts of Lichfield 83
Courts, Common pleas, 21
Courts, Ecclesiastical 28, 81
Courts, Leet 28
Courts, Manor/Manorial 28, 157
Coverdale Bible 96
Coverdale, Miles 99
Cowper, John 83
Cranmer, Thomas 37, 71, 96, 99
Crighton, Father, Jesuit priest 174
Croke, Sir John 43
Cromwell, Thomas 39, 67, 70, 96, 170
Crowche, William 63
Cuddington, Thomas 63, 149
Culham 105
Culpepper, Thomas 71

Daniell, John 71
Dannett, Goodwife 136-7
Darnley, Lord Henry 153
Daveley, John 82
Davy, Margaret 141
Dawson, George 169
Debasement of coinage 198
Dedham 169

Dekker, Thomas 120
Denman, Henry 63
Dereham, Francis 70-71
Dethrick, Eleanor 146
Devereux, Robert, Earl of Essex 72
Dewbeney, Oliver 84
Dido and Aeneas 77
Dissolution 68
Dogberry 123
Dowle, John 85
Drury, Thomas 77
Ducking Stool 52-53
Dudley, Edmund 27
Dudley, John 118
Dudley, Robert, Earl of Leicester 20, 28, 72, 85, 98, 188
Dyer, Roland 169

Eden, George 147-8
Edward I 32
Edward III 8, 143, 180, 187, 193
Edward IV 26, 102
Edward of Westminster 24
Edward the Confessor 5
Edward VI 17, 49, 89, 96-97, 116-119, 127, 162, 168-69
Egbert 5
Elgar, Edward 96
Elizabeth I ix, 62, 64, 72, 77, 96, 151-53, 162, 168, 181
Elizabeth of York 54, 131
Embracery 30
Emma of Normandy 13
Empson, Richard 27
Enclosures 68, 197
Enclosure Laws 24
Enclosure Riots 156
English, David 147
Engrossing 25

Index

Erasmus 216
Escheators (fraudsters) 138
Essex (witches) 204
Essex, Lady Frances 72, 74
Evans, Richard 138
Evidence in witchcraft trials 206
Evil May Day Riot 1517 211-13
Exchequer 27

Famines 199
Faversham 126-31
Ferdinand of Aragon 132
Field of the Cloth of Gold 215
Fish, Simon 168
Fisher, John 41
Fleet Prison 22, 89
Fletcher, John 106
Flodden 14, 172
Food Riots 199
Forensic science 122-23
Forest Law 140
Fortescue, Sir John 207
Foxe, John 95, 97
Francis I 15
Francis, Elizabeth 207
Freemason, Thomas 109
Freshwater 150
Frizer, Ingram 78
Fulthorp, Margaret 149
Fur (clothing) 181
Fynne, William 207

Gale, George 166
Galen, Claudius 122
Game Code 140
Gardiner, Stephen 18, 214
Garrard, Sir William 176
Gatehouse Prison 74
Gerard, Sir Gilbert 207
Gilbert, Guillemine 97

Gill, George 160
Gill, Margaret 160
Glass making 92
Glaston, Alice 114
Glorious Revolution 96
Glover, John 100
Gongfarmer 36
Goodwyn, Richard 114
Gosling, Richard 32
Gosselin, Helier 97
Grantham, Christine 109
Gray, Cecily 147
Gray, Richard 86
Great Malvern, Worcestershire 200
Greene, John 127
Greene, Robert 79
Guernsey 97
Guide to Grand Juryman, 1630 206
Guls Hornbook 120

Hackney Rectory 73
Hadrian's Wall 3
Hale, John 157
Hales, John 197
Halifax Gibbett 46
Hall, Edward 15, 212-13
Hall, Hugh 188
Hanging 46-48
Hanging in Chains 48-50
Hanging, Drawing and Quartering 50-51
Hare, Hugh, MP 174
Harman, Thomas 185, 202
Harrison, William 47
Hatton, Sir Christopher 176
Hayes, Catherine 46
Hayward, Richard 65
Hempnall, Norfolk 160
Henry I 6
Henry II 6

Henry III 6
Henry IV Pt 2 184
Henry VI 54, 131
Henry VII viii, 2, 26, 68, 96, 102-3, 131, 187
Henry VIII ix, 42, 64, 96-97, 108, 127, 168, 181, 204
Hepburn, James, Earl of Bothwell 116, 153
Herbert, William, Earl of Pembroke 173
Hereford 159
Heretic's Fork 210
Herle, William 176-79
Hext, Edward, MP 196
Hilley, Alice 109
Holbein, Hans 181
Holinshed Chronicles 127
Honorius, Emperor 3
Hooker, John 35
Hopkins, Gerard Manley 155
Hoppringle, Isabella 172
Horses Act 1540 64
Horses, Breed of, Act 1535 64
House, William 97
Howard, Katherine 40, 70
Hubert, Sir Francis 204
Hue and Cry 123
Hungerford, Edward 141-2
Hungerford, Walter 141-42, 170-71
Hunt, Francis 171
Hurt of Sedition 201
Hussey, Elizabeth 170

Ignes, William 142
Infanticide 123
Informing 92
Isabella of Castile 132
Isle of Wight 25, 150

James I and VI 90, 183, 204
James II 96
James IV of Scotland 172, 189
Jennings, Nicholas 186
Jersey 49-50
Jesuits Act 175
John 7
JP 30
Judge, Margaret 108
Julius Caesar 180
Jury of Matrons 108
Justice of the Peace Act 1361 33

Katherine of Aragon 15, 37, 96, 133, 190
Kent, Prince Michael 96
Kethulle, Jane van (later Daniell) 72
Kett's Rebellion 161, 201
King's Bench 55
King's College 183
Kings Lynn 46
Kingston, Sir William 37
Knevett, Sir Thomas 53
Knollys, Lettice 72
Kray Twins 23
Kyd, Thomas 77, 142

Ladislaus II 191
Lambeth Palace 204, 207
Lancaster, Henry of 34
Lanfranc 6
Langton, Christopher 57
Langton, Stephen 7
Languille, Henri 41
Lansdowne Manuscripts 136
Laxton, Nottinghamshire 156
League of Thievery 85
Leather making 92
Ledes, John, Abbot 201

Index

Lee, Thomas 165
Lesley, John, Bishop of Ross 177
Lewes, (Lewis) Joyce 99
Liberties 92
Lincoln, John 212
Lister, Dr Kate 81
Little Ease 178
Locard, Edmund 123
Lollards 95
Lovell, Francis 103-5
Luther, Martin 16, 96, 215
Lynstred (Lynsted), Anne 109

Mace, Isabel 165
Machlinia, William 15
Machyn 53
Magistrates 33
Magna Carta 7
Malice Aforethought 125
Man for All Seasons 214
Manox, Henry 70-71
Mantel, Hilary 214
Margaret of Burgundy 104, 190
Margaret Tudor 172
Marian Persecutions 97
Marian Statutes 126
Marillac, Charles de 171
Markby, Lincolnshire 200
Marlowe, Christopher (Kit) 76-78
Marriage laws 110
Marshalsea Prison 23, 176
Marwell, George 63
Marwood, William 47
Mary I, Mary Tudor, Bloody Mary 20, 38, 89, 96-97, 162, 164, 168, 181
Mary, Queen of Scots 39, 107, 116, 152, 162, 174
Massey, Perotine 97
Master, William 171

Mathewe, William 142
Matilda, Empress 7
Maximilian, Emperor 190
Meautys, John 212-13
Menville, Ninian 87-90
Mercers' Company 212
Miller, Anna 81-82
Mirfyn, Sir Thomas 127
Monastic charity 200
Monmouth, Humphrey 215
Montaigne's Essays 191
More, Sir Thomas 6, 68, 214-16
Morgan, Thomas 174
Mosbye, Thomas 127
Mote, Robert 31
Much Ado About Nothing 123
Mundy, John 212
Mutilation 53

Neck verse 22
Nelson, Frances 112
Nelson, William 112
Neville, Charles Earl of Westmoreland 153
Neville, Edward 175
Neville, John 102
Neville, Lord Henry 87-90
Neville, Sir Ralph 88
Newborough, George 146
Newborough, Mary 146
Newgate Prison 23
Nicea, Council of 99
Night-walking (poaching) 141
Norfolk Assizes 91
Norfolk, Duke of 70, 149, 213
North, Sir Edward 127
Norwich (plague effects) 198
Norwich Cathedral 91
Norwich Cathedral Priory 200

Oath of Supremacy 6, 49, 151-53, 187
Open field system 156
Orange, Prince of 178-79
Osenay, Richard 104
Owghan, Thomas 32

Paget, Lord 89
Palliards 57
Pamphlets 14-20
Parker, John 142-5
Parr, Katherine 96, 112, 116, 214
Parr, William, 112
Parris, George van 99
Parry, William 173-76
Paston, Mr (unidentified) 91
Paston, Margery 111-2
Pavia, Battle of 191
Peine forte et dure 51
Pennyrents 93
Percy, Lord Henry 102, 193
Percy, Thomas, Earl of Northumberland 153
Petty Treason 45
Petty, William, Marquess of Lansdowne 136
Peveril Castle 158
Philip II of Spain 16, 162
Philip, Archduke of Burgundy 191
Phillips, John 207
Philosopher's Stone 61
Phippes, Martha 166
Pierrepoint, Albert 47
Pilgrimage of Grace 49, 195, 200
Pilliwinks 210
Pillory 29, 56
Pious perjury 121
Plague 25, 198
Pleading the belly 22

Plot, Robert 55
Pole, Edmund de la 189-92
Pole, John de la, Earl of Lincoln 189
Pole, William de la 191
Poor, Able-Bodied 202
Poor, Impotent 202
Poor Law 29, 66, 199
Porter, Sir Nicholas 150
Pounder, Cicely 128
Prayerbook Uprising 161
Pressing 51-52
Pricking 210
Pringle, Janet 173
Psalm, fifty-first 22

Quesne, Bernabé Lé 49

Rack-renting 68
Rack, The 178
Raleigh, Sir Walter 74
Rape 164-6
Read, Margaret 46
Readshaw, Mary 112
Recusant 30
Reformation 133, 161
Rest, John 212
Reuters 135
Richard II 131
Richard III viii
Richardson, Thomas 65
Ridley, Bishop Nicholas 99
Ridolfi 153, 177
Right of Shack 158
Rivet 84
Rochford, Jane 71
Rogers, John 95, 99
Roman Law 2
Roose, Richard 41-43
Rosedale Priory 12
Rosimunde, Father 209

Index

Saint Edmund 10
Saint George 10
Salisbury, John Vane 125
Salisbury, Margaret,
    Countess of 133
Sanctuary 54-55
Saunders, Laurence 100
Savage, John 105
School for Pickpockets 139
Scold's Bridle 29
Scold's Bridle 55-56
Scrivener's Daughter 178
Sellett, Anne 165
Seymour, Edward, Duke of
    Somerset 98, 116-9
Seymour, Jane 36, 170
Seymour, Thomas 116-9
Shakespeare 29, 76, 78, 123,
    130, 184
Sharp, John 158
Shenfield, Essex 166
Sheppard, Jack 23
Shire moots 4
Shirt of Flame 98
Simnel, Lambert 104, 133, 189
Slyn, Edward 64
Smith, Thomas 171
Smyth, William 150
Smythe, Thomas 85
Somerville, John 188
Southampton 69
Southcote, John 207
Spacye, Robert 160
Speed, John 38
St Benet's Holm, Norfolk 200
St Peter ad Vincula 40
Stafford, Edward
    (double agent) 174
Stafford, Edward, Duke of
    Buckingham 215

Stafford, Sir Humphrey 55,
    103-5
Stafford, Thomas 55
Stanhope, Anne 116
Star Chamber 22, 27, 157-58
Statute of Artificers 33
Statute of Treasons 1352 143
Stephen 6
Stiles, Elizabeth 208-10
Stocks 36, 56
Stoke, Battle of 21, 189
Stracke, Mary 160
Street Literature 109
Strickland, Agnes 38
Stubbs, John 20
Sumptuary Legislation 180
Sunnyff, Thomas 28
Surrey, Earl of 212
Sydney, Sir Philip 74
Syon, Middlesex 200

Talbot, Mary 194
Tamburlaine 77
Taming of the Shrew 130
Tewkesbury, Battle of 24
Thews 35
Thirsk 149
Throckmorton Plot 178
Tort, law 135
Torture (witches) 209
Tower of London 23
Towton, Battle of 26
Trial by ordeal 13
Trypptt, Alice 42
Tuke, Sir Brian 181
Tumbrel 56
Tumor, Sara 166
Twain, Mark 184
Tyburn 48
Tyndale, William 17

Ulpian 3
Underwood, William 171
Utopia 216

Vagabonds Act 1572 203
Vagrants 196-203
Valor Ecclesiasticus 200
Velvet (clothing) 181
Vergil, Polydore 189
Vernon, Sir George 158
Vesalius, Andreas 122

Wade, Joan 82
Waits 32
Walden University 122
Walker, Gilbert 139
Walsingham, Francis 19, 85, 172
Walweyn, Richard 183
Wapping 48
Warbeck, Perkin 133, 189
Warham, Archbishop 194
Warner, Serjeant of the Admiralty 56
Warner, Simon 82
Wars of the Roses ix, 187
Warwick, Edward, Earl of 104, 131
Watchmen 29, 32
Waterhouse, Agnes 207-8

Watkins, Thomas 85
Weavers 211
Welles, Anne 143-5
Welyar, William 150
Wergild 4
Western Uprising 161
Westminster Abbey 54
Whalley, Lincolnshire 200
Whipping and Whipping Post 57
William I, conqueror 5
William II, Rufus 6
William III 96
Wilson, Thomas 168
Winchester, Marquess of 84
Wisdom, Gregory 87-90
Witchcraft 123
Witchcraft pamphlets 208
Witchcraft Statute 1542 205
Wolf Hall 214
Wolsey, Thomas, Cardinal 193, 215
Woodville, Elizabeth 54, 131
Worde, Wynkyn de 15
Wotton (cf Fagin) 115
Wright, Barnaby 169
Wyatt Rebellion 48
Wycliffe, John 76, 95

York 153-5